ADHD & the Focused Mind

A GUIDE TO GIVING YOUR ADHD CHILD FOCUS, DISCIPLINE & SELF-CONFIDENCE

D0036440

SARAH CHEYETTE, MD
PETER JOHNSON
BEN CHEYETTE, MD, PHD

SQUAREONE
PUBLISHERS

The information and advice contained in this book are based upon the research and the personal and professional experiences of the author. They are not intended as a substitute for consulting with a health care professional. The publisher and author are not responsible for any adverse effects or consequences resulting from the use of any of the suggestions, preparations, or procedures discussed in this book. All matters pertaining to your physical health should be supervised by a health care professional. It is a sign of wisdom, not cowardice, to seek a second or third opinion.

COVER DESIGNER: Jeannie Tudor
EDITOR: Caroline Smith
TYPESETTER: Gary A. Rosenberg

Square One Publishers

115 Herricks Road • Garden City Park, NY 11040
516-535-2010 • 877-900-BOOK • www.squareonepublishers.com

Library of Congress Cataloging-in-Publication Data
Names: Cheyette, Sarah, 1968- author. | Johnson, Peter, 1971- author. | Cheyette, Ben, author.
Title: ADHD & the focused mind : a guide to giving your ADHD child focus, discipline & self-confidence / Sarah Cheyette, MD, Peter Johnson, and Ben Cheyette, MD, PhD.
Other titles: ADHD and the focused mind
Description: Garden City Park, NY : Square One Publishers, [2016] | "How to use the successful coaching techniques of world class athletes to unlock your child's potential." | Includes bibliographical references and index.
Identifiers: LCCN 2015048284 (print) | LCCN 2016002068 (ebook) | ISBN 9780757004148 (pbk.) | ISBN 9780757054143 (Ebook)
Subjects: LCSH: Attention-deficit hyperactivity disorder. | Brain.
Classification: LCC RJ506.H9 C478 2016 (print) | LCC RJ506.H9 (ebook) | DDC 618.92/8589—dc23

Printed in the United States of America

10   9   8   7   6   5   4   3   2   1

Contents

*To our patients, students, sparring partners—
and their parents and families.*

Acknowledgments

To our patients, who have taught us more than we could ever learn in school; and to our colleagues at the Palo Alto Medical Foundation, UCSF, UCLA, and the University of Washington, who have shared their energy, talent, and enthusiasm: Together, you have inspired us.

Thanks especially to our children, our compass: When our attention is pulled in every direction, our love for you is constant.

From Sarah and Ben Cheyette

I would sincerely like to thank God for guiding my life. There are things that have happened to me that I can only describe as Grace. Without that Grace, I wouldn't be here writing this. For my family, the one I was born into and the family I chose to step into, I love you and my life is rich because of you. E, my favorite vowel and person in life, 4ever +1day. To the thousands of students and families I have had the chance to serve and the communities I've had the opportunity to positively impact, thank you for your lessons and your patience. To all my teachers and training partners, thank you for asking more of me than I sometimes asked of myself. Finally, I want to thank Mr. Bloom for igniting in me a love for learning and a passion for personal growth—the 10 pushups in front of the class made a difference!

From Peter Johnson

We are deeply grateful to Square One Publishers, particularly to publisher Rudy Shur and our wonderful editor, Caroline Smith.

From all the authors

Foreword

Had a book like *ADHD & the Focused Mind* been around when I was growing up with my learning difficulties, my family and I may have had a better understanding of what was going on. *ADHD & the Focused Mind* gives families hope. By incorporating the mental and physical difficulties for children with ADHD and other learning disabilities, parents have the opportunity to understand their children's thought patterns during the most difficult of times.

ADHD & the Focused Mind was co-written by Dr. Sarah Cheyette, Dr. Ben Cheyette, and Master Peter Johnson, a senior Tae Bo® fitness instructor. With Peter's knowledge of martial arts and its benefits for children with learning disabilities, as well as more than twenty years of teaching experience, he has provided parents with the fighting chance to show their children that they *can* conquer their difficulties. I was lucky enough to have martial arts introduced into my life at age eleven. Instead of having to search for the solution the way I did, *ADHD & the Focused Mind* provides parents and families with answers! If parents can incorporate these amazing tools, they will be giving their children an opportunity to be people, beyond their disabilities.

Billy Blanks
Creator, Tae Bo® Fitness

Preface

Sometimes it takes a challenging experience to forge strength. One of our authors, Peter Johnson, recalls such an experience from many years ago. He had been so excited to have the opportunity to train with the National Karate championship teams. But the end of the night found him with fractured ribs and a bloody broken nose. He felt sore all over his body. He wound up sitting on a bench, dejectedly overlooking the San Francisco Bay. He felt defeated at every level; at the top of his (sore) lungs he shouted, *"I've had it! I quit! I'm never doing karate again!"* But soon after those words left his body, he found a new perspective and the strength to continue his training. Now he is among the most elite and highly-ranked karate belts in the country. He still sometimes looks at his 7th Degree Black Belt certificate with a sense of disbelief, remembering that night long ago. The man on the bench could not have pictured himself becoming the successful sensei of today who has positively affected the lives of many students.

If you are reading this book, you or your child may be feeling defeated in the moment. But, just as Peter realized years ago in his own moment of defeat, success is defined not by your past but by the direction you choose to go in the future. You and your child can move forward and experience success that you may not yet have envisioned. We, as the authors of this book, don't know exactly what you are going through right now, but based on our collective experience that includes thousands of hours of study, research and training, and practical experience, we are positive this book can impact you, your child, and your entire family for the better.

If your child has been diagnosed with Attention Deficit Hyperactivity Disorder (ADHD, hyperactive or inattentive), you may be wondering if he "has to" start medication. The thought of starting their child on medication fills many parents with fear and uncertainty. This book is designed to address those feelings.

Fear not! Medication is *not* the only way to improve the behavioral challenges of an ADHD child: There are non-medication strategies that can help many children with ADHD. These non-medication strategies can be used alone or may be combined with medication.

As a parent, you have a key role to play: You can work with your child to improve his behavior. In this book, we will show you simple techniques that you or an outside ADHD coach can use to help your child become a high achiever despite a diagnosis of ADHD.

The ideas in this book are easy to understand and simple to follow. They will resonate with your child because they are based on the athletic mindset—the strategies and techniques that athletes use to stay focused on their goals. Most children are already familiar with this mindset as a standard part of sports practice. Even if your child does not participate in sports, he has been exposed to these ideas through routine participation in gym class, group sports at camp, or through other similar activities and organizations. Once your child realizes that the same ideas he has heard again and again—and has readily accepted from an athletic coach or group instructor—can be applied to the rest of his life, he will open his ears and listen. As an example, if your child with ADHD comes to realize that "keep your eye on the ball" can apply not only to when he is actually hitting a ball but also to when he is talking with someone else, he will be more open to that advice than if he is told for the umpteenth time: "Hey, look at me when I'm talking to you!"

By learning athletic-based strategies (including positive and strategic goal-setting techniques) that address the behavioral challenges of ADHD, your child will improve his ability to focus, reduce his tendency to procrastinate, and increase his organizational and planning skills. When trained with either your help or with the help of a designated ADHD coach, your child will be able to use the strategies in this book to become more successful at school and at home. Once internalized, these strategies can be applied to any situation in any setting, and will guarantee your child a winning season in every year of his life!

A Word About Gender

In an effort to avoid awkward phrasing within sentences, it is our publishing style to alternate the use of male and female pronouns according to chapter. Therefore, when referring to a "third-person" adult, child, healthcare provider, or caregiver, odd-numbered chapters will use female pronouns, while even-numbered chapters will use male, to give acknowledgment to people of both genders.

Introduction

Fifteen-year-old Andrew was extremely angry and frustrated. While he excelled at playing soccer, he wasn't doing well in any of his school classes. His parents didn't know what to do with him, and he didn't want to deal with them. They were in the doctor's office, the end of the line. His parents didn't really want him on medication for his ADHD, but they were at a loss. He was always in a bad mood and they suspected he was smoking marijuana. He was failing school, despite the fact that he was a smart kid. The one bright spot in his life was soccer, where he was the star player on his team. Was medication the only way out?

The doctor asked him one question, which Andrew later said changed his life: Can you apply what you have learned on the soccer field to school and to the rest of your life?

If you are a parent of a child with ADHD, the behavioral issues described above may sound all too familiar. ADHD, *attention deficit hyperactivity disorder*, is a condition in which people have greater difficulty than average focusing their attention, especially in situations they don't find interesting. This can cause challenges with functioning in daily life because to a large extent, accomplishment depends on the ability to focus on a task at hand, no matter whether the task is interesting or not. Everybody can have trouble focusing at times. However, ADHDers have a harder time focusing—and focusing in more situations—than average.

You can't control your child's in-born intelligence, and you can't control whether or not your child has good teachers, the way your child's school assesses its students, or how difficult a teacher makes a test. However, with the right advice, training exercises, and practice, you *can* improve your child's motivation, organization, time management, perseverance, attitude, and social skills—and your child *will* be more successful in all of these areas and more.

The goal of this book is to give ADHDers and those who want to help them the tools they need to achieve excellence in any area they choose. We believe that our approach will help virtually every child with ADHD without side effects, and for the minimal cost of this book and the time and effort you and your child put into it. The training we advise can be accomplished on your own time and on your own schedule—as fast or as gradual as you want. It is designed to create a process for success that you can help your child apply to whatever he wants to accomplish in life.

Our approach involves using the training techniques of world-class athletes. Not the physical training techniques—this book is not about coaching ADHDers to run a four-minute mile, shoot winning baskets, or land the perfect "ten" in gymnastics. Instead, this book is about teaching ADHDers how to develop the same intense focus and commitment that athletes use to attain their performance goals. This is called the *athletic mindset*. By doing this, the ADHDer can take these skills and apply them to any aspect of performance in his life.

Just as athletes improve their athletic skills through proper coaching and training, ADHDers have mental skills that they can improve through proper coaching and training. Both ADHDers and athletes need to identify challenges, set goals, and train hard with a coach. A person with ADHD who does this can break away from a cycle of underachievement or outright failure to become a world-class success story.

Many kids with ADHD already participate in sports; they already understand the athletic mindset that includes trying your best, participating fully, and constantly setting new goals for achievement. Many kids with ADHD become willing to make changes and confident in their ability to make these changes once they understand that all they have to do is take their "athlete self" and apply it to their "school self." They realize quickly that if they can do it for their coach or their team, they can do it for themselves as students, sons, and daughters.

Nevertheless, we emphasize that this book is *not only* for athletes who have ADHD. You can also easily apply the techniques in this book even if your child has no interest in sports. Our message is that *anyone* can use the *attitude* of competitive athletes to overcome the obstacles that ADHD throws in the way of success.

Athletes identify their weak areas and work on them in training. Athletes measure how they are doing today and set specific goals for what they want to improve in tomorrow's workout. Athletes work with coaches to help them through their rough spots and keep them motivated until they reach their long-term goal. They give their all to achieve that goal and they give their all to excel.

In this book, we show you how to use these same tools to strengthen your child's achievement. How can your child become faster at accomplishing tasks at school or at work? How can your child keep from getting distracted—i.e., how will he "keep his eye on the ball?" How do you keep his motivation going if he has a setback? The principles are the same whether one is talking about performance in sports or in other areas, including school, work, or personal relationships.

In the coming chapters, you will learn about how the ADHD brain works. We begin in Chapter 1 by defining ADHD and identifying common symptoms and behaviors associated with it. We also explain some of the biology behind the brain with ADHD.

Then, in Chapters 2 through 4, we discuss the importance of goals: how to fully commit to a goal, what criteria are important for setting a goal, and how to stick with that goal until it becomes a reality. Having a goal gives your child something to focus on. When a goal is achieved, the child feels an important sense of accomplishment and pride, which encourages him to continue setting bigger goals. We discuss how to organize goals and how to set up a clear, step-by-step, and realistic timeline for achieving them.

In Chapters 5 and 6, we discuss *how* an ADHDer can learn to focus and achieve, and apply these skills to his everyday life. We present fundamental exercises to help ADHDers concentrate better. These include techniques to focus the eyes, mind, body, and spirit, which all work together to create motivation in your child.

Chapter 7 invokes how your child can best utilize the help of those around him—for example, his teachers, friends, and even his "competitors" in the classroom. Some children with ADHD have trouble working with a team, especially if the other team members do not fully understand ADHD. This chapter provides strategies for your child to use in order to succeed when working with others.

Improvement sometimes comes in two steps forward and one step back. Just as an athlete is going to lose sometimes, an ADHDer is going to have times where he doesn't feel things are going well, or doesn't reach his goal. Many kids give up when they are faced with failure, even if you think they should respond in a different way. Changing this attitude of dejection in response to setbacks is essential for a successful life. You will learn strategies for dealing with, and recovering from, disappointment and failure—strategies that allow your child to go forward and continue to reach for his goals—in Chapter 8.

Chapter 9 discusses the growing practice of working with an ADHD coach, and how to find the perfect coach for your child. In some cases, parents decide to coach their own children. Wouldn't it be great if your child viewed you as part of the team—instead of the enemy? As a parent, you will learn what strategies are important for coaching ADHDers. How much do you push? When do you hold back criticism because of ADHD? We also provide tips for finding an outside coach.

Finally, in Chapter 10, we discuss some of the issues ADHDers and their parents weigh when deciding whether or not to take medication. We will explain the benefits and the potential side effects of the most common ADHD medications.

If you are reading this book, you are probably looking for an answer to the challenges posed by ADHD in your child. With this book, we not only hope to energize you and your child on that journey, but to do more. We want this book to jump off the page and shift your spirit. We want this book to kick you in the pants and give you confidence about helping your child. We want this book to be the means by which your child has an excellent—not just an average—life!

We three authors approach this from different backgrounds, which contribute to the uniqueness of this book. Ben and Sarah Cheyette are physicians. Ben is a practicing psychiatrist, but he also has a PhD in Molecular Biology and runs a lab that researches brain development. Sarah is in clinical practice as a neurologist and sees many patients (both kids and adults) with ADHD. Peter Johnson is a seventh-degree black belt in Okinawan Karate. His connection to ADHD comes from training many people with ADHD in his dojo (school) and his dedication to teaching them martial arts. Ben and Sarah connected with Peter at Peter's dojo and we all realized that the mental techniques Peter uses to teach people how to be better athletes could be more widely applied to all aspects of ADHD. All of us share a passion for helping people to be their best.

We aim to give you a novel, easy-to-understand approach that is about changing both mindset and behavior. We will introduce simple but powerful concepts that will motivate your child and keep him on the road to success.

Having a desire for success is good, but achieving success takes more than desire—it is a task that requires effort to actually make it happen, and practice to make it a habit that happens again and again. We believe that the spirit that develops in athletes through their training, and that your child can develop with the help of this book, can link desires to long-term success. We want your child to develop and to use this winning spirit to combat the challenges of ADHD. Not everyone can become an Olympic-level athlete. But *everybody* can develop the mindset that an Olympic athlete uses to achieve his goals, and everybody can apply that mindset to their own personal arena of performance and achieve a gold medal in life!

1

Understanding ADHD

Although ADHD behaviors have been observed by physicians for at least 200 years, the term *ADHD* is fairly new; it was first officially used by health professionals in the 1980s. The biology behind it is not yet fully understood. Opinions about ADHD vary widely—some view it as a quirky but harmless personality trait, while to others, it is a disruptive disorder. Despite these differing opinions, most people agree that while ADHD can contribute to creativity and intellect, it can also inhibit success at school or at home, frustrating children and their parents alike. Understanding what goes through the mind of your ADHD child is the first step to managing the condition.

This chapter will present you with a general definition of ADHD, as well as typical behavioral symptoms that must be present for an official diagnosis. We will provide examples of the different ways ADHD may present in a child or teenager. Finally, we will briefly review current treatments for ADHD.

WHAT IS ADHD?

ADHD stands for *attention deficit hyperactivity disorder.* It is a behavioral condition that affects millions of children and often persists into adulthood. The term covers an assortment of behaviors, including difficulty paying attention, hyperactivity, impulsive behavior, distractibility, forgetfulness, and disorganization.

People often wonder: What is the difference between ADD and ADHD? The answer is that there isn't much difference. They are two variants of the same thing. Typically, *ADD* (*attention deficit disorder*) has been applied to people who have difficulty with attention but who are not hyperactive. Meanwhile, ADHD has been applied to people who are predominantly hyperactive. Many people have a combination of inattention and hyperactivity. Currently, both variants are referred to as ADHD. In this book we will accordingly use the term ADHD and refer to anybody with ADHD as an *ADHDer*.

As an aside, we don't particularly like the name "Attention Deficit Hyperactivity Disorder" because it appears to imply that children with ADHD can't ever give their full attention to anything. The name also includes the word "disorder," implying disease, and we (and many others) do not see it as a disease. Instead, we see ADHD as a condition in which attention and energy are hard

> **Coaching Corner**
> This chapter provides you with basic information about ADHD, while later chapters focus on our unique approach to improvement.

for an individual to manage. ADHDers may feel more distracted and hyperactive than other children, but they *can* be trained to work optimally when and where it is important.

WHAT CAUSES ADHD?

There is a theory that the symptoms of ADHD are becoming more common in our society because the modern environment is faster-paced, with more stimuli coming our way from every direction. For example, at the turn of the twentieth century, the height of transportation technology was the horse and buggy; six miles was considered a long trip that could take over an hour. Now, we can cover that same distance in a few minutes by racing around in cars that contain a dozen different gauges, dials, and electronic gadgets to distract our attention. Children used to be stimulated from playing outside; now they have flashing screens in front of their faces from toddlerhood on. All of these different stimuli simultaneously compete for our attention—for better or for worse—in a way that previous generations did not have to cope with.

There are those who feel that, considering all the distractions that kids have, ADHD is not a real condition so much as it is a normal response to our fast-paced environment. However, there are many scientific studies that validate the existence of ADHD. It tends to run in families and has some genetic basis. There is evidence that environmental factors, such as exposure to cigarette smoke or high levels of lead during pregnancy or childhood, can also contribute to the emergence of ADHD. ADHD is *not* caused by bad parenting, bad teachers, bad diet, or too much screen time—although all of those factors could play a role in making it worse. ADHD is not a label, an insult, or a joke—it is a condition that is treatable.

In the United States, considerable research, money, and effort has been expended in studies of ADHD using brain magnetic resonance imaging (brain MRI) to look for differences in brain anatomy. Although differences in many brain areas (including the hippocampus, frontal and temporal cortices, basal ganglia, and cerebellum) of ADHDers have been reported by individual groups of investigators, there is little agreement across this area of research because these structural differences are very small. No single brain region has consistently been found to be affected by ADHD across many imaging studies. However, the prefrontal cortex (located behind the forehead) is widely thought to play a part because of its important role in planning and decision-making.

On the other hand, there is substantial evidence that one underlying biological issue in ADHD is with the chemicals (*neurotransmitters*) that are responsible for communication between brain cells. For example, as discussed very briefly below and further in Chapter 10, every major class of medication that has proven effective in treating ADHD enhances one of two neurotransmitter systems—dopamine or norepinephrine. This supports a link between ADHD and the function of these chemicals in transmitting signals among brain cells.

But although neurotransmitters seem to play a significant role, the explanation for ADHD is certainly not as simple as "too little dopamine" or "too little norepinephrine." For one thing, these neurotransmitters are involved in many different regions of the brain that do very different things. For example, although dopamine is involved in ADHD, it's also involved in Parkinson's disease, which has nothing to do with ADHD. Similarly, some antidepressant medications also raise the level of norepinephrine in the brain, even though depression and ADHD are very distinct behavioral conditions. In short, the human brain is extraordinarily complicated: Different brain regions use the same neurotransmitters to contribute to many different behaviors. Therefore, it is difficult to pinpoint an exact brain area or neurotransmitter that is responsible for ADHD.

Some genes have been associated with ADHD, and although much work still needs to be done in this field, genetic research is progressing at a rapid rate. In the coming decades, modern genome sequencing studies will revolutionize our understanding of the molecules and genes that contribute to ADHD and to other behavioral conditions. This will provide new and powerful opportunities to dissect and understand the most basic biology at the root of these conditions.

> **Coaching Corner**
> Although we don't yet fully understand all of the biology behind it, ADHD does reflect an underlying biological condition.

WHAT IS THE DEFINING FEATURE OF ADHD?

The core issue with ADHD is that an ADHDer has to work harder to focus in a situation that is not inherently interesting to her. Take the example of a student in a class who is supposed to pay attention to the teacher explaining a lesson at the front of the room. Non-ADHD students will generally pay attention in this situation, not necessarily because they are inherently interested in what the teacher is saying, but because it is more "automatic" for them. In contrast, a student with ADHD *needs* the teacher to be talking in a vitally interesting way or about a subject that she finds deeply fascinating in order to focus and maintain the kind of attention that comes naturally to most other children. Unless she really remains interested, her attention will quickly shift away from the teacher.

Reading this example, you may object that everybody—ADHD or no ADHD—pays better attention in a stimulating, interesting environment. That is true. The difference is that ADHDers *only* focus well in a situation that is *inherently* (naturally) interesting. Otherwise, they have great difficulty focusing at all. It takes a greater effort for an ADHDer to turn her attention "on" and maintain it in the "on" position when things are not naturally interesting to her. She may start with one idea, but then "follows the bright shiny penny" wherever it goes.

Many times we have heard parents object, "Oh, my kid can't have ADHD—she can play video games for hours!" Well, video games are very stimulating to most people who play them, and gaming companies spend a lot of time and money figuring out how to make their games more attention-grabbing and addictive. Watch a child with ADHD engage in video games, or another activity that interests her, and you will be amazed by her ability to concentrate. In contrast, studying high school chemistry, doing chores, and completing homework are considerably less inherently stimulating to her—very few of us would describe them as "addictive" in any way! However, schools (and later in life, employers) will ask your ADHD child to focus on these types of tasks, which are often outside her band of intense interests. Since she may not be able to do that very well, this results in repeated failure and beats down the self-esteem of a child who has the potential to be successful in other ways.

When their attention *is* turned on, many ADHDers focus very, very well—some to an almost obsessive degree. In fact, ADHDers sometimes have difficulty *not* concentrating on details that the rest of us can more easily set aside (this is called *hyperfocus*), and this too can cause challenges. Take the example of seventeen-year-old Eric, who had to do a project for school that involved analyzing data and presenting it in a table. He focused so much on how the table should be organized and how the cells of the table should look that he didn't get to analyze the data in time to turn in a completed project.

Daniel was a fifteen-year-old boy who was extremely gifted in visual arts. He made movies that professionals admired, and he was largely self-taught. He launched several visual arts businesses over the Internet and made money through all of them. However, he failed a number of his classes in high school. He just could not make himself do the homework he needed to pass, and was in danger of not graduating.

Another distinctive feature of ADHDers is that they often process a broad range of incoming pieces of information simultaneously, in contrast to most non-ADHDers who focus solely on the task at hand. As a result, ADHDers often notice things that may escape the notice of non-ADHDers. For example, a 1984 study compared ADHD children with non-ADHD children. Each group was given cards to memorize. Not surprisingly, the ADHD children did a poorer job of memorizing the cards.

However, they were much better than the non-ADHD children at remembering details of the posters on the walls, which was not a part of the test.

Given this example, one can understand why ADHDers often describe feeling overwhelmed—there are so many incoming perceptions and thoughts running through their minds that it's hard to figure out what to prioritize first. As one patient said, "It's like spaghetti in my head." With so many loose ends jumbled together, it's hard to disentangle and follow just one thought. Or, an ADHDer often may feel that she is daydreaming—again, this reflects that the things she should be focusing on, the ones right in front of her, don't grab her attention. Instead, her mind wanders to other ideas and fantasies.

DIAGNOSING ADHD

You now know that the main issue with ADHD is that an ADHDer has trouble paying attention unless the subject is very interesting to her. But everybody can be inattentive at times. Everyone knows that kids get bored, and that kids who get bored get wiggly—so what? This surely does not mean that every kid has ADHD. ADHD should *only* be diagnosed when there are serious patterns of inattention that interfere with the child's ability to perform well at major life tasks, such as in school or in forming relationships with friends and family.

> **Coaching Corner**
> *Don't worry about whether your child has "ADD" or "ADHD." Both conditions are called ADHD. Some kids are more inattentive; some are more hyperactive. Medications are the same for both, and coaching interventions should be directed toward your child's individual tendencies.*

Estimate percentages for children ages four to seventeen who *do* have ADHD range from 5 percent (according to the American Psychiatric Association) to 11 percent (according to the Centers for Disease Control and Prevention).

There are professionals who feel that ADHD is overdiagnosed in the United States, and it is true that the diagnosis of ADHD has become more common over the years. However, it is important to note that even today, the vast majority of kids are *not* diagnosed with ADHD.

For a person to be diagnosed with ADHD, symptoms have to be present in childhood (although they may not significantly impact the child until her teen years). The symptoms have to be present for at least six months prior to diagnosis. They have to cause challenges with functioning in different settings, not just school or home.

Here are some examples of behaviors commonly seen in children with ADHD (adapted from DSM-5, the most commonly used set of criteria for behavioral diagnosis in the United States).

ADHDers who are mainly *inattentive*:

- Often fail to give close attention to details; they make careless mistakes in schoolwork or with other activities.

- Often have trouble keeping their attention on tasks or play activities.

- Often do not seem to listen when spoken to directly.

- Often do not follow through on instructions and fail to finish schoolwork, chores, or duties in the workplace—they become sidetracked.

- Often have trouble organizing tasks and activities.

- Often avoid, dislike, or are reluctant to do tasks that require mental effort over a long period of time (such as schoolwork or homework), and thus procrastinate.

- Often lose things necessary for everyday tasks and activities, such as school materials, pencils, books, tools, wallets, keys, paperwork, eyeglasses, and cell phones.

- Are often easily distracted.

- Are often forgetful in daily activities. For example, they frequently forget to do their chores.

ADHDers who are prominently *hyperactive-impulsive*:

- Often fidget with or tap their hands or feet, or squirm in their seat.

- Often leave their seat in situations when remaining seated is expected.

- Often run about or climb in situations where it is not appropriate (adolescents may be limited to feeling restless).

A New Perspective
on ADHD

In this chapter, we talk a lot about the ADHD child. In case you're still not sure you understand the ADHDer, let's think outside the box and imagine a dog interacting with a cat. Most dogs' brains will automatically "turn on" and focus intensely when the dog sees a cat: "Cat cat cat cat." Other thoughts ("I'm hungry," "That grass sure smells sweet," "Hey, what's that thing behind me? Time to chase my tail!") fall lower in priority and do not interfere with "cat cat cat cat." (See Figure 1.1.) The dog's brain automatically prioritizes "cat" above all other potentially competing thoughts and won't think about anything else until the cat is out of sight.

But if the dog had ADHD, he might think "cat" only briefly before it quickly sails out of his consciousness. The "cat" thought doesn't stick: It isn't interesting enough to maintain his focus. If you looked at the dog during this time, it might appear that after momentarily noticing the cat he stares out into space, daydreaming. This is analogous to a human ADHDer who is mostly inattentive *without* hyperactivity. As one ADHDer put it, "I feel like I have a whiteboard in my head and the words appear on it but erase themselves quickly." (See Figure 1.2.)

Figure 1.1. A Dog that Does Not Have ADHD.

Figure 1.2. A Dog with Inattentive ADHD.

Figure 1.3. A Dog with Inattentive and Hyperactive ADHD.

Another dog with ADHD might have difficulty prioritizing "cat" above other competing thoughts. Since this dog doesn't hold one thought above all others as the most important, his brain perceives a jumble of non-prioritized thoughts all at once. (See Figure 1.3.) To this dog, the "cat" thought is no more important than "I'm hungry," "That grass sure smells sweet," or "Hey, what's that thing behind me? Time to chase my tail!" Because this dog has many thoughts of equal priority, he has trouble choosing one thing to do and sticking with it. So what happens?

This dog starts to chase the cat, but is distracted after the first few steps by a whiff of grass; he forgets the cat and starts to sniff the ground. A moment later, perceiving something attached to his rear end, he chases his tail around in a circle. A few seconds later he starts to chase the cat again. . . . and so on. Such a dog might earn the label "ADHD" not only because of his inability to focus, but also because of his inability to sit still and attend to one activity at a time. This is comparable to a human ADHDer who shows symptoms of inattention *and* hyperactive behavior.

Sound familiar?

- Often are unable to play or take part in leisure activities quietly.

- Are often "on the go," acting as if "driven by a motor."

- Often talk excessively.

- Often blurt out an answer before a question has been completely asked.

- Often have trouble waiting their turn.

- Often interrupt or intrude on others by butting into conversations or games.

   Your child also could have combined inattentive and hyperactive-impulsive characteristics.

HOW ADHD LEADS TO PRACTICAL CHALLENGES

Even the most intelligent people in the world won't be successful if they don't have the skill set needed to bring their wonderful ideas to fruition. Similarly, ADHDers often trip themselves up because they don't have the skills they need to focus on, set, and reach goals. The following section highlights some of the symptoms of ADHD and explains why they can lead to challenges. For practical tips on how children with ADHD can overcome these challenges at home and at school, see pages 75 and 169.

Disorganization and Procrastination

These are huge challenges, both at home and at school. For example, ADHDers often have trouble turning in homework. They may forget they have to do it or forget when it is due (writing things down in a planner is a step they often skip). They may not bring home the books they need to do it. When they get home, they may get distracted or procrastinate and never do it. If they do complete it, they may leave it at home or lose it (in the mess of their room or backpack), or bring it to school but forget to turn it in. Issues with the "homework cycle" often lead to huge fights between parents and children. Parents find it so frustrating—it seems like such a simple thing to do homework and then turn it in!

Lack of Planning and Not Following Directions

Kids with ADHD often have challenges with planning. As a related issue, they tend to not fully think their actions through (see section "Hyperactivity and Poor Impulse Control" on page 18). Reading or listening to instructions is naturally boring to most ADHDers, who have a tendency to skip right to the "doing" part of the task at hand. However, by skipping the instructions, ADHDers tend to make more mistakes even if they understand the big picture of the work they are supposed to do. Lack of planning and inadequate reading of directions naturally leads to poor time management, especially when combined with general disorganization. ADHDers frequently underestimate how long a project will take to complete because they aren't thinking about all the steps involved in getting from point A to point B.

Slower Work with More Mistakes

If your child's attention shifts from one task to another, each task will take longer and will contain more mistakes. Shifting from task to task means that your child not only loses momentum on the task at hand, but in addition must repeatedly refocus whenever she resumes work on a previous task. As a result, when children with ADHD *do* complete tasks, the product of their efforts often doesn't reflect their full ability.

Faster Work with More Mistakes

Not all ADHDers work slowly; some fly through tasks recklessly and make many mistakes along the way. In children with ADHD, this frequently occurs in math, where a single careless error can torpedo an entire problem. For example, if your child absentmindedly adds when she should subtract, she will get the wrong answer even if she understands the math concepts involved in the problem perfectly well.

Incomplete Projects

At the onset of a project, a kid with ADHD may display an intense burst of enthusiasm and creativity that reflects her raw energy and intelligence. But in the face of even normal setbacks, the ADHDer has a tendency to turn away and seek satisfaction in more immediately stimulating and gratifying activities. The result is that the ADHDer is more likely than average to move on from an unfinished project and never return to it.

Hyperactivity and Poor Impulse Control

Children with the hyperactive variant of ADHD can have loud and disruptive behavior, including interrupting others or talking out of turn. Some children with ADHD are fidgety, move around at inappropriate times, and have trouble keeping their hands to themselves. Younger ADHDers often "look with their hands," not with their eyes, so they may wind up touching everything and everybody, which at a minimum is

Another Take on ADHD:
The Difference Between Hunters and Farmers

Thom Hartmann, who has written several books about ADHD, has promoted the idea that ADHD is better understood as a behavioral "difference" rather than as a behavioral "disorder." He makes the analogy that ADHDers are more like traditional "hunters," whereas non-ADHDers are more like traditional "farmers." The genes for behavioral traits that benefited people when their lives depended mostly on being good "hunters" (e.g., in pre-historic times and in hunter-gatherer societies) remain present in modern people living in industrialized societies. However, not everybody in industrialized societies views these persisting "hunter" behavioral traits as beneficial. How do these (partly) genetically-driven behavioral traits look in a modern industrialized society? To Hartmann, they look a lot like ADHD. See the table on the facing page, adapted from Hartmann's book *The Edison Gene.*

As this suggests, ADHD has probably been around for as long as people have been around, with its traits being prevalent in hunters. But society has changed, and ADHD traits that were advantageous in previous societies are not always perceived as advantageous in today's society. If your child is sitting in class trying to learn algebra, her hunter's instinct to turn around at the sound of a bird at the window is not beneficial. But take heart—those ADHD traits definitely will do your child some good in other ways, especially once they have been properly trained and harnessed. (See "ADHD Can Also Contribute to Success," page 21.)

off-putting to other children. More seriously, children with ADHD may impulsively hit other children or adults, while teens with ADHD are more likely to get into serious fights with legal consequences. Besides the possibility of hurting others, children with ADHD often put themselves in dangerous situations. These are the children seen teetering across the tops of jungle gyms, darting out into the middle of the road, and skiing down slopes out of control. As they grow into teenagers, they

Table 1.1. Comparing ADHD Characteristics with Those of Hunters and Farmers

HUNTER (ADHD)	FARMER (NON-ADHD)
Constantly monitoring the environment.	Not easily distracted from the task at hand.
Able to throw himself into the chase instantly.	Able to sustain a steady, dependable effort over a longer period of time.
Ready to change strategy at any time; flexible.	Uses long-term strategies; purposeful.
Tireless; capable of sustained drives, but only when "hot on the trail."	Conscious of time/timing; paces himself, has good "staying power."
Results-oriented; acutely aware of whether the goal is getting closer now.	Patient, aware that results take time; willing to wait.
Thinks in a visual/concrete way.	Is okay with pursuing abstract goals.
Acts independently.	Works in a team.
Becomes bored by mundane tasks; enjoys new ideas, excitement, and "the hunt."	Tends to details, follows through, and "takes care of business."
Is willing to take risks and face danger.	Careful; assesses situation before acting.
Does not excel at socializing; is always "on the run."	Nurturing; creates and supports community values.

may be more likely than the average teen to drive too fast. Lack of impulse control can lead to a violation of social norms, such as stealing. Similarly, ADHD increases the risk of early and unprotected sex.

When Practical Challenges Become Psychological Issues

The challenges encountered in ADHD described above can interfere with personal productivity and achievement, and therefore directly interfere with success. They can also interfere in another, more insidious fashion: Together, they lead to a damaging perception of the ADHDer, coming both from within herself and from others around her.

At a psychological level, ADHD often causes kids to feel like underachievers. Grappling with recurring underachievement makes even smart people *feel* dumb. This leads to serious self-esteem issues: If you feel like you can't do anything right, then, of course, you become less likely to even attempt a project. Over time, an ADHDer may lose motivation to work at all on a task (such as homework) that she knows from experience is difficult for her to do well. As Henry Ford succinctly put it, "If you think you *can* do a thing or think you *can't* do a thing, you're *right*."

Beyond the psychological damage they can do to themselves, ADHDers often irritate the people around them. As we know, ADHDers are easily distracted away from activities they must do by activities they naturally find more interesting. This often results in the necessary activities not getting done, and is frequently perceived by others as laziness or a lack of motivation. In the eyes of an ADHDer's peers, the inattentiveness of ADHD is often taken to be a choice. Someone who is constantly losing things, procrastinating, or not finishing projects will naturally annoy anybody who depends on her. Also, ADHD kids may not be aware of or pay attention to social cues, leading to further difficulty in relating to their peers. As a parent, you of course want to help your child, but that can be hard to do when even you are frustrated with your child and she seems to ignore your advice. Kids with ADHD tend to get yelled at a lot—and neither they nor their par-

> ### Coaching Corner
> *Don't let your child call herself lazy or use that as an excuse to avoid work. If she says she is lazy, she will become lazy.*

ents enjoy the yelling. But it is important to remember that the distractibility of ADHD is an unconscious shift; an ADHDer doesn't intentionally decide to shift her attention any more than anybody else. In fact, because of their low threshold for shifting attention, ADHDers have to work harder than others to maintain focus on non-stimulating tasks. From this perspective, rather than being lazy, many kids with ADHD actually work longer and harder than non-ADHDers in order to accomplish the same amount of work.

> **Coaching Corner**
>
> *ADHD can be an outlet for creativity and an antidote to the mundane. Tell your child: "It's about perspective and not about being defective. You are in control of how you look at this."*

ADHD Can Also Contribute to Success

So far, you've received a lot of bad news about ADHD. But we have good news, too! There are aspects of ADHD that can help your child succeed and don't need fixing or treatment. For example, ADHDers often are creative. This may be because the ADHD brain tends to maintain lots of different ideas simultaneously, so it has the ability to group ideas and to connect concepts in new and different ways. This differs from people with more "linear" brains, who tend to focus on one idea at a time.

People with ADHD think outside the box more easily and tend to come up with innovative solutions to challenges. Moreover, ADHDers can harness their hyperactivity to muster immense energy and put their ideas into effect. In line with this, a number of inventors and trailblazers have been diagnosed with ADHD. These include David Neeleman, the founder of JetBlue Airlines, and Paul Orfalea, the founder of Kinko's. They both credit their success in part to their ADHD: "If someone told me you could be normal or you could continue to have your ADHD, I would take ADHD," said Neeleman in a 2005 issue of *ADDitude* magazine. "I knew I had strengths that other people didn't have, and my parents reminded me of them when my teachers didn't see them. . . . I can distill complicated facts and come up with simple solutions. I can look out on an industry with all kinds of problems and say, 'How can I do this better?' My ADHD brain naturally searches for better ways of doing things." Orfalea said, "Because I have a tendency to wander, I never spent much time in my office. . . . If I had stayed in my office all the time,

I would not have discovered all those wonderful ideas to help expand the business. . . . My biggest advantage is that I don't get bogged down in the details, because of my ADHD."

This is not exclusively a subjective perception that ADHDers like to hold of themselves. The advantages of ADHD are often noticeable to non-ADHDers around them as well. For example, here's a quote from a woman we saw in the clinic regarding her husband's ADHD:

> *Despite the difficulties with ADHD, it has brought me and our family a lot of benefits. He has a lot of energy and can be very driven in pursuit of a goal. He has a lot of ideas which keep on coming, and he is not stopped by inhibitions that would stop others, which is good for his work as well as ourselves.*

So ADHD can be an advantage in many situations.

CURRENT TREATMENTS FOR ADHD

Although ADHD can have its advantages, for the most part, many children affected by ADHD find that it can disrupt their lives significantly (and, in fact, a significant disruption in important life tasks is a necessary criterion for the formal diagnosis of ADHD—see "Diagnosing ADHD" on page 12). But it is often difficult to find an affordable, simple solution that both parent and child can agree on. The two most common solutions to managing ADHD are to give a child medication and to utilize a professional therapist. However, if you are reading this book, you are probably interested in trying other methods to help your child address challenging ADHD behaviors. Despite a diagnosis of ADHD, it is possible to change thoughts, feelings, and behavior patterns—and even though there are biological underpinnings of ADHD, medication is not necessarily required to make these changes.

Treating ADHD with medication is a relatively modern concept. Some people are concerned that it may be influenced and promoted by pharmaceutical corporations who financially profit from the sales of these medications. The rise of the "pill cure" also parallels a financial cutting back across the American medical system for non-medication-based mental health services.

That said, it cannot be denied that medications for ADHD provide many ADHDers with significant help. Medications are easy to use; some of them act instantly. Medications can be very effective at temporarily improving attention. Still, nobody absolutely needs to take these medications to live; unlike diabetes or high blood pressure, nobody dies directly from her ADHD because she didn't take her medications (unless an impulsive decision or inattention leads to serious injury or death). So, should your child take these medications?

Many ADHDers and their families may decide that they do not want to take medications for a variety of reasons. All medications have potential side effects and can make your child feel worse in some ways. You may worry about physical side effects, such as effects on blood pressure, pulse, height, and weight. Medications can also cause insomnia and lack of appetite. They can even cause your child's moods to worsen—for example, your child may become more prone to anger, sadness, or anxiety. A common fear that parents and children have is that medications will result in a "zombie effect," where the medicated child becomes jarringly docile and quiet. Even if you are desperately seeking help with behavioral modification for your child, nobody wants their child to change or lose other beloved aspects of her personality.

Certainly, no parent starts a medication for their child hoping that the child will be on it forever. So once your child starts a medication, you naturally want to know when she will be able to get off the medication. What happens after that? Will your child's behavior continue to improve? She needs to have some behavioral strategies to fall back on. (For more information about medications, including different drug classifications and how the chemicals in medications affect the brain, see Chapter 10.)

To learn these behavioral strategies, you may have been advised to take your child to a professional therapist. Such therapists can include psychiatrists, psychologists, and social workers. If you can find the right therapist to motivate your child, help her strategize, and get her through the rough spots, this assistance can be invaluable. However, it is often hard to find the right therapist. The therapeutic relationship takes time to cultivate. Some people have unrealistic expectations for therapy: Kids with ADHD may go into therapy after years of doing things the "ADHD way" and either they or their parents expect that after just a few sessions, everything will be fine. A parent will sometimes drag an unwilling, uncooperative child in to see a therapist and then get angry with the therapist (or the child) when the child is not "fixed" quickly. Finally, therapy can be very costly, especially if not covered by insurance (as is often the case, in whole or in part). This cost issue puts therapy out of reach for many families. But, as you'll learn in Chapter 9, there is a less costly and increasingly popular alternative—an ADHD coach. Whether you decide to be your child's ADHD coach or find somebody else to do it, you can help your child improve her concentration and willpower by practicing the techniques we will describe in this book.

SUMMARY

In this chapter, we explained what ADHD is, how it is diagnosed, and the potential causes and biology behind this condition. Theories about ADHD's causes, as well as its potential effects on a child's life (both good and bad) were discussed. We have also explored the two most common treatments for ADHD: medication and professional therapy. But we strongly believe that there is an alternate way to help your ADHD child—a way that is medication-free and highly affordable. In Chapter 2, we will begin to delve into our unique management plan of applying professional athletes' mental training techniques to the challenges faced by your ADHD child. The first step will be teaching your child the importance of setting a goal and fully committing to it. Turn the page and let's begin!

2

Own the Goal and Play to Win

"What grades are you getting, David?"

"C's."

"What grades do you think you can get?"

"A's."

*"Are you willing to commit to do whatever it takes
to reach your goal?"*

Most likely, you are reading this book because you want to help your child be successful. But that's not enough: Your child needs to want success himself! For success to happen, the ADHDer must *commit to making an improvement.* But there may be some obstacles in the way of this first step: Your child may find it easier to *externalize,* or blame the outside world (including other people), for the challenges he is facing; or he may recognize that he is responsible but be *ambivalent* (hesitant) about changing his thinking and behavior.

In this chapter, we discuss each of these issues and provide exercises that you can do with your child to identify the obstacles he faces. Then, we will provide a table that can be used to categorize goals so that the most important ones receive your child's best efforts. We will also examine the importance of commitment to the process of change. By the end of this chapter, your child will be ready and eager to own his goal.

WHAT IT MEANS TO OWN THE GOAL

When we say that somebody "owns a goal," we mean that he both acknowledges the need for change within himself *and* he has set aside any excuses or ambivalence he may harbor about changing himself. Together, these create the desire and ability to successfully attain a goal and a willingness to move beyond the inevitable challenges along the way. The importance of "owning the goal" to achieve success holds true for anybody, but especially for ADHDers.

Why Owning the Goal Is Vital to an ADHDer

As discussed in Chapter 1, ADHDers don't have an absolute deficit in attention; what they have is difficulty in maintaining attention in circumstances that are not vitally important to them.

In the context of goal-setting, what this means is that while a child without ADHD may reach for and attain a goal that he doesn't personally care much about (e.g., because he is told to do so by a parent or teacher), a child with ADHD will find doing that far more difficult. If a child with ADHD doesn't personally care about a goal and doesn't see the goal as relevant or interesting, he won't be able to maintain a consistent focus on achieving it.

It is often harder to be successful when pursuing long-term goals compared with short-term goals. The attainment of a long-term goal is the product of a string of successful actions pursued over time—and so maintaining focus over time is even more essential. The long-term goal of overcoming the obstacles of ADHD is like a journey: What you and your child are seeking is not a single win followed by more failures. What you are seeking is repeated success, even in the face of occasional setbacks. That journey can't be taken unless your child comes to see ADHD as a challenge that he is committed to undertaking.

Throughout this book, we emphasize that the challenges of ADHD are similar to challenges that athletes face; that is why training techniques that work for athletes can also be applied to those with ADHD. Two contrasting examples that demonstrate the importance of "owning the goal" in athletics come from the American Olympic team. Bode Miller, an American alpine skiing champion, was not personally dedicated to win at the 2006 Olympics. His coaches and millions of American viewers wanted him to win, but Bode himself was less personally interested in that goal. He explained: "My quality of life is the priority. I wanted to have fun here, to enjoy the Olympic experience, not be holed up in a closet and not ever leave [my] room." The result was that Bode did not ski up to his potential in 2006. In a sport where he was a favorite to medal in at least five events, he won no medals at all. Instead, he decided to "party and socialize at an Olympic level."

In contrast, speed skater Apolo Ohno took home multiple medals in the 2006 Olympics— and then decided to take his game to an even higher level for the 2010 games. In the run-up to 2010 he went on a strict training regimen. Here is what he said about it: "Come these Games, there's no one who's going to be fitter than me. There's just no way. Whether I can put it together on the ice or not and feel good, that's a different story. But I know, from a physical training standpoint, nobody's even close. . . . I've never prepared like this in my life—for anything. I want to leave nothing on the table." The result of Apolo's personal dedication to success was that he won three additional medals in 2010—in a sport in which it is rare to even return to compete in a second Olympics.

The differing attitudes of Bode Miller and Apolo Ohno demonstrate that when someone, whether he is an athlete or not, strives his hardest to reach a goal, he will feel inner validation and pride in his work. But as we discuss in this chapter, a child with ADHD may be reluctant to start working toward his goal. Exercise 2.1 presented on page 28 will help identify obstacles, while serving as a physical demonstration of "putting away excuses."

Extraordinary things can be achieved when an individual owns his goal. For example, Peter Johnson, one of our authors, has done fire-walking exercises. To walk over hot coals, he had to make a firm decision and focus on his goal (the end of the path). When he did so, the coals became less important; they were just something he had to get through to reach his goal. Similarly, if your child owns his goal, excuses that previously prevented him from starting will just become things he has to get through ("hot spots") that won't stop him.

Give your child more responsibility to make decisions as he gets older. If things go wrong, resist the urge to solve the challenges for him. Instead, ask him, "What are you going to do about it?" Let him know that you are there to help him, but that he needs to work on increasing his independence over time. Then enjoy watching him achieve triumphs on his own.

EXERCISE 2.1

REACHING A DECISION AND OWNING THE GOAL: WILL YOU CROSS THE LINE?

During this exercise, you and your child will work together to establish commitment to a goal.

Tools Needed

- A rope
- A partner
- A goal you want to achieve
- A file folder (labeled "Excuse Folder")

Directions

1. Lay the rope horizontally on the floor in front of your child.

2. Say the following to your child: "If you are committed to (name of goal), step in front of this line."

3. If he is unable to step in front of the line, you might try and rephrase the statement and say, "If you are committed to (name a reward or benefit that comes with achieving the goal) step in front of this line."

4. If he is still unable to step in front of the line, ask him to write down on a piece of paper what is stopping him.

5. Repeat the exercise until he has written down every excuse that prevents him from stepping over the line. Put each excuse into the Excuse Folder.

6. Now, open the Excuse Folder and with each excuse, say something along the lines of, "If (read an excuse out loud) were *completely* solved and not a problem, step in front of this line if you are committed to achieve (name of goal)."

7. Repeat (if necessary) until your child is able to step over the line!

The Importance of Long-Term Commitment

The decision to own a goal can be made either deliberately or impulsively. Either way, it is *commitment* that creates the conditions for real transformation over time in the face of obstacles. This is what your child needs to practice to overcome ADHD.

You may need to remind your child (and yourself) that progress is a process—not an instant makeover. It takes time to change old habits and start new ones. During that time, you and your child will learn more about what he wants and what he is willing to work for. During the process he will become stronger. Think of the difference between one person training over many weeks with successively heavier weights to reach his ultimate goal of bench pressing 200 pounds, versus a second person with the same goal who makes one quick effort to press it. They might both bench press the weight—but the first person will come out of it with a strong body, determined to take on new challenges. The second person will have a bad back and a determination to lie in bed until he feels better. If we again think about Apolo Ohno's strict training regimen for the 2010 Olympics, we see that even if he hadn't won any medals that year, he still would have personally benefitted from his perseverance and from building good habits. In these examples, the process of training is more important than the short-term results. Things that are hastily built tend to fall apart.

> **Coaching Corner**
> If your child doesn't "own" goals, he won't commit to reaching them. Without that commitment, sustained improvement is not possible.

Often, a parent decides to help a child with ADHD during a time of crisis—e.g., the child is flunking out of school, or he is on the verge of getting kicked out because of poor behavior. If you are reading this book in "crisis mode," that's okay. But we want your child to not only become successful, but *stay* successful. The mindset for sustained progress must be proactive and not reactive—it cannot be "make a change because of the crisis." This doesn't work because crisis is an emotional time, and emotions are transitory. Many people respond to a crisis by trying to make a lot of changes very quickly. Unfortunately, if "crisis mode" is the only thing supporting the changes, and "crisis mode" disappears, so will the changes.

A decision to change is nothing without a plan in place to make those changes. But following a plan is hard work, especially in the face of setbacks, and setbacks are an inevitable part of any long journey. Without commitment, a plan will evaporate once challenges appear, and a journey will end at the same place it began—the starting line. Kids with ADHD tend to be impulsive and do things without a lot of thought behind them. That trait can be an initial advantage when it comes time to make a change—it can get the ball rolling—but the challenges come when the initial impulse is not sustained. Your child can use his impulsiveness to start working at a goal, but that will only take him so far.

> *Basketball player Stephen Curry, the NBA's Most Valuable Player in 2015, wasn't always a standout. "When it comes to basketball, I was always the smallest kid on my team. I had a terrible, ugly catapult shot from the time I was fourteen because I wasn't strong enough to shoot over my head, and I had to reconstruct that over the summer. . . . I wasn't ranked," he said in his MVP acceptance speech. But despite his challenges, he devoted himself to persevering and making changes until he achieved success: "You have to realize that there is always work to do, and you want to be the hardest-working person in whatever you do. . . . And you have to have a passion about what you do. Basketball was mine, and that's what's carried me to this point."*

We want you to help your child make meaningful changes that *will* be sustained. For a list of small, easy, but helpful steps to take, you and your child can take a look at the "Tips for Parents of ADHD Children" sections on page 75 (tips for home) and page 169 (tips for school). Whether the decision to make changes has been reached in "crisis mode" or deliberately, it is critical to make a commitment to stick with this decision. By putting his intentions into writing, Exercise 2.2 on page 31 will help your child remember the type of commitment he is willing to make to reach his goals.

RECOGNIZING ATTITUDES THAT PREVENT CHANGE

Once your child learns the importance of owning his goal and is prepared to make a commitment, he has started on the path toward success. He has put himself in a position of control and has cleared the way for

EXERCISE 2.2

MAKING A COMMITMENT

On a separate piece of paper, your child should write in his own words the commitment he is willing to make to overcome the obstacles of ADHD and reach for success.

Examples

- I am willing to give up television on weeknights in order to study, to ultimately raise my grades to A's.

- I am willing to spend an hour every Sunday morning organizing and cleaning my room, so I will spend less time later in the week trying to find my homework and school supplies.

action. The next step is to evaluate any excuses your child may have for not reaching his goal.

The two main types of excuses that can prevent your child from achieving his goal are *externalization* (blaming others or outside circumstances for his troubles) and *ambivalence* (holding strong, conflicting feelings toward change, which causes indecision). Once you can identify the reasons behind your child's excuses, you can then find a way to eradicate them. Below, we will explain how externalization and ambivalence are detrimental to an ADHD child's success.

Externalization

Externalization is the blaming of outside forces for your shortcomings. It is a way to avoid accountability for a challenge and prevents you from having to face responsibility for making a change. Externalization happens because it is far easier for most people to blame something else for their difficulties than to accept that they themselves are at fault. People with ADHD are not the only ones who externalize—almost everyone at one time has made an excuse such as, "I wouldn't be having this problem if it weren't for (an outside person, situation, or thing)."

Athletes can fall victim to externalization, as well. For example, members of a losing sports team can acknowledge that they lost the game because they didn't play up to their potential, or they can complain instead about unfair play by the other team or bad referee calls. A player can attribute a missed shot to his own lack of preparation, or he can blame the spectators for being too distracting or the stadium for being too hot.

When an individual blames his difficulties on someone or something else, he is finding a way to escape responsibility for doing anything to change his behaviors. This type of thinking can make a bad situation even worse: If your child does not view himself as personally responsible for results, he will not learn or develop from setbacks. For example, a student may say that he would behave better in class if it weren't for the fact that his teacher "has it in" for him. Even if there is some truth to that, it is more than likely that some elements of the student's behavior contribute to the teacher's approach. Upon reflection, how likely is it that the student's behavior is *not* adding to the conflict? Blaming the teacher colors the student's perception of the teacher's actions, affects the student's responses and the effort he makes in class, and likely will create a vicious downward spiral of disrespect and slacking off. As long as the student externalizes his issue, there is not only no incentive for self-improvement, but there is likely to be momentum going in the opposite direction.

External difficulties exist, of course—the issue is when a child believes there is nothing he can do to overcome these difficulties. Exercise 2.3 below serves to provide you with an idea of what external issues are bothering your child.

EXERCISE 2.3

FRUSTRATION STATION

This exercise will help you identify some of the external stressors in your child's life that fuel negative emotions.

What (or who) are you frustrated with? List your frustrations in ascending order on a separate piece of paper.

1. Kind of annoying

2. Pretty darn frustrating

3. This *really* gets on my nerves

4. The most *horribly aggravating* thing I have to deal with

A child with ADHD might externalize by saying he is kind of annoyed with his mom because she is always asking if his homework is done. He might be pretty frustrated with his teacher for having too many rules that he cannot remember. His little sister may get on his nerves because she is always "doing the right thing" and making him look bad. He may be horribly aggravated by friends who are talking behind his back. In short, naming things that annoy him highlights ways the child might attribute the sources of all his challenges to things on the outside.

But a child cannot force his mom, teacher, sister, or anybody else to change! The only person who he has any real power to change is himself. In the above examples, the ADHDer can acknowledge his frustration with these people, but his larger focus should be placed on what he *can* control. Instead of blaming his mom for always asking about his homework, he can work on ways to set clear boundaries with his mom. Instead of blaming his teacher for having too many rules, he can categorize rules in the classroom and choose to carefully obey the most important ones. Instead of blaming his sister for making him look bad, he can identify his own strengths and then "up" his sister in those specific domains—engaging in healthy familial competition instead of a destructive and angry sibling rivalry. By redirecting frustrations in this way, the child moves not only the source of the frustration, but also its solution, from the "outside" to the "inside." This puts him in charge. This simple shift in perspective can make all the difference between taking charge of a bad situation and improving it, versus using an external excuse to escape responsibility and making a bad situation even worse. The exercise below takes your child's stressors and turns them into situations that he can control.

EXERCISE 2.4

SHIFTING THE LOCUS OF CONTROL

For each of the frustrating items listed in Exercise 2.3, rephrase it as an "I can" statement that can address the situation.

Example

KIND OF ANNOYING: My mother always asks me if I've done my homework. Rephrased as an "I can" statement: **I can** consistently get my home - work done before my mother asks about it. (Then she will eventually stop asking me about it.)

Ambivalence

We have discussed externalization, and how behaviors can become worse if a child with ADHD avoids responsibility for his challenges. But what if your child has acknowledged his responsibility, yet never takes the first step toward change? Your child may say that he wants to change, but his actions (or lack of actions) may say something else. This demonstrates that he may be *ambivalent*. The word ambivalent is derived from two roots: "ambi-," meaning "both," and "-valent," meaning "strong." A child who is ambivalent harbors strong conflicting feelings within himself that prevent action—part of your child might agree that making changes is a good idea, while the other part of him fights equally strongly against those changes.

Making a change first involves coming to a decision. The word decision also has two roots: "de-" means "to go away from," and "-cision" means "to cut." A "de-cision" therefore means "to cut away from"—that is, to cut something out so that you can take your life in a new direction. To use a sports analogy, in baseball a runner has to take his foot off of first base if he ever wants to get to second base. Runners usually "lead off" of first base—they move a few strides off the base, but return to the base many times before finally making a run to second. In the same way, it may take a whole lifetime and many false starts before some people reach "the moment of decision." Actions from then on define a new course. An ambivalent base runner will never get to second base, and will lose the opportunity to score. Likewise, if your child is ambivalent and never decides to commit to a goal, he will remain where he currently is in life.

Ambivalence is a common feeling and can arise for many reasons. Most people naturally resist change because it is risky; it involves the unknown. Most people prefer "the devil they know to the devil they don't." As with any fear, the fear of the unknown may have a trivial or completely irrational basis, and yet it still can have a very forceful impact on behavior.

> **Coaching Corner**
>
> *If your child can't commit to a goal because of emotional issues such as blaming others or having mixed feelings about it, go back to square one and talk to your child about what's going on.*

For example, at some inner level your child may understand that one result of going from a B student to an A student may be jettisoning old friends and finding some new ones. As the parent, that may not seem like such a big deal to you (it may even seem like a good thing to you!), but it might seem huge to your child. Even if he wants to do better in school and doesn't completely like all of his current friends, some part of him will still be afraid of a change that can mean giving friends up. That part of him will resist this change, consciously or unconsciously.

Besides being a nearly universal fear, change also requires work, and nobody really likes to go through the hard work of developing new habits and skills if he can avoid it. It is much easier to keep doing what he has always done. So even if your child is not afraid of change and part of him really wants to change, another part of him might resist putting in the work necessary to achieve it.

If proper decision-making skills are not learned, your child may fall into the trap of "wait and see." That is, he may just mentally drift along, waiting to see what happens instead of controlling the outcome himself. This thinking is a setup for failure because it prevents action. If your child is of a "wait and see" mindset, excuses become roadblocks. Without a plan to reach the end goal, ambivalence will reinforce this "do nothing" attitude and the goal will not be reached. Any challenge that comes up will be used as an excuse for not making changes.

As a parent, you have to find a way to decrease your child's ambivalence toward change, whether the ambivalence arises from oppositional reasons, from fear, or from a lack of motivation. Exercise 2.5 on page 36 helps your child understand how ambivalence prevents him from reaching his goals.

THE GAME MATRIX

We have spent some time discussing the obstacles and attitudes that can prevent your child from striving for his goal. Another important consideration to take into goal-setting is to evaluate which situations empower your child's best efforts—we call this "playing to win."

We've borrowed the concept of "playing to win" from athletic philosophy. Most children would never go out for a competitive soccer match intending to lose the game. They understand what it means to put out their best effort on the field to achieve the goal of winning. Playing to win can be applied to any situation in which it is important for your child to reach a certain goal. The following game matrix concept lays out

---

EXERCISE 2.5

LEARNING TO IDENTIFY AMBIVALENCE
AND HOW IT SABOTAGES DECISION-MAKING

On another piece of paper, have your child list three decisions that may not have come to fruition because of ambivalence, and what the ambivalence was about. By identifying sources of ambivalence, you and your child can then discuss what steps need to be taken to move forward instead of staying in the same place.

Examples

- Your son said he wanted to study more to improve his grades, but it conflicted with his equally strong desire to just hang out with his neighborhood friends in the evening. He kept putting off the decision to start studying and hung out with his friends instead, and as a result, his test scores stayed the same.

- Your daughter said she would be more punctual. She really did want to get to school on time, but she also wanted to stay up late texting and to spend time doing her hair every morning. Since she was reluctant to go to bed or wake up earlier, she still found herself late to school every day.

---

three other levels of effort your child can give in any situation—although these may not lead to the desired result compared with when your child plays to win. Knowing what mindset your child is working from can help you determine how best to approach him with setting a goal. Understanding the game matrix will help your child achieve a winning performance when it's important. Better yet, the winning performance will come from a desire to be at his personal best!

What Is the Game Matrix?

Fariborz Azhakh, founder of Team Karate Centers and a respected teacher of the martial arts, devised the concept of the game matrix. It is a way to measure an individual's level of engagement, as well as the level of adversity or hardship he is willing to endure to win his "game." We have slightly modified his matrix to more closely relate to ADHD and have reproduced it below. The game matrix states that any situation can be defined as a game, and there are four choices your child will always have:

*To gain a **positive** outcome*	*To avoid a **negative** outcome*
Play to win	Play not to lose
Play only for fun	Choose not to play

Playing to win means to have an internal locus of control that guides performance. It's the place where standout performances and personal bests come from; it is a focus on being the very best self possible. Your child should play to win when he is faced with what's important now, whether it is better organizational skills, meeting all deadlines, or getting better grades. This game matrix serves to remind him that there will be different outcomes depending on how he approaches the "game."

A person who plays to win will commit more fully than somebody who chooses to "play not to lose." Playing not to lose signifies that a person is putting in the minimal amount of effort required to do an okay job. He is not striving for excellence; he is only avoiding failure.
Think of the difference between someone who is aiming for A's versus someone who aims only to avoid getting F's.

The next option, "play only for fun," may result in your child having a good time trying to achieve his goal—but he is focusing only on having fun, and not on putting forth his best efforts. For example, maybe your child's goal is to improve his social skills by joining an after-school art club. However, he has too much fun painting by himself and ends up not talking to the other students in the club. He will have a positive outcome because he will have a positive experience, but he may not have made a lot of progress toward achieving the original goal.

The last option is "choose not to play," which is exactly what it sounds like. If your child chooses not to play, he is backing out of his commitment to a goal. Choosing not to play is not an ideal choice unless the goal is impossible to achieve or reaching the goal is no longer personally relevant or important to your child. A negative outcome is avoided by choosing not to play, but a positive outcome is also avoided.

A person with ADHD who plays to win is going to have more success than one who plays not to lose, plays just for fun, or chooses not to play. Think back to the examples of Bode Miller and Apolo Ohno earlier in this chapter: Miller played for fun, while Ohno played to win. Both athletes achieved what they wanted to achieve, but only Ohno walked away with pride in his effort and work ethic, respect from his audience and fans, and awards for his performance. Your child must choose to focus if he is going to play to win, and in order to make that choice, he has to be mentally, physically, and spiritually committed to that goal. (More about mental, physical, and spiritual commitment is discussed in Chapter 5.)

Think of two great tennis players battling it out on the court. The one who plays to win will work harder and bring all his talents together in order to win—and he will have his greatest performance. He would not have as great a performance if he chose to "play not to lose"—this implies that he is engaging in the game with only as much effort as is required to not be outdone by his competitor. In any situation where your child plays to win, that is where you will see him at his best.

Should Your Child Always Play to Win?

We are not saying that your child should play to win all the time. Not all games are for winning; there are times when he *should* just play for fun! Nobody should (or could) force themselves to go "all out" in everything that they do—it's not practical or possible. The other boxes in the game matrix are all valid choices at times. For example, there may be times when your child is competitive in his sport, playing to win the game, and other times when it's fantastic to just kick the ball around with his friends at recess.

There also will be times when your child may decide not to participate at all. It may be appropriate for your child to consciously choose not to take the harder class or to choose not to go after the extra credit. There are times when it's okay for your child to decide that he doesn't want to pursue a place on a competitive team. These are all fine, so long as in each case your child's true goals and everything he has been working for is represented and taken into account. But if it is a situation where being fully successful and achieving the highest level in that particular activity matters to your child, then "choosing not to play" is not the right choice—that is when he should play to win.

Likewise, "playing not to lose" is okay in some situations but not in others. We mentioned the example of a tennis player—if he knows he will need to conserve energy and stamina for the next match in the tournament against an even stronger player, perhaps all he *should* do is play well enough not to lose. Similarly, some children may decide to go after all A's. That may not be realistic for all students, and if they have other major goals outside of school, maybe they only want to make the GPA needed to be able to stay on the varsity sports team, for example. Sometimes, even the most academically talented kid may need to just get a particular assignment done quickly and adequately (rather than do his best job) in order to get enough sleep at night, so he can perform well on tomorrow's important exam. It all depends on your child's goals and where an activity fits into his "big picture." Playing not to lose can be a justifiable choice, but as with choosing not to play, it is not a choice that will maximize success for a significant goal.

Coaching Corner

Having a successful, fulfilling, healthy, and happy life is about balance. Use the game matrix to help you and your child think strategically about how a particular short-term activity or goal fits into achieving long-term goals and into a well-balanced life. Is this a place where he should commit to "playing to win," or is it more appropriate in this particular instance to "play not to lose," "play just for fun," or even to "choose not to play"?

You need to help your child think consciously and carefully about which box of the game matrix he needs to be in for any particular situation. Use the language given in the game matrix to talk about how he views his goals. For goals that are important for him to achieve, he must play to win, and he must take the decision seriously. If your child says he is playing to win but doesn't put in his best effort, he may become overconfident if he does manage to win. This could lead to failure later on when he faces a more difficult opponent or situation. If he doesn't give his best effort and loses, on the other hand, he may become discouraged. In short, playing to win is not something one can pretend to do. It requires the highest level of commitment, focus, and effort, but the outcome carries the highest benefit compared with the other options in the game matrix.

SUMMARY

In this chapter, you learned how to help your child set and "own" a goal. The first steps are to eliminate externalization, ambivalence, and excuses; make a firm decision that it's time for internal change; and fully commit to that decision and reach for success. We also discussed the situations that will require your child's best efforts—playing to win—and the ones where just having fun and relaxing are suitable, and how to sort out which situations are which.

The next chapter will discuss how your child can establish the goals for which he will "play to win." Any major goal your child sets for himself should follow the S.M.A.R.T. criteria—specific, measurable, attainable, realistic, and time-defined. S.M.A.R.T. goals are more likely to be achieved, which helps increase your child's self-confidence and diminish the issues of externalization and ambivalence that we have identified in this chapter.

3.

Setting S.M.A.R.T. Goals

Erica, an almost-fourteen-year-old girl about to start high school, was brought into the doctor's office by her mom, who wanted her to start taking medication because of chronic problems with not turning in her homework. After some discussion, it was revealed that Erica had not really applied herself to school since kindergarten, although she was "bright and enthusiastic" in preschool. She also did not give much effort in her sport (volleyball) or in any other aspect of her life. She was a smart kid who did not feel smart. However, after working on setting specific goals, she started to take on more challenges and put in more effort. In high school, she was much better at turning in her homework.

Having completed the last chapter, your child has set aside external excuses and ambivalence, owned the goal, and made a commitment to play to win against any obstacles ADHD throws her way. In the following sections, we will discuss how to take this dedication and apply it to the goals that are most significant for overcoming ADHD. In order to do this, your child needs to learn the S.M.A.R.T. (Specific, Measurable, Attainable, Realistic, Time-Defined) strategy for setting goals.

Intelligent goal setting is the key to breaking a negative cycle of repeated failures and to entering a positive cycle of repeated success. Whether you are an athlete or an ADHDer, goal setting and achievement require planning, hard work, and persistence. Goal setting is an important part of the athletic mindset. Without goals, athletes do not have anything to work toward; having a goal causes them to work harder.

There is good evidence that *specific* goals are better than vague goals (e.g., "just do your best"). Athletes find that setting specific goals and targets improves their training and leads to success.

In this chapter, you and your child will create goals that fit the S.M.A.R.T. criteria. But before we talk about *how* to set S.M.A.R.T. goals, we will talk about *why* S.M.A.R.T. goals are important: Repeatedly obtaining manageable goals leads to greater achievement, higher self-esteem, and happiness over time (what we call the Positive Cycle of Success). If you can teach your child to set goals and follow through with them like an athlete does, your child will be motivated to keep on achieving.

THE GOAL-SETTING CYCLES

There are two cycles that can affect your child's goal-setting patterns: the Positive Cycle of Success and the Negative Cycle of Failure. The idea behind these two cycles stems from the fact that behaviors and thought patterns that are rewarded are automatically reinforced and become more likely to happen on a regular basis. Think of the circuits in your child's brain as muscles in her body: If they are trained through exercise, they become stronger. This is what happens in the Positive Cycle of Success. Conversely, behaviors and thought patterns that are not trained or used very much—the brain circuits that are not rewarded or that are punished, including by neglect or criticism—are negatively reinforced and become weaker (less likely to happen). This is demonstrated in the Negative Cycle of Failure.

The Positive Cycle of Success

The Positive Cycle of Success is about accomplishing smaller goals before tackling big ones. Satisfaction from accomplishing a goal, even a small goal, creates a positive feedback loop; that is, it provides you with encouragement to repeat that success. Once a person has experienced success and the satisfaction that comes with it, she is more likely to set additional goals and to want to stick with them. This is because she knows that a reward (internal satisfaction) will come when success is achieved again. Using an example from sports, an athlete is more likely to train hard if she knows from previous experience that the training leads to improving her skills and winning games. We call this feedback loop the Positive Cycle of Success (see Figure 3.1).

Figure 3.1. The Positive Cycle of Success.

Edwin Locke, a psychologist who researched goal setting for over thirty years, published a paper summarizing much of his work. One of Locke's findings was that "Goal setting is most effective when there is feedback showing progress in relation to the goal. . . . when provided with feedback on their own performance or that of others, people often spontaneously set goals to improve over their previous best. . . . simply as a way of challenging themselves." Meanwhile, those who receive negative feedback (and lose confidence) "tend to lower their goals, decrease their efforts, and lessen the intensity and effectiveness of their strategy search." These findings support the theories of the Positive Cycle of Success and the Negative Cycle of Failure. Whether someone is an athlete or an ADHDer (or both!), she will find motivation upon successful achievement of her goals and will strive to outperform herself as the goals become more challenging.

The Negative Cycle of Failure

What if your ADHD child does not currently set goals, or makes plans that frequently fall through? This may be an issue of motivation. The root of "to motivate" is "to move." Many ADHDers have a hard time *moving* toward their goals, and this lack of motivation can cause a negative feedback loop.

There are many ways in which the common symptoms of ADHD can interfere with the Positive Cycle of Success we described above. Disorganization can make your child lose sight of a goal she was hoping to achieve. Other times, procrastination is an obstacle. Your child might procrastinate if she does not really own the goal (for example, her teacher's goal is for her to complete homework—okay, she knows she has to do it, but she puts it off to work on her personal goal of writing a really cool iPhone app). Sometimes ADHDers are not motivated because of self-esteem issues: If your child doesn't believe in her ability to achieve something, she won't even try.

Another hurdle some ADHDers face when making goals is their impulsivity. You may have noticed, for example, that your ADHD child is often quick to set a goal *at first,* but loses her motivation and abandons the goal just as quickly when she fails to achieve it right away. Your child may be enticed by tales of "instant success" in the media—stories of people who become successful through luck, or by being seen with the right people, wearing the right clothes, or driving the right car—which contradict the notion that hard work is necessary for success. ADHDers have a tendency to be more impulsive than average, so messages of "instant" roads to success are especially appealing to them. People who are naturally more cautious and deliberative are more immune to these messages because they tend to assume the opposite—that achieving any goal will require careful planning and hard work.

And, of course, that is truly the case: Closer examination of the majority of apparent overnight success stories shows that these achievements were actually years in the making. "You hit home runs not by

> ### *Coaching Corner*
> *Upon closer inspection, most "overnight success stories" turn out to be the result of years of preparation and training. Repeated turns of the Positive Cycle of Success set your child up for ultimate success over time!*

chance but by preparation," said New York Yankee Roger Maris, who knew a lot about hitting home runs—with sixty-one home runs in 1961, he broke Babe Ruth's thirty-four-year-old single season record. In other words, if you are not prepared to swing that bat many, many times in practice, expect to strike out during the game.

The challenges of ADHD can short-circuit the Positive Cycle of Success. If that has happened to your child, she may stop trying, stop setting goals, and stop succeeding. We call this contrasting feedback loop the Negative Cycle of Failure (see Figure 3.2). A child caught in this cycle will have low motivation and poor self-esteem.

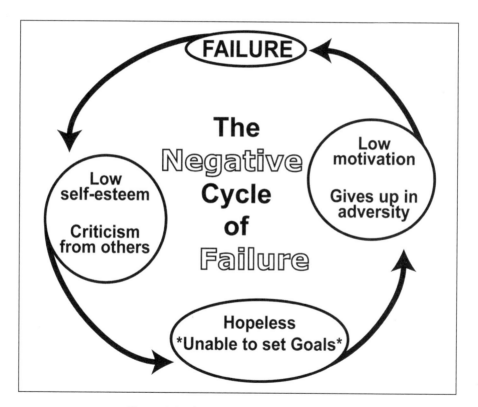

Figure 3.2. The Negative Cycle of Failure.

If your child has repeatedly engaged in the Negative Cycle of Failure, her brain circuitry has become reinforced to drive this negativity. Conversely, brain circuitry that could drive the Positive Cycle of Success in your child has atrophied from disuse and lack of conditioning.

Feeding platitudes or offering general advice, such as "put a smile on your face," "you could succeed if only you tried harder," or "you can do it, you're so smart" to a child in this situation doesn't work. The words may be true, but they won't be effective if the child doesn't have the success "muscles" (i.e., the proper brain circuitry) to believe them.

To train your child's brain circuitry to work with the Positive Cycle of Success, let's examine the key point of overlap between the Positive Cycle of Success and the Negative Cycle of Failure. As noted by the asterisks in Figure 3.3, *goals* are integral parts of both cycles. What this means is that by working on goal-setting, your child can learn to jump from the Negative Cycle of Failure to the Positive Cycle of Success.

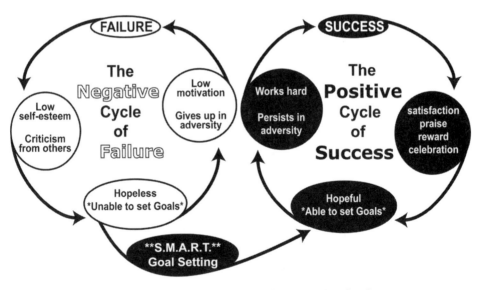

Figure 3.3. Jumping From the Negative Cycle of Failure to the Positive Cycle of Success.

S.M.A.R.T. goal setting involves taking your child's general ideas and turning them into goals that are specific, measurable, attainable, realistic, and time-defined. It is much easier for an ADHDer to work on a small but concrete goal than to only have a vague goal in mind without any plans on how to achieve it. The next sections in this chapter will help you and your child think of and narrow down some goals for her to work on.

WHAT ARE YOUR CHILD'S GOALS?

As we have stated, it is important for children with ADHD to have clear, achievable goals. Often, coming up with goals is *not* the hard part. A lot of children with ADHD are great at coming up with ideas for goals! After all, ideas come to them more quickly and creatively than for many people without ADHD. However, it's crucial to generate not just ideas, but also comprehensible and appropriate goals. Picking out *one* goal to focus on, and keeping that one goal a consistent priority over time, is critical. This can be a challenge; ADHDers often have many goals that all seem equally important. Remember the example of the dog and the cat from Chapter 1? The dog without ADHD could easily prioritize "cat" over other thoughts (Figure 1.1), but the dog with ADHD gave the "cat" thought equal importance to "chase my tail," "smell grass," and all other thoughts (Figure 1.3). Thus, the dog without ADHD could chase the cat without distraction, whereas the dog with ADHD ran from thought to thought and ended up just lying in the grass, getting nothing done at all.

> ### Coaching Corner
>
> *Identifying goals is a crucial way to "jump" from the Negative Cycle of Failure to the Positive Cycle of Success. But it is important that the goals be S.M.A.R.T.: In the following sections, we explain how your child can set a S.M.A.R.T. goal.*

Action is a root in the word "distraction." When your child is distracted, she moves away from her intended action. The key to all goal-setting is the ability to take action without distraction. As Les Brown, motivational speaker, said: "You don't have to be great to get started, but you have to get started to be great." How does your child start? How does she take her ideas and make them work?

Exercise 3.1 on page 48 will get your child thinking about her many ideas for goals.

Once your child has a list of goals, how does she narrow them down? Some are going to be better to pursue than others, for a variety of reasons—more practical, more achievable, more timely, and maybe even less expensive! We will next go into detail about the S.M.A.R.T. strategy for helping your child refine her goals.

EXERCISE 3.1

GOALS TO GO FOR

On a separate piece of paper or on her computer, ask your child to write down some ideas about what she'd like to accomplish. They can be anything. She should write down what she'd like to do at work or at school. She can write about personal development goals or relationship goals. She can write about becoming more organized or more reliable. She can write about where she wants to be physically (for example, stronger or faster). She should write her ideas down even if they seem completely silly or crazy. The important thing is for her to keep her pen moving (or her fingers typing). When your child is done, she should have at least a dozen different goals written down.

THE S.M.A.R.T. STRATEGY FOR SETTING GOALS

The S.M.A.R.T. strategy was first developed in 1981 by Dr. George T. Doran, and has since been reproduced and revised in a number of books and articles about goal setting.

This concept states that to be successful, your child's goals must be:

S   Specific

M   Measurable

A   Attainable

R   Realistic

T   Time-Defined

Below, we will go through each attribute and explain why it is important. At the end of this section, we will help you and your child apply these principles to the goals she wants to set.

Specific Goal Setting

To work well, a goal must be *specific*. For example, on New Year's Day, you might resolve to "lose weight." If that's your goal, and you lose one pound, you have met your goal—however, losing a single pound is not going to make a meaningful difference in your life. If you want to lose ten or twenty pounds, you must make the specific number a part of your goal. That way, you will keep working on your goal (assuming you are motivated) until you reach that number. Then you have made a meaningful change in your life—success!

A good coach knows this. She doesn't just say to her team: "Win!" She gives a precise goal—for example, "win forty games so we can get to the playoffs," and then she asks for specific contributions from each player. The coach might ask an offensive lineman to learn and perfectly execute a specific, designated play in order to win the game, instead of just telling the lineman to "make a good play."

Sure, coaches also say things like "try your best"—but the athlete is expected not just to try, but to achieve a certain, measurable goal or a set of goals. *Trying* isn't the same thing as *accomplishing*. If you try over and over again without accomplishing a task, you will give up and stop trying, thereby enforcing the Negative Cycle of Failure. On the other hand, if trying is accompanied by succeeding at the task, then you will keep trying for other goals.

Arnold Glasow, a twentieth-century writer, said, "In life, as in football, you won't go far unless you know where the goalposts are." To succeed, ADHDers must have specific goalposts to work toward. If you are reading this, you are interested in helping your child make some positive differences. But it is not enough to just set a vague goal of "better grades" or "a more organized room" for exactly the same reason that it is not effective in the athletic arena to set vague goals like "run faster" or "score more points." *Specific* goals are what your child needs to carry her to what she *really* wants to achieve.

The direction you want your child to move toward is the target, and her specific goal is the bulls-eye. She needs to know what she is aiming for so that she can repeatedly hit the bulls-eye!

Measurable Goal Setting

Effective goals are *measurable*. When your child measures progress that is made in a task or a skill, she sets up an opportunity for improvement. In other words, once she measures where she is and compares it to where she wants to be, she will know when she is halfway to her goal, 90 percent to her goal, and so on. Whether it is raising her GPA from a 3.0 to a 3.5, having ten less missing assignments, or going a month without significant procrastination, there should be an objective and concrete yardstick by which to measure how far away your child is from reaching her goals.

Once your child has the ability to measure where she is in relation to her goal, she can then use that measurement to break down her larger goal into smaller, more specific measurable goals. For example, if her goal is to stop procrastinating and doing things at the last minute, and she has a five-page paper due at the end of the week, she can break it down into writing one page a day. This makes writing and completing the paper more manageable.

Measuring how your child is doing along the way helps her understand how she is moving overall toward reaching her goal. This allows her to make corrections that improve her methods as she goes along.

Jason's parents were dismayed at the grades their son (age 14) was getting—when they found out about them. He had hidden them because a lot of them were really bad! Although he was smart, he only seemed to do well in classes where he liked his teachers. If he didn't like his teacher (and evidently he didn't like most of them), he didn't make an effort—and he blamed the teachers for his poor grades. Going into high school, Jason acknowledged that his grades needed to come up. He set a goal of B's in every class. As part of achieving his goal, he "checked in" with his parents every two weeks to see where his grades were at the time. By staying on top of his grades before he got too far behind, he surprised even himself by how well he did.

The mind absorbs information that is broken down into pieces better than it can assimilate larger chunks. It is also much easier to stay focused on a series of short-term goals and accomplish them one by one than it is to remain focused for a long time on a larger goal that has no smaller steps. Your child can celebrate every small goal reached and feel like she has accomplished something!

Consider again the Positive Cycle of Success versus the Negative Cycle of Failure. A big benefit of breaking up a larger long-term goal into a series of smaller short-term goals is that as each incremental goal is reached, your child gets to experience the cycle of success and all the positive reinforcement and forward momentum that it generates.

So instead of your child trying this:

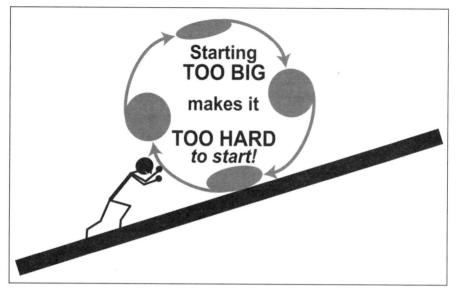

Figure 3.4. Setting an Unachievable Goal.

She should try this:

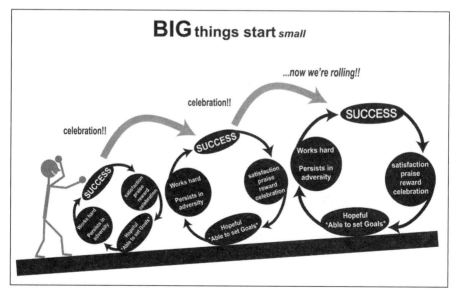

Figure 3.5. Setting an Achievable Series of Goals.

It is easier to push the "small wheels," or the smaller goals, forward a few times and to use each Positive Cycle of Success to feed the next cycle (Figure 3.5) than it is to push the "big" wheel forward once without intermediate positive feedback (Figure 3.4).

It's similar to bike riding. To start a bike from a standstill, you would use the low gear. This is the easiest gear to push; it provides power, but only moves you forward a short distance each time it turns. You use this gear to build up momentum—then you can shift into higher gears that accelerate you more and more quickly. Everyone who rides a multi-speed bike learns quickly to never start in high gear—that doesn't work because you can't get the forward process to start.

Once the forward process gets going, it is critically important to complete each achievement (i.e., to push the wheel all the way around) by *celebrating* the success! Only then should your child pick the next short-term goal. As she builds up her confidence and ability to reach goals (building up momentum with each turn of the wheel), she can then "shift" into higher gears by setting successively loftier, harder-to-reach, long-term goals. Professional athletes realize the importance of this process—they don't begin training one year and expect to be in the Olympics the next. They often have multi-year plans, each with their own measurable goals. These smaller plans build strength, skills, and experience over time as the athletes work toward their overall goals.

> ### Coaching Corner
> *As with shifting from "low" to "high" gear in a vehicle, it is important to build momentum by setting small goals early and building up to bigger goals over time. Big or small, each goal must be measurable so that progress toward the goal can be tracked, and achievement of the goal celebrated!*

Eventually, your child will be able to take on bigger and bigger goals and challenges without the need for so much intermediate short-term reinforcement. As the brainpower behind the Positive Cycle of Success gets used more and more, it will become stronger, while the brainpower that drives the Negative Cycle of Failure will fade from disuse. On the other hand, if your child sets large goals too early (starting in "high gear"), it's a setup to fail, which will only reinforce the Negative Cycle of Failure.

Everyone has setbacks, and the capacity to engage both the Positive and Negative Cycles exists in everyone. At times, a child who has been making good progress may slip back into her old habits, and the Negative Cycle will kick in again. If that happens, it is important for your child not to get frustrated or give up, but to reset and begin again by re-engaging that Positive Cycle; it may even be necessary to start in a "lower gear" again and rebuild. This is similar to a bike rider that has stopped after previously moving in high gear. To get going again, she needs to downshift and start moving again in low gear to rebuild momentum. Your child can stay on the Positive Cycle of Success by thinking in advance about what she will do to start moving again if she encounters challenges.

A time like this (when the bicycle has come to a standstill) is when your child will benefit the most by having an ADHD coach—someone outside of herself who can perceive what is happening and push her back on track. (Picking an ADHD coach is discussed further in Chapter 9.)

Attainable and Realistic Goal Setting

For goal-setting to work, the chosen goal must be *attainable* and *realistic*. Attainable means that the goal is reachable and achievable. To return to the weight loss example, losing fifty pounds overnight is a goal, but it is an impossible goal that nobody could achieve (except with a chainsaw, setting up the next goal of not bleeding to death). You have to "inspect what you expect." Are your child's goals improbable "pie in the sky" objectives?

"Realistic" means that your child needs to have a reasonable plan, one that works within the context of her life, to reach her goal. That is, the goal must not only be attainable, it must also be sustainable. Again, using the weight loss example, I could set a goal to lose forty pounds, and this might be attainable over time through a healthy diet and exercise regimen. However, if instead I set a goal to lose this weight through a strict water-and-avocado diet, I probably will only last a day or two. The odds of my sustaining this diet until I reach my goal are slim.

> ### Coaching Corner
> Just like in sports, if your child's goals are unrealistic or if the goals are not meaningful to her, she will miss her target.

Similarly, your child may set a goal to keep everything on her desk in alphabetical order and cross-filed by date—but if she tries to do this while she is also focusing on homework, then that is not a realistic (sustainable) goal. "I'm never going to have a messy desk again" is also not a realistic goal for most people. In contrast, a goal of "Once a week I will sort through my desk and throw away all the junk I no longer need" might be much more attainable *and* realistic.

Time-Defined Goal Setting

Your child's goals must be *time-defined*. Your child has chosen a goal that is specific, measurable, attainable, and realistic—but how can she keep a consistent focus on completing the goal? The motivational speaker Brian Tracy noted, "Goals in writing are dreams with deadlines." To make progress in achieving goals, it's important to set a due date for them—or else they are likely to remain dreams forever. A due date makes the goal more urgent, and when something is urgent, you pay more attention to getting it done. Your child must commit not only to the goal itself, but also to the due date for *when* she wants to achieve it.

Most athletes' goals are time-defined: The championship game, the Olympics, and other important matches all have unchangeable dates. If an athlete is told to play the game "sometime" or "whenever you're ready," she would not train with as much urgency or purpose. Likewise, you and your child need to consciously put a "time stamp" on her goals to maintain a level of intensity.

Now that we've explained what S.M.A.R.T. goals are, you and your child should go through the list of ideas from Exercise 3.1. In Exercise 3.2, have your child select and/or rewrite goals from this list as S.M.A.R.T. goals. Refer back to the paragraphs above as needed to remind yourself and your child of what makes a goal S.M.A.R.T.

EXERCISE 3.2

S.M.A.R.T. GOALS TO GO FOR

On a separate piece of paper, have your child select and/or rewrite goals from Exercise 3.1 on page 48 as S.M.A.R.T. goals.

Now, ask your child to compile all the ideas from Exercise 3.2 into different lists: long-term goals and short-term goals. More specifically, for each goal, your child should write down the length of time she thinks it should take to be achieved. In Exercise 3.3, she will sort them into categories such as "one to three months," "three months to a year," or "a year or more."

EXERCISE 3.3

A TIMELY MANNER

On another piece of paper, have your child write down the following categories, leaving some space underneath each heading:

1. Goals that can be completed in one to three months:

2. Goals that can be completed in three months to a year:

3. Goals that can be completed in longer than a year:

Then tell her to organize the S.M.A.R.T. goals from Exercise 3.2 into these categories based on estimated time to completion.

Once your child has finished assigning deadlines to her goals, she is ready to go on to the next chapter about achieving each of her goals using the "Super-S.T.A.R." method. As part of that, she will temporarily put everything aside except the "one to three months" list of goals. But she should keep the whole list—this section has not been wasted! She's going to come back to the full list in the future.

SUMMARY

We discussed the importance of having your child set the right goals—goals that are specific, measurable, attainable, realistic, and time-defined. Using this S.M.A.R.T. strategy is key to your child's success because it makes it easier for her to achieve her goals; whenever she achieves a goal, that contributes to the Positive Cycle of Success. If your child is on the Negative Cycle of Failure, teaching her how to set appropriate goals can help shift her back onto the Positive Cycle. Each of these cycles is self-reinforcing and responds to training.

In the next chapter, we will take your child's short-term goals and use the Super-S.T.A.R. method as a way to practice accomplishing her goals and making them a reality.

4.

Super-S.T.A.R.
Turning Goals Into Reality

An expert was speaking to a group of business students and, to drive home a point, he used an illustration those students never forgot.

As this man stood in front of the group, he said, "Okay, time for a quiz," and pulled out a one-gallon, wide-mouthed jar and set it on a table in front of him. Then he produced about a dozen fist-sized rocks and carefully placed them, one at a time, into the jar.

When the jar was filled to the top and no more rocks would fit inside, he asked, "Is this jar full?" Everyone in the class said, "Yes." Then he said, "Really?" He reached under the table and pulled out a bucket of gravel. Then he dumped some gravel in and shook the jar, causing pieces of gravel to work themselves down into the spaces between the big rocks.

He smiled and asked the group once more, "Is the jar full?" By this time the class was onto him. "Probably not," one of them answered. "Good!" he replied. And he reached under the table and brought out a bucket of sand. He started dumping the sand in and it went into all the spaces left between the rocks and the gravel. Once more he asked the question, "Is this jar full?"

"No!" the class shouted. Once again he said, "Good!" Then he grabbed a pitcher of water and began to pour it in until the jar was filled to the brim. Then he looked up at the class and asked, "What is the point of this illustration?"

One eager beaver raised his hand and said, "The point is, no matter how full your schedule is, if you try really hard, you can always fit some more things into it!"

"No," the speaker replied, "that's not the point. The truth this illustration teaches us is: If you don't put the big rocks in first, you'll never get them in at all."

In the previous chapter, your child learned to "get S.M.A.R.T."—to create Specific, Measurable, Attainable, Realistic, and Time-Defined goals. In this chapter, we will discuss how to turn S.M.A.R.T. goals into reality. It is not enough for your child to have goals if he never reaches them. Despite what we may like to believe, reaching goals is not a matter of luck; it's a matter of deliberately using a process to achieve objectives. Successful people have such a process incorporated into their skill set and use it routinely.

The name of the process we will teach your child in this book is "Super-S.T.A.R." "Super" stands for your child's "big rock"—the most important goal out of all of his S.M.A.R.T. goals. "S.T.A.R." stands for Slice the goal, Take Action, and Review the process. We will take a closer look at this method below.

THE SUPER GOAL

What is your child's "super" goal? "Super" signifies your child's most important goal. It would, of course, be great if your child accomplished everything on his list of S.M.A.R.T. goals from the last chapter. But it is also important to keep in mind the ADHD dog from Chapter 1 who had so many ideas in his head that he could not prioritize "chase the cat" (Figure 1.3). This dog spent a few minutes on each of his goals, but did not complete any of them because he did not think about which one was the most important. When one goal is not prioritized above the others, your child will be more likely to get distracted and not accomplish any of the goals. This is why it is essential to identify his most important goal. What does he value above all else? Exercise 4.1 on page 59 will help your child identify which goal from the previous chapter's one-to-three-month goal list should be his "super" goal.

Selecting a "super" goal and making it stand out from his other goals will naturally increase your child's focus and make him more likely to achieve it. He might enjoy thinking about and pursuing what he values most. Once your child has selected his "super" goal, it will be time to begin learning a process to achieve it. We abbreviate the process here as S.T.A.R.

EXERCISE 4.1

WHICH IS YOUR "SUPER" GOAL?

In Part One of this exercise, ask your child to think about three of his one-to-three-month S.M.A.R.T. goals from the previous chapter. How is he going to decide which one is the most important one? Have him write down the goals again on a blank piece of paper.

In Part Two of this exercise, your child should consider the "big rocks of life" story at the beginning of this chapter. Tell him to think carefully about his answers in Part One and identify which of them is the "big rock" goal (the goal that he should put in the "jar of his life" first).

Part One

1. First one-to-three-month goal

   (a) Why is this goal important to you?

   (b) How would your life be different if you achieved this goal?

   (c) Would you *love* to achieve this goal? Or is it just a little important to you?

2. Second one-to-three-month goal

   (a) Why is this goal important to you?

   (b) How would your life be different if you achieved this goal?

   (c) Would you *love* to achieve this goal? Or is it just a little important to you?

3. Third one-to-three-month goal

   (a) Why is this goal important to you?

   (b) How would your life be different if you achieved this goal?

   (c) Would you *love* to achieve this goal? Or is it just a little important to you?

Part Two

Underneath the answers to Part One of this exercise, write down what you have decided your first "super" goal will be.

SLICE THE GOAL

Your child has chosen his most important short-term S.M.A.R.T. goal. One to three months may seem like a short time frame, but it is both enough time to achieve a meaningful result and also enough time to lose sight of a goal and get derailed. To keep from getting lost, your child must slice his goal down into smaller, achievable goals based on an even shorter time scale. Luckily, he has created a S.M.A.R.T. goal, and one component of S.M.A.R.T. goals is that they are measurable. Therefore, it should be easy to split this goal up into smaller pieces.

For many people with ADHD, it is challenging to break down a large goal (I want to lose fifteen pounds) into smaller goals (I want to lose three pounds per month for five months). This is because ADHDers tend to be "big picture" people. The ultimate result may be captivating, but the details of how to achieve it are boring for them. Alternatively, some ADHDers over-focus on the details, making it hard to finish a project on time. In general, a sense of time and how long things take to achieve is a frequent weak point in those with ADHD—that is precisely why these exercises are so important!

What if your child's goals are too low? For example, what if your child aims for grades that you think are lower than what he is *capable* of achieving? (Note: This is different from grades lower

> **Coaching Corner**
> *The longest journey starts with a single step. To start down the road to success after a history of frustration, slice the most important S.M.A.R.T. goal into the smallest achievable steps. Then take (and celebrate!) each step—one at a time.*

than what you *want* him to achieve.) One possible reason for setting goals too low could be an inability to see past where he is now. If he is in a "down" place, it may be hard for him to visualize himself as successful. If this is the case, it may be important to return with him to Chapter 2, in which we discuss overcoming externalization, ambivalence, and other psychological traps, as well as the importance of making a commitment to change. Keep the Negative Cycle of Failure in mind; over time, many kids with ADHD may develop low self-esteem if they have been unable to attain their goals. They may have concluded that they are "just dumb," and so in order to achieve anything, they would have to become a completely different person. If your child thinks this about himself, he is likely to conclude, "That is impossible, so why bother even trying?" He has to change the false vision he has of himself, and to do that, he must keep trying. Your child may be correct to set low goals, at least initially, in order to gain confidence and build forward (positive) momentum. (Refer to the Positive Cycles of Success in Figure 3.5.)

If your child has a negative self-image, what can he do to overcome it? That's precisely the question he must ask himself: What *can* I do? When any goal seems too big and unattainable, he must ask himself: What part of it (no matter how small) *can* I do in the short term? The idea is to identify small, isolated tasks that will move your child toward a long-term goal—these are key for getting started. For example, to move up a grade point in class, maybe a first step would be to "make sure there are no missing assignments *this* week." Your child does not necessarily need to start studying thoroughly for every test; that may be a later goal, one that he will set once he has enjoyed initial successes, established good habits, and achieved some momentum.

Here are some other examples of slicing up the "super" goal. Your child can come up with his own in Exercise 4.2 on page 62.

- If your child's goal is to do all of his math homework, but that seems too big, what *can* he do? Can he at least start the first problem?

- If your child's goal is to organize his desk, but he just doesn't know where to start, what *can* he do? Can he clean out just one drawer?

- If your child's goal is to be on time to school but it seems daunting because he has never done that before, what *can* he do? Can he start by waking up ten minutes earlier than he usually does?

The idea is not for your child to just make smaller goals and lower his sights permanently; he has to determine which actions can take him on his way to bigger long-term goals. Taking the first step can be challenging, but it is the most important step. If he doesn't take the first step, he certainly won't take the second step. So, it is critical to make the first step one he *can* take.

It is important to have these intermediate goals set for many reasons. For one thing, it can feel overwhelming to look at a long-term goal without knowing what short-term steps are needed to get there. Think of the

EXERCISE 4.2

THE SECRET TO GETTING AHEAD IS GETTING STARTED

Break down the Super S.M.A.R.T. goal chosen in Exercise 4.1 into even smaller, shorter-term chunks. We recommend that each chunk be something that can be achieved in no more than a week. Kids who have severe trouble focusing may need to slice even smaller at the beginning—perhaps setting goals that can be met in a single day.

Examples:

- *"Lose fifteen pounds in three months"* becomes *"Lose five pounds per month (for three months)."*

- *"Improve my final grade in class by one letter this semester"* becomes *"Study for my next test so that I improve on my last test score by 10 percent."*

- *"Complete all my homework this month"* becomes *"Complete and turn in all my homework on time this week."*

person in the previous chapter who struggled to push the "big wheel," compared to the person who started with smaller wheels and celebrated periodic successes to gain strength to push the big wheel (Figures 3.4 and 3.5). These celebrations of accomplishments are important in learning to succeed! They can be as simple as a high five or a pat on the back. We all learn best when we are having fun and enjoying ourselves. Many people make the mistake of waiting to celebrate only until after their *big* goal is achieved and then wonder why they cannot stay motivated over the long term. Short-term celebration is a critical factor that leads to long-term accomplishments.

It is easy for ADHDers to get distracted while working toward a long-term goal. This is a further reason why interval goals are so important. These smaller steps will give your child the rewards of reaching a goal quickly, which will keep him motivated and eager to achieve more goals. A short-term goal is more urgent and receives priority in your child's brain. Finally, being able to measure his progress in small chunks can provide your child with a reality check. For example, if a weightlifter sets a three-month goal to increase the amount of weight he can bench press by ten pounds a week, but finds that he cannot keep up with this goal after a couple of weeks, that is a strong message that his goals were set too high to begin with. Perhaps a twelve-month goal of increasing the weight by two pounds a week is something he can more realistically and consistently accomplish.

A final reason to break longer-term goals down into intermediate steps is to defuse procrastination. The word "procrastination" comes from the Latin roots "pro," meaning "forward," and "crastinus," meaning "tomorrow." So it literally means to "forward something on to tomorrow," instead of taking action "here today." ADHDers tend to procrastinate for many reasons, one of them being that a long-term goal feels overwhelming and the gratification is not immediate enough. Most people, ADHD or not, are more likely to put off a large task whose outcome is in the distant future than a small task with an instant result. Having short-term goals reduces the sensation that there is a big, overwhelming project to complete. The natural prioritization that occurs when you have an immediate goal helps counteract the tendency to "put it off til tomorrow."

TAKE ACTIONS TO REINFORCE THE GOAL

At this point, you have helped your child identify his top-priority ("super") S.M.A.R.T. goal that can be achieved in one to three months. You and your child have sliced it down into smaller chunks that can be accomplished in even shorter periods of time, thereby allowing you (both) to celebrate each interval success along the way. Now, what actions can your child take to proactively increase his ability and incentive to achieve these interval goals?

As you go through these steps, remember to think small! Small actions repeated over time will add up to big changes. The key is to get started—any action taken toward your child's goal creates action toward its accomplishment.

Write Down the Goal

To keep goals in the forefront of your child's mind, it is useful to write them down and keep them in plain sight. If your child's first interval goal is to get all his homework turned in *this month*, he should write down "My goal is to get all my homework turned in this month" and post that prominently, perhaps in more than one place. Some locations for him to post his goal could be over his desk, next to his bed, on the refrigerator door, inside the hall closet, or any other place in the house that he frequently sees. This will help him remember his objective, maintain his motivation, and keep him constantly reaching for that goal.

Writing down goals is an important step in turning something that initially exists as only a thought or abstract wish into something concrete and attainable. We recommend Mark Victor Hansen's (author of *Chicken Soup for the Soul*) maxim: "Don't think it, ink it." To use a professional sports example, world-renowned swimming champion Michael Phelps (who was diagnosed with ADHD as a child) stated that if he ever felt like quitting, "My mom would ask me 'Are you sure that's the best decision?' And I'd think, think, think. . . . I wrote down the goals that I had so I could always see what I wanted to accomplish. And I would look at that goal sheet and think 'I still want to do this.' So I'd decide 'I'm not quitting.'" Writing down his goals motivated Phelps to keep training because he could better visualize those future accomplishments.

Mental and physical connections to a goal are created by writing it down. A 2007 study by Gail Matthews of Dominican University demonstrated the importance of writing down goals. This study followed 149 people who were split into five groups and asked to achieve their stated goals. The first group had unwritten goals. The second group wrote their goals down. The third group also wrote their goals down, but added a specific *action plan* to achieve the goals. The fourth group further added telling a supportive friend both about the goals and about the action plan they had written down. The final group had written goals, an action plan to achieve those goals, and not only told a supportive friend

> **Coaching Corner**
> There is a huge difference between saying you have a goal and actually taking steps toward that goal. Each step your child takes toward his goal builds his self-esteem and transforms him from a talker into a doer.

about these, but also made weekly progress reports to that friend. The results of this study were clear: The members of the final group were about 33 percent more successful in accomplishing their goals than those in the other groups. In general, all those who wrote down goals performed better than those in Group 1, who did not write down their goals.

If your child is not comfortable with writing his goals down, or if you want to further emphasize what he has already written, ask him to say his goals out loud. Stating goals out loud reinforces commitment. Moreover, saying them frequently helps affect how he thinks. Ask him to repeat his particular goal (or his reason for having that goal) every day, several times a day if necessary. For example, if he has an interval goal to put his house keys away when he gets home from school every day this week, ask him to repeat "I want to put my keys in the cupboard by the window every day this week" or "I really like it when I am able to find my keys right away whenever I need them." Ask him to say it each time he puts his keys away, or each time he finds himself looking for his keys when he didn't put them away properly. The more he says his goal and his reason for having it out loud, the more committed he will become to achieving it.

Create a Schedule

In general, ADHDers will be more productive when their time is scheduled. We want to start by saying that we are big believers in unscheduled time, too: Everybody needs downtime, and that includes ADHDers. However, if there is a certain block of time in which your child is supposed to be getting things done, it's helpful to structure out the time in small chunks. So for example, "Homework from 4 to 5:30 p.m." can be broken down into:

- 4 to 4:20 p.m.: Study language arts.

- 4:20 to 4:40 p.m.: Study math.

- 4:40 to 4:45 p.m.: Exercise break.

- 4:45 to 5:05 p.m.: Science homework.

- 5:05 to 5:25 p.m.: Work on history project.

- 5:25 to 5:30 p.m.: Exercise break.

This is particularly important during the transition from high school, which tends to be very structured, to college, which tends to have less structured "assigned" study and class times.

Many ADHDers perform much better in settings where there are clear expectations. They may be able to function well, for example, at a school where the schedule is: 9 to 10 a.m.: math, 10 to 11 a.m.: science, 11 a.m. to 12 noon: art, and so on. But at a more free-form school or at home, where there is much less structure, ADHDers may have a harder time getting things done. Picture a few unstructured hours at home, during which time there are tasks (clean room, do homework, set the table) that should get done "at some point"—but don't have assigned times. The same ADHDer who can accomplish a lot in a structured school environment can come home and get nothing done. Making and keeping a detailed schedule for this otherwise unregulated time can help. Once again, we recognize that everybody deserves and benefits from some free time, and this includes kids with ADHD—so don't try to program your child like a robot! That said, when it's important for your child to focus on and complete a task, work with him to create a schedule as specific and detailed as necessary.

Visual calendars also can be really helpful in breaking long-term goals into short-term interval goals. Your child can use a regular paper calendar or planner to map out a timeline for him to achieve his goal(s). Electronic calendar methods such as Google Calendar, Apple iCal, or Outlook Calendar are also helpful, particularly because they can be set up to send automated reminders to your child's email or phone. However, a downside to this method is that your child can easily get diverted by games or other apps while accessing an electronic calendar, so be sure to keep an eye out if he has been on his phone for too long!

Keep a Checklist and Progress Log

As your ADHD child sets goals for himself and trains to achieve them, he should keep a log to record how he is doing. A log is helpful for many reasons. Writing in it every day motivates your child to take daily action toward his goals; builds your child's confidence by becoming a written collection of his accomplishments; and helps identify which strategies do and don't work for him.

Just like ADHDers, athletes must work hard to reach their goals. They also frequently endure a great deal of pain and hardship to get there, especially at the highest levels of athletic success. As he trains, a serious athlete tracks how he is doing by writing his training regimen as he accomplishes it (e.g., "Bench pressed 100 pounds: ten reps, three sets"). He also records progress toward his goal by measuring interval improvements (e.g., "I pressed one more set than last week").

Steve Magness, a former coach of Olympic runner Ciaran O'Lionaird, published O'Lionaird's training logs written from 2011 to 2012, during the runner's buildup to a 3:54 mile. The logs helped Magness adjust the regimen when necessary: "Whenever I get in a bind in figuring out what to do with an athlete, I always go back and read the basics of training again and then look at past logs and experience." Progress logs are reminders that can be reviewed in the future and used to renew commitment or choose new goals and strategies. (See the discussion "Review and Renew" on page 70.)

Writing down goals, posting them in prominent places, and keeping to a training schedule are great ways to remind your child of the goal he is reaching for and keep him on track toward that goal. It is important for your child to record his actual training activities as he accomplishes them, as well as his progress toward achieving his interval goal. This is as simple as keeping a list of activities on your child's schedule, where he can check off completion of each scheduled task. As with writing down goals, keeping a checklist turns an abstract commitment (e.g., "4 to 4:20 p.m.: Study language arts") into a concrete reality (i.e. "✓: I *did* study language arts from 4 to 4:20 p.m. as planned").

If your child's goal is to turn in all of his homework for a week, he can write down his progress at the end of each day: "Monday night—20 percent there!" Additionally, he could add a quick note: "I was going to play Xbox but didn't and finished homework early!" Make it simple, or it won't get done!

An example of a completed checklist/progress log for the week is on page 68. For your convenience, a blank copy for you and your child to photocopy and fill in can be found on page 230.

Stay in Good Company

When your child is around people who are doing the tasks he himself needs to do, he is more likely to do them, too. If your child knows people who tend to encourage and support him, make spending time with them part of his goal. This could be a coach (see Chapter 9), a family friend, or any adult you trust, respect, and with whom your child feels comfortable. Find a way to integrate such people into your child's planning. For example, if your child's goal is to turn in all homework on time this month, a contributing sub-goal might be to ask someone your child trusts to check in with your child about his homework every week.

Table 4.1. Example of a Checklist to Track Your Child's Progress

Example of a checklist for a child whose goal is to complete homework and study every night.

Task	Sun	Mon	Tues	Wed	Thurs	Fri	Sat
Language Arts (20 MINUTES)	✓	✓	✓	✓	✓	Off	Off
Math (20 MINUTES)	✓	✓	X	✓	✓	Off	Off
Break (5 MIN POGO STICK)	✓	✓	✓	✓	✓	Off	Off
History (20 MINUTES)	✓	✓	✓	✓	✓	Off	Off
English (20 MINUTES)	✓	✓	✓	✓	✓	Off	Off
Break (5 MIN HULA HOOP)	✓	✓	✓	✓	✓	Off	Off
Science (20 MINUTES)	✓	✓	✓	✓	✓	Off	Off
Break (10 MIN SKATEBOARD)	✓	✓	✓	✓	✓	Off	Off
Review for quiz (TUES/THURS)	n/a	n/a	✓	n/a	✓	Off	Off
Backpack (READY FOR AM?)	✓	✓	✓	✓	✓	Off	Off

PROGRESS

Mon	Tues	Wed	Thurs	Fri
Felt great!	Left math homework in locker. Check before leaving next time!	Back on track! Did extra math to make up for yesterday.	Just have a few things left to do before the weekend.	Got 90% on pop quiz in math class!

Also see the section, "Tips for Parents with ADHD Children: At Home," on page 75 for more tips regarding checklists, progress logs, and calendars.

Encourage your child to hang out and study with other students who also want to get better grades. Conversely, suggest to your child that he avoid people who distract him or who don't see the importance of what he wants to achieve. Tell your child: If the people around you don't see your mission as important, they will not support your mission. It will be much easier for your child to accomplish his goals if he surrounds himself with supportive, like-minded people—and much harder if he surrounds himself with distracting people who push him off track.

Optimize the Environment

Environment is also important. If your child is going to get work done, he needs a place with few distractions. Sometimes a child will work best in a place where a parent can supervise him and remind him to stay on task; this may be a common area of the house and does not necessarily need to be the quietest spot. However, the workspace should at least be kept neat and clean. Eliminating physical clutter helps prevent your child from getting distracted, and also teaches him what a workspace should look like. A neat and organized workspace makes it less likely that assignments will get lost.

Coaching Corner

If your child is having trouble giving up his phone or wants to watch TV when he is doing his homework, you can ask him this: When he goes to soccer practice, is there a giant TV screen next to the field? Does the coach encourage him to check his texts between plays in the middle of a game? What is the difference between trying to score a goal with the TV on versus trying to do homework with the TV on?

Electronics (phone, TV, Internet) are often the biggest distractions of all. Do *not* expect your child to concentrate on his homework if there is a TV on nearby. Fortunately, there are a number of ways to minimize electronic distractions. (See Chapter 6 and "Tips for Parents of ADHD Children: Home" section on page 75.) Consider the idea that "proximity is power." Things that are closer have a greater pull. Align your child with people and places that move him closer to his goals, and have him write them down in Exercise 4.3 on the next page.

EXERCISE 4.3

PROXIMITY IS POWER

On a separate piece of paper, your child should write down the people and places that inspire him to focus on what needs to get done.

1. Who are three people I spend time with who support my desire to get stuff done?

2. Where are three places that bring me incentive to work?

REVIEW AND RENEW

During your child's journey to achieve his goals, recalibration will be required. In the same way one workout does not create a lifetime of health, one plan to achieve a goal isn't enough to create a lifetime of success. Like the weightlifter who set his bench press goals too high in the example earlier in this chapter, it is vital to regularly review progress made in the plan and to make adjustments as needed over time. When your child does this, the important question to ask is not "Am I doing everything right?" but "Are the steps in place for me to make progress or should I make further adjustments to my goals and plan?"

Encourage your child to adopt the mantra "progress, not perfection." Just as a rear-view mirror in the car aids your perspective, a look back on your progress to see how far you've come is one of the best ways to create new goals and stoke excitement to achieve them. If your child is focused only on the end goal,

> ### Coaching Corner
> It is much easier to get a child to set a smaller goal compared with a larger goal. But if your child sets small goals, and adjusts both the goals and the eventual target as he goes along, he will accomplish a great deal—without fear of the process.

he may forget to review the process that is supposed to get him there. This is an important function of the progress log we mentioned earlier in this chapter. After reviewing the log (at the conclusion of some intermediate interval—a week or a month), you and your child may conclude

Kaizen
The Practice of Continuous Improvement

One formalized version of review and improvement is known as Kaizen, developed in Japan following World War II. Kaizen is a Japanese term that means "continuous improvement." It is a practice that many companies around the world (most famously Toyota) use to improve their production process. The process is systematic, based on all workers constantly making small changes for the better, wherever possible.

While a company like Toyota might use Kaizen to improve productivity or to reduce cost or waste, it can be applied to any goal-setting situation. This includes personal goals set by individuals. In fact, as originally intended, the concept was meant to be applied to all aspects of life—professional as well as personal.

If you were to ask a group of random people on the street if improving something 100 percent was possible, most would answer no. However, if you were to ask this same group if a one-percent improvement were possible, the majority would say yes. The idea behind Kaizen is to make many one-percent changes that add up to a very significant improvement over time. Once again, the idea is to focus on sequential small steps that get you to your goal in the end.

that his schedule or process needs to be adjusted in some way. The best time to make adjustments is as your child is actively engaged in following his plan to reach his interval goal.

As your child starts achieving interval goals, together you and he should continuously review and adjust them as needed. In the process of reviewing goals, your child will gain a greater understanding of how important they are to him. When your child reviews a goal, he is deciding if attaining that goal is in alignment with his values—who he is and where he wants to be. While some goals are worth pursuing over time, your child might realize that other goals are no longer aligned with his values and can be discarded.

Consider Marietta, a sixteen-year-old junior. She was the captain of the swim team while running three high school clubs, and she additionally enjoyed going out with her friends. In the midst of deciding if she was going to join the robotics team, she realized that being involved in so many things didn't actually make her happy. It wasn't worth the whirlwind she always found herself in. Instead of adding activities, she decided to cut back to a couple of clubs that really mattered to her.

Setbacks may disrupt your child's process. During your child's review of where he is, he may mistake a challenging goal for a challenging process (or vice versa). Try to help your child discern: Is it difficult for me to reach the goal because the goal itself is not worthwhile? Or is it my *process* that needs to be tweaked or made more realistic in some way? Remind your child that the setback should be a cause for consideration of the challenges he faces, not an opportunity to quit and abandon a worthwhile goal. Thomas Edison had to try many, many times to invent the proper filament for the incandescent light bulb. Some people would have regarded all the trials that didn't work as failures—but Edison resolutely pressed forward. Rather than a failure, he viewed each unsuccessful attempt as part of his road to success. "I am not discouraged," he said, "because every wrong attempt discarded is another step forward. . . . I have not failed. I've just found 10,000 ways that won't work." (See Chapter 8 for techniques on pressing forward after a setback.)

Say that one morning you wake up after your usual good night's sleep and enjoy a healthy breakfast before leaving for work. However, your normal route to work offers you a detour sign. So you follow the detour. But that detour takes you to another detour. When that happens, do you follow that detour sign too? What if you keep seeing detour signs? At what point do you give up and turn back? If the route to get to work becomes too challenging, you may start thinking about whether you really need to go to work today, or if you should try to get there a different way. If, upon reflection, it is really important for you to get to work, you will press on until you get there—one way or another.

This detour analogy can be compared to the Kaizen process mentioned in the inset on page 71. Kaizen is a series of small questions that help improve a path to an ultimate goal; these questions can help your child consider *why* he is aiming for that goal. As your child encounters challenges (detours) along his path, each detour offers him an opportunity to reevaluate his goal and the route he is taking to get there. As your child reviews his log, he should remind himself that each potential detour along the way provides an opportunity to recommit to his original goal, as well as to reconsider the process. Maybe he remains committed to both the goal and to the process he wants to use to get there. In that case, he simply has to keep trying—maybe the process needs just a slight improvement or tweak to make it better. On the other hand, maybe the detours are a sign that there is a different and better route your child can take to his goal. After evaluating the detours, he might decide he no longer wants to get to that goal, because it no longer is what he values.

> ### Coaching Corner
>
> *Each challenge your child encounters while stepping toward his Super S.M.A.R.T. goal is an opportunity to re-evaluate the goal, re-evaluate the plan to achieve the goal, and to recommit or to change the goal based on his core values.*

As a parent, you probably have had many experiences that did not go exactly the way you had planned. Exercise 4.4 below asks you to think back to times in your life when you had to adjust your plans in order to achieve your goals. Going over this exercise with your child is a great way to share your experiences and bond with him, while also reassuring him that even if the road to his goal is disrupted, he can still reach it by finding a new way to get there.

EXERCISE 4.4

LEARNING BY EXAMPLE: TEACHING YOUR CHILD TO REVIEW AND RENEW HIS GOALS

On a separate piece of paper, write down three goals in which you (the parent) encountered difficulty *more than once* but persevered until you reached your goal. Then, look at the goals you have written and circle any or all of the goals that required you to modify your initial plan of action. See, you've done this already—so can your child!

SUMMARY

In this chapter, you learned how to take S.M.A.R.T. goals and turn them into reality. The Super-S.T.A.R. method helps your child prioritize one "super" goal and then slice that goal into smaller chunks. Your child also learned to take action on a goal by surrounding himself with positive influences and writing down what motivates him. The last step in the Super-S.T.A.R. process is to consistently review your child's action plan, preferably by maintaining a checklist or progress log, and adjusting either the goal or plan when necessary.

The idea is to celebrate progress, not perfection. Improvement happens over time, not overnight; rather than strive for a 100 percent change, look to make one-percent improvements in 100 ways. By accomplishing smaller goals and making progress toward his "super" goal, your child's confidence will continue to grow!

In the next chapter, we will discuss how to use your child's mind, body, and spirit to help him stick to his goals. The mind, body, and spirit work together to achieve success, and each is fueled in a different way. Once your child understands what motivates him and why, he can understand mistakes he has made in the past and how he can make better decisions in the future.

TIPS FOR PARENTS OF ADHD CHILDREN
AT HOME

So far, you have read about the basics of ADHD and how your child can set and commit to a S.M.A.R.T. goal. Your child has also learned how to turn his "super," or most important, goal into a reality. But what about daily goals, such as getting enough sleep and behaving well? How can your child put these concepts into practice in his everyday life? The following tips are actions you and your child can take at home to make his days a little easier. Many children with ADHD do well in school, where there is a structured schedule, only to come home and forget about their homework and responsibilities. While children should have free time to play, these tips can help you and your child keep his momentum from school going at home when it's time to get to work.

DOING HOMEWORK

- Divide work into smaller segments, with breaks between segments as needed. (See Table 4.1 in Chapter 4 for an example of a homework schedule.)

- Intermittent deadlines for long-term assignments help break big projects down into manageable chunks.

- If your child seems to get stuck, ask him specific questions such as: "Which part is confusing?" "What do you understand?"

- Highlight key words in instructions before beginning projects.

- Hiring a tutor can help prevent frustration between the parent and child.

- If your child has a hard time remembering to bring textbooks home, or often brings the wrong books home, get a second set of textbooks to keep at home. (Easier on the back, too!)

- Keep distractions to a minimum. Make sure the area your child is working in is not messy, or near a TV or other electronic distractions. Put cell phones in another room.

- To minimize being overwhelmed, sometimes it is helpful to present just a page of homework (or part of a page, with the rest folded down) at a time. Or, if your child has to read an entire chapter from a textbook, he can use a sheet of paper to block all text besides the paragraph he is currently reading. This can prevent distraction and "jumping around."

- Establish a "homework comes first" policy (although exercise before homework is okay). Set limits on TV watching and phone or computer use.

- For most people, doing the harder assignments first makes the most sense. Some children do better "warming up" by starting with something easy.

- Your child should work in short but effective bursts. Tell your child to concentrate intensely for a set amount of time, and then take a short break.

- Use a timer. Ask your child how long a particular assignment (or portion of an assignment) should take him, then set the timer. Have your child see if he finished in the amount of time that he stated. This has a number of benefits. It teaches your child how long something should take. It may keep his interest level up, since he is "competing" against himself. Also, if there is time left over, he can use the time to double-check his work. However, make sure he does not rush through the assignment to "beat" his stated time.

- Have your child work on his own as much as possible. Your child has to learn to work independently at home because he has to learn how to work independently in other situations as well.

- Insist that teachers use School Loop, PowerSchool, or other computerized tracking programs so you and your child will know about missing assignments. They have to be updated in a timely manner (best every day, at least every week). You may need to discuss this with the principal if needed.

- iHomework is an iPhone app that helps manage homework schedules.

HEALTH AND WELLNESS

- Getting good sleep is important. If there is a concern regarding your child's sleep, either not enough hours or poor quality sleep (kicking a lot, snoring, waking a lot, etc.), please let your child's doctor know.

- Always make sure your child eats breakfast before school. Make sure there is some protein in it.

- Exercising before going to school and/or before doing homework can be helpful for your child.

- Work with your child on goal setting.

- Talk to your child about what his strengths are, not just his weaknesses. How does he use his strengths to compensate for his weaknesses?

KEEPING A ROOM ORGANIZED

- Schedule time for your child to organize his desk at home and at school (e.g., always clean up before bed; get to school ten minutes early on Fridays).

- Slow down! Tell your child not to just throw things down when he is done with them. Come up with habits and routines that result in his putting important things in the same place every day (e.g., a place for keys).

MINIMIZING ELECTRONIC DISTRACTIONS

- There are a number of apps that will block distracting websites. For Mac computers, SelfControl is one of the best (www.selfcontrolapp .com). For Windows, try Cold Turkey (www.getcoldturkey.com) or StayFocusd (www.stayfocusd.com). Qustodio (www.qustodio.com) is parental software that allows you to monitor and limit your child's use of the Internet on both the computer and smartphone. Programs, apps, and electronic devices are constantly being developed and the best ones change frequently. Consult a web search engine for up-to-date information about the best electronic/computer-based aides available for your child.

ORGANIZATION

- Checklists kept in a prominent place can help your child focus on what he needs to be doing.

- Have your child organize his backpack for the next school day before he goes to bed. Put Post-it notes on homework that's supposed to be turned in so it is easier to see—the Post-its will stick up out of the top of the folder that the homework is in.

- Use visual calendars to keep track of your child's long-term assignments, due dates, chores, and activities. Be sure to use the calendar for more than just due dates or tests; write down "study for test" on the days before the tests, or use the calendar to break down the different steps of a project.

- Getting chores and simple tasks, even just getting ready in the morning, finished can be a challenge. Keep things as simple as possible. Use a timer to challenge your child to work faster. Think about using positive rewards for motivation. Organize as much as you can the day before. There is an app for iPhone called "30/30" that can be very helpful as a visual organizer, because it is a task manager that uses a timer.

RELAXATION TRAINING

- There are a number of apps designed for achieving mindfulness—the state of active attention to the present moment. These apps include Buddhify, Take a Break, Headspace, Calm, Smiling Mind, and Starflight VR.

REWARD PROGRAMS

- Reward programs can be vital for shaping behavior. Use a point system for both positive and negative behavior (give points for good behavior, take away points for unwanted behavior). When the child gets to a pre-set number (10 points), he can put the points "in the bank" for a toy or another reward. This can be useful for results (such as "you have a clean desk—3 points!") or shaping behaviors (such as

"I saw you get frustrated but you didn't lose your temper—good job—5 points!"). Take away points for negative behaviors ("I saw you hit your sister—minus 3 points"). You can adjust this program depending on your child's age or motivations.

- Note when your child is doing well and praise him for it. It's the difference between saying "don't run" and "great walking." Children with ADHD hear "no" all the time. Encouragement is important!

- There are a number of behavior modification apps—for example, Chore Pad or iRewardChart.

SAFETY

- If your child likes to ride his bicycle or skateboard, always make sure that he wears a helmet. He may be tempted to just jump on his bike and go, but your child should establish a habit of placing his helmet right on top of his bike's handlebars or the seat when he puts it away. That way, the next time he takes his bike out, he will remember to put on the helmet.

- *Talk to your teenager about sticking his cell phone in the trunk while he is driving.* A distracted teen driver is a danger to himself and others on the road.

TEMPER TANTRUMS

- Taking a video of unwanted behavior with your phone and showing it to your child later can be helpful: "Be the person you want to see on YouTube."

- When your child says "No," ask him to add a "because": "No, because. . . ." While young children are used to impulsively saying "no" as a response to a request, as they get older, children should stop, think, and reason it out. This decreases the number of reflexive "no" answers.

5

Mind, Body, and Spirit
The Three-Part Model of Motivation

James, age sixteen, was overweight, inactive, unmotivated, and failing his classes. His parents were worried he might never get back on track. After talking with his doctor, James realized he had a problem and became willing to work on it. He started tagging along with a friend to karate lessons. The teacher at the dojo helped him realize the importance of good nutrition: He couldn't do what he wanted to do physically until he changed his diet. A sleep study showed that James had sleep apnea, which was additional incentive to lose weight. He started to spend more time away from video games, which was easy to do because in the dojo, he was surrounded by motivated students and teachers who truly believed in what they were doing.

James started training with everything he had in him for his green belt. It was a hard test, so he practiced at home for hours and asked higher belts for advice. Though still overweight, he started to feel proud about what he was able to achieve physically. He made green belt and was thrilled. His karate teacher asked him about what he learned to get through the green belt test. James realized that it wasn't enough to just be in shape physically—or even mentally—to want to pass the test. He also had to put his heart and spirit into the test.

James was able to take the lessons he learned from karate and apply them to his academics. He transformed from a kid who could barely be bothered to do his homework into one who did all the extra credit and participated in class. He made new friends and enjoyed feeling more attractive and energetic. Now it was clear to himself, his parents, and everybody who met him that he was definitely on the right track—the track to success!

I n the last chapter, your child learned the importance of splitting a large goal into smaller, easily attainable goals. She also learned the benefits of keeping a log to review and improve her goal-achieving process over time. However, if your child still finds it difficult to practice these techniques and put them in motion, she may fall off track before reaching her goal. If this repeatedly happens, she is not only wasting her time and energy, but she may become more discouraged. How can we prevent this?

Here again, think about athletic training and performance. Athletes routinely face motivational challenges when striving to reach their goals. For example, a basketball player might set a goal to improve her free throw percentage by her next game, but then finds herself too fatigued after regular practice to do extra drills; when game day arrives, she hasn't improved her free throw percentage at all. An Olympic hurdler may resolve to do extra squats daily in order to increase her leg strength and shave another second off her time, but then finds that she can't keep to that extra training commitment. In contrast, successful athletes stick to their training regimens and consistently put in the work to get better and reach for their goals. Having a training schedule, checklist, and progress log are external factors that can help with this, but what internal qualities do successful athletes use to accomplish this feat?

Athletes sometimes use a three-part model of the self as a simple way to understand and harness major internal forces that, when they work together, can keep the athlete on track to her goals. This model of the self is: mind, body, and spirit. When these internal forces don't work together, success is sabotaged. We believe this same model can be helpful to ADHDers when training themselves to reach for their goals.

WHAT IS THE THREE-PART MODEL?

It is important for your child to understand the three parts of the model so she can utilize them to make smart decisions about her goals. The first part, *mind,* denotes the cognitive aspect of the self. The mind is the planner, the goal setter, the part of your child that charts her course; it is the "decider." The mind decides what is best to do and how to go about doing it. The mind is the brainpower that rationally assesses where she is and compares it to where she wants to be.

Body denotes the physical aspects of the self. Nourishing the body is what causes the self to be ready to train and make beneficial changes. For your ADHD child, this means getting enough sleep, eating nutritious foods, and generally being in proper physical shape to accomplish her goals. Feeling good physically lifts the whole self up in every way: Developing healthy habits for the body fuels brain biochemistry. In contrast, feeling only so-so physically drags the rest of the self down and can prevent your child from accomplishing anything that requires effort. To paraphrase motivational speaker and author Jim Rohn, many people don't *do* well because they don't *feel* well. Your mind and spirit communicate with the external world through your body.

Spirit is an immeasurable aspect of self. It corresponds to emotional, from-the-gut motivation. It is the part of the self that pushes your child to perform even better than her mind alone might think possible. The spirit also is the part of the self that most deeply registers a sense of fulfillment after reaching a goal. Of course, "spirit" has religious connotations for some people—but believing in a religious spirit is not necessary for the model that we are advocating here. In the context of this book, the spirit embodies determination, emotional energy, and competitiveness. If the mind is the intellectual force and the body is the physical force, the spirit can aptly be described as the energy force within us.

Getting these three parts of the self to work together is not just a suggestion—it is *essential* if your child is going to play to win. In addition, it is essential not only to *make* good decisions, but to *stick with them*. That won't happen without all three parts of the self working together. When all three parts are working together, your child creates an opportunity for greatness.

Let's provide an example of a simple goal that cannot be achieved when the three parts of the self do not work together: Say you are debating whether or not to take a walk outside. Your mind might say: "I think it's a good idea to take a walk around the block." But if your body isn't ready (e.g., you are tired or dehydrated), and if your spirit is saying "Nah, it's too hot outside, I don't feel like it, maybe another time," you won't get off the couch and out the door. In this case you literally take one step forward and two steps back! In contrast, when the three parts of the self are in agreement, you not only might walk around the block but walk a mile or even farther. To use a professional sports example, when an athlete is described as "being in the zone," you can be sure that all three parts of herself are working together in unison. In a study, elite athletes were questioned about what words they would use to describe being "in the zone." The research found that the athletes agreed on the feelings that represented "the zone": "Athletes describe salient features of the [zone-like] experience—total concentration and involvement, control, a unity of mind and body and a sense of personal fulfillment at an optimal level of performance—with remarkable similarity when asked to reflect on how it feels when their experiences are most positive." The success that comes with the unity of mind, body, and the "sense of personal fulfillment" (spirit) is demonstrative of the three-part model of motivation.

You can help your child get "in the zone" to overcome ADHD by helping her identify these three parts of herself and keep them working together. The next few sections describe the role of each of these parts of the self in more detail and provide some exercises to bring out their qualities in your child.

THE POWER IN YOUR CHILD'S MIND

When athletes train, it's not just about getting bigger muscles. It's also about training their minds. They must train themselves to persist, even when they are tired or in pain. They must train themselves to set goals and to give their best efforts, focusing during training. They must train themselves to listen to their coach, even when the coach is telling them things they don't want to hear. This is the athletic mindset. An athlete who can develop this mindset, plus the physical skills needed to deliver, will go far.

Without this mindset, an athlete is at a major disadvantage. If she starts to hurt in training and is not equipped with a powerful mindset, she will quit. If she hears criticism from her coach, she may take it personally rather than use it to get better. She may start thinking about other things that distract her during practice, preventing

> ### Coaching Corner
> Ask your child to think of times when she was "in the zone": During a sports game? While painting in art class? Helping out a friend? What a great feeling that was! This chapter is about how your child can get in the zone when it doesn't arise naturally. When mind, body, and spirit work together, your child will be empowered.

her from fully engaging in the moment and improving her performance. If the athlete's mind is not engaged, her performance is at the expense of whatever else is going on that day.

The same concerns apply to your child with ADHD. Your child's mind must be fully engaged for her to reach her goal. If she is actively thinking about what she wants to accomplish, she will deliver a performance to be proud of. To do this, she needs an understanding of three things: what she doesn't like about what she is doing now; why she wants to reach a new goal; and how she can get there.

What does your child not like about what she is doing now? Maybe your child's messy room doesn't bother her, but she admits that she doesn't like to waste time looking for things in her room. That might be enough to motivate her to put at least a few things away in the correct place. Similarly, your child might not like doing homework—but she may acknowledge that she doesn't like it when missing homework brings her grades down. Is she always running late? She might not like the idea of waking up earlier, but she might be okay with it if she thinks about the embarrassment she feels when she walks in late and sees the other students looking at her.

Identifying the things that bother your child can help her become motivated enough to take steps to change them. The negatives in life can drive us forward when they are paired with the positives. Without a negative pole, a car battery won't work and the car won't move forward. Negatives in life have a value! These experiences can build a positive person, provided that they are viewed and utilized correctly—that is, so long as the negatives are eventually paired with a positive action. Exercises 5.1 and 5.2 on page 86 will evaluate *why* your child wants to achieve a goal.

Once she identifies the things that bother her, your child can decide what she wants to change. What does she want to move toward and why? Knowing what the reward will be will help anchor the direction she takes. Here, we focus on clearly identifying the rewards she will get when she reaches her goals.

Have your child visualize how she will benefit from the change she is thinking about making. If she is thinking that her room should be neater, she should visualize how great it will be to easily and quickly find things. If she is thinking that she should turn in her homework more regularly, she should think about how much better her grades will be as

EXERCISE 5.1

NEGATIVES THAT POWER YOU UP!

This exercise reminds your child of why she wants to make changes by listing the negative consequences of her current actions.

On a separate piece of paper, have your child fill in the sentences that apply to her, and write down some of her own.

Examples

- *I don't want to lose things because I hate looking for them.*
- *I don't want to leave projects incomplete because . . . .*
- *I don't want to be late to school because . . . .*
- *I don't want to interrupt when other people are talking because . . . .*
- *I don't want . . . . because . . . .*

EXERCISE 5.2

POSITIVES THAT POWER YOU UP!

This exercise will help your child think about why she wants to reach her goal by listing the positive consequences of making changes.

Help your child fill in the sentences that apply to her, or encourage her to write down some of her own.

Examples

- *I want to work faster because then I won't have to spend so much time on my homework and will have time to do some other fun things each evening.*
- *I want to be a better listener because . . . .*
- *I want to get better grades because . . . .*
- *I want to be on time because . . . .*
- *I want to . . . . because . . . .*

a result. If she is thinking that she should work on arriving to school on time, then she should visualize how it will feel to be seen as responsible, instead of having her classmates see her as "the late one." Having her picture these benefits and positive outcomes in such a detailed way allows her to really envision herself in a successful position. (See Chapter 6 for more on how visualization techniques can help your child achieve her goals.)

Together, Exercises 5.1 and 5.2 define a negative and a positive pole—a negative beginning and a positive ending. Your child begins by identifying reasons to stop bad habits and declare, "I don't want to do this anymore." She ends by saying, "I will feel much better when I gain my reward." But how does she get from the beginning to the end? She must go via a pathway that contributes to the ultimate goal. This is where your child says: "I can find my shoes better if I put it them in my closet when I take them off," "I can get my homework done if I put my phone in a different room while I'm doing it," "I can be on time by timing my morning shower so it takes only five minutes instead of twenty-five."

Establishing these good habits will help crystallize the goal setting that we talked about in previous chapters, but additionally, they will help your child focus on her motivations. If she can clearly explain *why* she is doing something and engage her mind in the journey to her declared reward, her attention will improve. If she has clarity about what she wants to do and why, she will be more motivated to do it. Remember, anything that increases motivation or interest for an ADHDer will help prioritize and focus her attention naturally. In Exercise 5.3 on page 88, your child can practice coming up with different approaches she can take to achieve her goals.

THE POWER IN YOUR CHILD'S BODY

The second part of the self, the body, has to be in good physical condition to support the goals that are set by the mind and pushed for by the spirit. Three of the most important contributors to physical health are sleep, nutrition, and exercise. These three contributors to physical well-being are like the three legs of a stool—they support the body. Your child will perform optimally when she establishes habits that improve these components of physical health.

EXERCISE 5.3

LET THE ENERGY FLOW:
THE CIRCUIT FROM NEGATIVE TO POSITIVE

This exercise helps your child think about the things she can do differently in order to achieve her goals.

The next important question to get the mind in gear is: *What can I do to achieve my desired result?* Help your child to fill in the sentences that apply to her, or have her write down some of her own on another sheet of paper.

Examples

- *I can get faster at my work by blocking Facebook while I'm working.*

- *I can be a better listener by not interrupting, and by remembering that thinking of what I'm going to say next is not the same as listening!*

- *I can get better grades by . . . .*

- *I can keep my desk organized by . . . .*

- *I can be on time by . . . .*

- *I can be more successful if I can . . . .*

- *Learning how to . . . . will allow me to . . . .*

- *I can . . . . by . . . .*

Sleep

Nobody knows exactly what the function of sleep is, but experts agree that it is a necessary process for optimal brain function and for general health. Without enough sleep, your body shows signs of stress, and increased amounts of hormones like cortisol (often called the "stress hormone") are produced. Sleep plays an important role in mental functioning. Many people think of learning and remembering information as "daytime, waking" activities, but what they don't realize is that sleep is critically important for learning and remembering. While you sleep, information that you have learned during the day become consolidated in your memory. When researchers measure consequences of sleep deprivation, they see negative impacts on impulse control, planning, and memory. So the functions of the brain that are already "weaker" because of ADHD become even more impaired by lack of sleep.

We can all temporarily push on with less sleep, but too many people believe they can do so without consequence. Experts have studied how a "sleep deficit" builds up if your child chronically gets less sleep than she needs, in the same way that your bank balance goes into deficit if you withdraw a little too much money every month. There are two common traps that lead children into a sleep deficit. One is too few hours of sleep. The second is poor sleep quality. That is, your child might get the right number of hours, but her sleep is fragmented because of snoring, obstructive sleep apnea, restless leg syndrome, or other problems that keep her from sleeping deeply. Some kids get into sleep deficit in both ways: They don't get as many hours of sleep as they need, and they also suffer from poor sleep quality.

> **Coaching Corner**
>
> *With busy schedules, it is hard to get enough sleep. So many things can get in the way, such as college prep for high schoolers. At the least, make sure your child is getting as much sleep as she can; don't let anything unnecessary (e.g., electronics) intrude on sleep time.*

Sleep is regulated in large part by a naturally secreted hormone called melatonin. The "blue light" (light from the blue part of the visible spectrum with short wavelengths around 450 nanometers) found in many electronics can be disruptive to melatonin production. This is one reason to curtail electronics a few hours before bedtime. Another reason is that the games played on electronic devices are designed to be difficult to put down, so they keep you awake!

Your child may not always feel tired the next day, but lack of sleep affects both body and brain regardless. In the world of sports, some notable athletes have fallen from grace simply by arriving for the game having partied too much the night before and not getting enough sleep. For an ADHDer, every day is "game day," and good sleep every night is a must. Think honestly about how you function when you are tired— not well! Even when a person without ADHD gets behind on her sleep, it becomes more difficult for her to follow instructions. The consequences of a sleep deficit are magnified in a child with ADHD.

How much sleep your child needs depends mostly on age. Below is a table that details average sleep needs according to the National Sleep Foundation.

Average Sleep Needs

Age	Optimal Sleep Needed
5–13 years old	9–11 hours per night
14–17 years old	8–10 hours per night
18 and up	7–9 hours per night

It must be noted that these are *average* numbers; individual needs and circumstances may vary the amount of sleep needed. Depending on what she has been doing, sometimes your child will need more sleep than at other times. For example, if she has been exercising a lot, she will need extra sleep. If she is under a lot of stress at home, in her personal life, or at school, she will need more sleep. Also, if she is coming off an extended period of time where she hasn't had all the sleep she needs, she will need extra sleep to make up for sleep that she missed.

Tips for Your Child to Get Better Sleep

- Exercise during the day (but not right before bedtime).

- Finish dinner at least two hours before bedtime.

- Avoid electronics (any screens) in the two or three hours before bed. The light emitted from electronics disrupts circadian rhythms.

- Avoid all caffeine products, *especially* in the evenings.

- Turn the lights down about an hour before bed—nothing over forty watts. In the morning, get sunlight or bright light on your child's face when she wakes up.

- Go to bed at the same time and get up at the same time, even on weekends.

- Create a regular, relaxing bedtime routine. Examples include taking a bath, reading, or knitting.

- Use the bedroom only for sleep. Do not read or watch TV in bed; do not do work in the bedroom. This trains your child's body to know automatically that it's time for sleep when she walks in the bedroom.

- Sleep in a quiet, dark room with comfortable bedding.

- If she can't fall asleep within twenty minutes, she should leave the room, do a boring activity, and then try again. She should avoid lying in bed awake.

- If she is bothered by thinking about something, she should write it down in a notebook she keeps near the bed. She can then be assured she won't forget and can deal with it in the morning.

Sometimes, your child may not feel tired because ADHD makes her feel "on the go." For this reason, how tired she *feels* subjectively is not necessarily a good gauge for how much sleep she *needs*. If your child is running a sleep deficit and were to be objectively tested on attention or memory, she might do poorly—even if she "feels fine." The mental consequences of sleep deficit include a lowered ability to perform daily tasks.

Emily, 13, a busy soccer player and an "A" student, had ADHD. With a chaotic, busy life, she burned the candle at both ends. She was very tired and often felt like she could not think clearly, especially in the later afternoons, when she usually fell asleep unintentionally. Simply adding on another hour of sleep at night made a huge difference, despite initial protests that she could not fit it in her schedule! She found that by getting more sleep at night, she became more productive during the day, with the result that she actually had more time left over.

Nutrition

Another basic requirement for the body is good nutrition. Proper nutrition is vital to everybody—athletes and people with ADHD alike. Too often, people with ADHD try to accomplish a great deal without adequate nutrition. They may be running late and leave the house without breakfast at all, or rely on quickly processed simple carbohydrates (e.g., snack bars, sugary cereal, or a pastry/muffin) for energy. These foods tempt us all in part because they provide a high amount of energy very quickly—but unfortunately, the energy leaves the body just as quickly and can lead to a "crash." The quick "highs" and "lows" that come from eating a diet of simple carbohydrates are bad for the body, as well as for the mind and spirit.

There is little evidence that anything in food directly causes ADHD symptoms. In 1975, Dr. Benjamin Feingold, a pediatric allergist from California, proposed that ADHD was caused or worsened by several artificial substances in the diet: artificial colors and flavors, salicylates (anti-inflammatory chemicals), and preservatives. A few studies provided some weak support for this, but many others did not back it up. In the 1980s, some studies did seem to suggest that there could be benefits from the elimination of some artificial additives; however, elimination of sugar was not as effective. In 2011, another study was performed, in which subjects adhered to a strictly supervised elimination diet. This diet consisted of hypo-allergenic foods like rice, meat, vegetables, and pears. Water, some potatoes, other fruit, and wheat were also allowed. Although beneficial effects were recorded in more than half of the children tested, it is possible that the expectations of the participants influenced the outcome of the study. It is also unclear if the results of the study could be implemented in real life; most children and families would find this diet way too stringent to put into consistent practice.

We recommend a healthy diet and believe in the computer software engineering adage "garbage in, garbage out." Like a computer, your child's body is an amazing high-tech performance machine, so treat it like one! A diet high in protein will fuel her body more steadily than a diet high in sugar, so she should eat protein-rich foods. When she does eat carbohydrates, she should go for whole grain, fiber-rich varieties (avoid "white" carbohydrates). Whole grain carbohydrates take more time to digest, leading to more consistent blood sugar levels, and the natural fiber present in them has the added benefit of making her feel "full" for a longer time. Your child's brain is the most metabolically active part of her body: Pound for pound, it needs more fuel than any other part, including her muscles. She shouldn't skip meals. Studies have shown that eating a healthy breakfast will improve school performance in and of itself.

Annabel was always busy. A sixteen-year-old dynamo taking three Advanced Placement classes and playing sports year-round, she never had a spare moment and was always on the go. She felt low in energy during much of the day. She figured she was just tired from everything she had to do. However, she felt much more energetic after starting to eat smaller high-protein meals every three hours during the day.

Exercise

Many children with ADHD find that their energy is difficult to contain in a quiet setting. Exercising is an appropriate way to release this energy, while improving your child's mood, concentration, and health. There is strong evidence to support the importance of exercise in overcoming ADHD symptoms. Several recent studies have investigated how exercise biologically impacts the brain in ways that are relevant to ADHD. For example, a lab rat model of ADHD was created in an experiment published in 2013. In this experiment, scientists forced some of the "ADHD rats" to exercise on a treadmill.

A different group of ADHD rats was given a common drug treatment for ADHD, Ritalin (methylphenidate). Both the exercise-treated and the Ritalin-treated ADHD rats improved in terms of hyperactivity, and they also improved in terms of spatial learning tasks. Moreover, both groups of rats showed increases in the same brain chemicals. For example, there were increases in enzymes related to dopamine, a neurotransmitter involved in attention and reward (and, as we mentioned in Chapter 1, a possible biological link to ADHD). There was also an increase in Brain-Derived Neurotrophic Factor (BDNF), a chemical that supports the growth and health of brain cells, in both groups. Lowered levels of BDNF have been linked to ADHD.

Exercise has been shown to affect mood. Exercise releases endorphins (natural opioid proteins that affect receptors in the prefrontal and limbic areas of the brain), which connect our minds and emotions with our bodies to produce feelings of success, accomplishment, and happi-

> ### Coaching Corner
> *Exercise causes chemical changes in the brain that improve focus. When your child takes a break for homework, suggest she do something physical (sit ups, pushups, jumping jacks, walking, running).*

ness. In terms of achieving internal satisfaction, it can take hours in a classroom to do what can be achieved in thirty minutes of physical exercise. This internal satisfaction can be a foundation for additional successes, inside or outside the classroom.

Ryan, age thirteen, never felt right at school. He was always fidgeting and his teachers remarked that his hands and feet were never still. He often had a hard time sitting down to start his classwork. He found that he performed much better when he started to do a two-mile run before school. Although that added time to his morning schedule, he found that after a run he was much more efficient at getting ready for school. He arrived at school each day feeling focused, happy, and confident. What a great way to start the day!

ADHD and the Martial Arts

The martial arts have been shown to be helpful for managing ADHD. Learning to focus is an intrinsic part of the martial arts curriculum, in contrast with many other sports, where the emphasis may be placed more on strategy or technique. In a martial arts classroom (dojo), "focus" and "control" are interchangeable concepts.

In a dojo, a child is encouraged to concentrate not only on her own moves, but on the moves of others around her. The dojo balances high energy with personal accountability through the practice of self-control. The structure of the group gives a child clear expectations of how she should behave. Three tenets taught in a traditional dojo are respect of elders (and peers), perseverance through adversity, and development of character. These all positively influence the martial arts student and can benefit an ADHDer as well. Through respect of their seniors and peers in the dojo, students learn to demonstrate respectful behavior in speech and action toward their parents, teachers at school, and even their classmates and siblings. Training toward the goal of earning a black belt is a means for learning perseverance through adversity. This teaches students to commit to accomplishing

Any type of exercise your child likes to do will be beneficial, whether it is a sport or running around on a playground. Some ADHDers do not do well in sports; for example, if a child is inattentive on a soccer field, she will not be ready when the ball is passed to her because her mind is elsewhere. Other children with ADHD may have trouble in a sport like baseball, where they have to wait for their turn.

However, many ADHDers make great athletes in any sport. Sometimes, a playing field is where they feel the *most* focused. No matter what the situation with your child, try to encourage some type of physical activity, even if it is something she had never considered before (e.g., fencing, badminton, or rock climbing). Some children with ADHD will do best in a group sport or activity, because the other members of the team will motivate them; other ADHDers may do better with an individual sport, because there are fewer distractions.

---

goals, regardless of the challenges. The martial arts' powerful influence on character development means that a child training in martial arts will grow to possess self-control—a habit that can benefit her for the rest of her life inside and outside the dojo. She will learn to choose what is right, even when no one is looking.

In addition to the numerous non-physical benefits of studying the martial arts, the physical benefits of strength, flexibility, and balance contribute to the creation of a body that is more resistant to fatigue. But at its best, training in martial arts is not simply physical—it is like a "moving meditation" for students because it improves concentration and attention span. Attentiveness develops because students must look carefully at where they are going while performing the physical techniques. Learning to think proactively in competitive combat develops control over impulsive urges (which are often associated with ADHD). In short, when a student learns the "rules of the game" in a dojo, a strategy for success in the world beyond begins to emerge. Outside of the dojo, black belts often exhibit a quiet confidence and an increased ability to patiently attend to themselves and to others. The development of these skills can be invaluable to children with ADHD.

THE POWER IN YOUR CHILD'S SPIRIT

Spirit is the third part of the self. As stated earlier, it can be summed up as the willpower or energy force within us all. But what do we mean by that? As we use it here, "spirit" corresponds to a more emotional part of the self than "mind"—but it is not merely emotional. What we are referring to by the term "spirit" are the forces within your child that get her going, fill her with inner purpose, and provide meaning to her life: This is her "spiritual intent."

In athletics, an example of spiritual intent carrying the day was the stunning performance by Jason Lezak, who swam in the men's 400 freestyle relay during the 2008 Beijing Olympics. Lezak swam his relay leg faster than anyone would have believed. It was the fastest relay leg in history for a come-from-behind victory. At the last fifty meters, he was still far behind, and briefly thought, "There's no way [to win]."

But then: "I changed. I thought, 'That's ridiculous. I'm at the Olympic Games. I'm here for the United States of America. I don't care how bad it hurts, I'm going after it.' I just got a super charge." His spirit took over and pushed him to swim at a speed that, according to all of his previous trials in training or competition, he never should have been able to reach. This was truly his spirit in action!

What does your child strive for? What are her dreams? What powers her? A great performance in the face of adversity requires a spiritual drive that exists beyond the present moment. Getting the spiritual part of your child on board with the goal of overcoming ADHD is a critical piece of the puzzle, because the positive emotions generated by that spirit can carry her above, beyond, and through the journey, even in the face of setbacks and challenges.

ADHDers often make impulsive efforts to improve, but have trouble sticking with them when they get distracted by other tasks or when things get tough. If your child is an impulse-driven person, it is especially important to help her develop a positive spirit to carry her over bumps in the road or lapses in her own will, and enable her to maintain her original intentions over time. Lasting change is made when the changes are anchored to a positive spiritual intent.

Another feature of "spirit" is that it is enhanced when working with others. Spirit makes the biggest contribution to success when an activity serves a larger purpose and is being pursued not only for one individual, but also for others. This is one reason why athletes often perform at a higher level when they compete as part of a team compared with when they are competing solo. An outstanding athletic endeavor in team sports is powered by an athlete's ability to align his spiritual intent with a "we" and not just a "me" philosophy. Synergy is the unison of different energies and is powerful evidence that the whole can be greater than the sum of the parts. (See Chapter 7 for more on how working with a team enhances spirit.)

Take the previously mentioned example of Jason Lezak. While swimming for the University of California Santa Barbara, he was kicked off the team for a lack of effort and for exhibiting a "me first attitude." After Lezak wrote a "commitment contract" and apologized to his teammates, his coach allowed him to rejoin the team. Jason's newfound character and dedication led to more wins and qualifications. Before his astonishing 2008 Olympics win, he gave a pep talk at the team meeting, which undoubtedly contributed to the team's spirit—as well as his own.

Coaching Corner

Spirit is the component of self that contains within it the ability to strive for something greater than "self" and to inspire those around us. Whether it's the real-life Jason Lezak swimming faster than ever before to make Olympic gold, or the fictional Rocky Balboa fighting to stay up in the boxing ring to prove he's not "just another bum from the neighborhood," it's the human spirit that drives personal performance from ordinary to extraordinary and stirs us all.

In all areas of life—not just in athletics—people can accomplish more when their actions contribute to something greater than themselves. With regard to your child with ADHD, if she thinks about how negative actions affect those closest to her, she will be more likely to make a commitment to changing those actions. To reverse the roles, if those closest to her are positive spirits who share the same (or at least a similar) goal, she will also perform better. If she is surrounded by people who operate negatively or are fragmented in their goals, her spirit will suffer and so will her performance. Exercise 5.4 on page 98 will ask your child to think about incidents where she has either lifted or lowered the spirits of those around her. Because positive and negative attitudes are both contagious, the chance of achieving success or failure is also contagious, based on our interactions with those who surround us. We discuss this further in Chapter 7.

EXERCISE 5.4

ME VS. WE

This exercise is meant to help your child evaluate: When does she contribute positive energy to those around her? When does she contribute negative energy? Have her write down the answers to the following questions on a separate piece of paper.

1. Are you a giver? Name two occasions when your spirit lifted those around you.

2. Name two occasions when working as part of a team helped lift your performance.

3. Name two occasions when your negative spirit brought those around you down.

4. How do your actions contribute to something beyond yourself (for example, the team, the coach, the classroom, the community)?

SUMMARY

In this chapter, we discussed how important it is for your child's whole self to support the decision to improve and manage her ADHD symptoms. A useful model is to consider the self as three parts that need to work together: the mind (the rational motivation), the body (the physical strength), and the spirit (the emotional willpower). When all three parts work together, the goal becomes easier to reach. In the next chapter, we will help you add "focus" to your child's mind, body, and spirit—and you will see how powerful your child can become with this combination!

6.

The Will to Win Is Nothing Without the Will to Train

"I run on the road, long before I dance under the lights."
—MUHAMMAD ALI

In the last chapter, we presented a three-part model of the self designed to help your child conceptualize the mind, body, and spirit. Understanding and appreciating contributions from these three parts of himself will help improve his performance. In this chapter, we build on this model, providing techniques and exercises that will help your child strengthen each of the three parts. When your child sharpens his mind, body, and spirit, he will be able to maintain his attention and achieve his goals—in other words, he will be able to concentrate on "playing to win."

How can your child with ADHD concentrate enough to achieve any goal, even one that he does not find interesting? One way is by using the same holistic approach to performance found in many martial arts, which simultaneously involves engaging the mind, body, and spirit. This approach applies well to ADHD, as the guiding principle is *focus*. Focus here is synonymous with "control" or "concentration." To concentrate on achieving his goals, all parts of your child's self need to be focused—i.e., controlled—to harness energy to achieve a win.

Although we presented a three-part model of the self in the last chapter, concentration is a recipe with *four* ingredients:

1. Focus your eyes.   3. Focus your body.

2. Focus your mind.   4. Focus your spirit.

The reason for the extra ingredient ("focus your eyes") will become apparent as we discuss it below. The eyes are a crucial connector: When the eyes are focused, the mind and body tend to follow suit. As with any recipe, omitting an ingredient will make the outcome less desirable.

THE IMPORTANCE OF TRAINING

Your child currently does not concentrate easily. To be able to "win" (succeed at his goal), your child must first "train" his concentration skills. Training means practicing and learning how to focus well. To train is to acknowledge that accomplishing any worthwhile task—especially learning a whole new way of thinking—won't happen without hard work. Training is important to athletes as well. Without training, an athlete won't win his game.

Athletes who don't train rely on luck to carry them to victory—sometimes it works and sometimes it doesn't. Athletes who do train *create* reliable winning situations for themselves. A winning athlete or team may seem "lucky" to a fan who only watches them on game day, but what that fan hasn't considered is all the training and preparation that goes into that winning performance. As Arnold Palmer said, "It's a funny thing. The more I practice, the luckier I get." Training creates what may *appear* to be luck to somebody who doesn't think about the training behind the success.

Even naturally gifted athletes achieve more when they train; they use training to supplement their natural abilities and to overcome any deficiencies. To increase endurance, speed, accuracy, and strength, athletes routinely employ training strategies that get their mind, body, and spirit to work together. If an athlete is unable to do so, he will have a diminished performance and be less likely to win.

Just as an athlete must train to win in sports, children with ADHD must train to win their personal battles in life. Remember that ADHDers find it naturally more challenging to prioritize one task above other tasks; they find it difficult to stick with the most important thing they need to accomplish. As a result, they scatter their energy and efforts in many different directions—remember the dog from Figure 1.3 in Chapter 1, who had many thoughts but did not prioritize one over the others. The training principles that apply to athletes also apply to ADHDers. Athletes train endurance, speed, accuracy, strength, and other physical and mental skills; what do children with ADHD need to train? Well, first and foremost, an ADHDer must train his ability to *focus.*

Maybe you are saying to yourself, *"But my child can't focus! That's the whole issue!"* Remember, ADHD doesn't mean your child *can't* focus. It means it's harder for him to focus when he is not interested in something. Everybody *can* focus on some things. In fact, many children with ADHD have the ability to focus very intensely if they are interested in something. The challenge for these children is to maintain an appropriate level of focus when performing a task that they are "supposed" to do, but in which they are not very interested. Many athletes face a similar challenge—an athlete may be naturally very gifted in one aspect of his sport (jumping in basketball, for example), but unless he is willing to train hard in other areas (shooting from the free-throw line, making a fast-break, etc.) he will only take his game so far. Training takes talents and turns them into skills. The top athletes in any sport train constantly to perfect *every* aspect of their performance, including aspects in which they are not innately gifted or that they do not naturally enjoy. In the same way, an ADHDer must learn how to maintain focus on completing a task, any task, even one that is uninteresting to him. The eyes are the first part of himself that an ADHDer must train; focusing the eyes is a key ingredient in concentration.

FOCUS YOUR EYES

"Focus your eyes" simply means to look at what you are intending to do. In sports, the common sayings "keep your eyes on the ball" or "look for the open receiver" are two examples. The eyes connect mind, body, and spirit; there is a reason they are called the "windows to the soul." When focused, the eyes connect every part of the self to the task at hand. Eye contact is often a meaningful, powerful, and deep way to communicate with somebody else. Where the eyes go, energy flows.

The eyes are direct anatomical and developmental extensions of the brain. In the embryo, each eye develops from the same starting tissue as the brain, and the retina (the rear part of the eye that serves as a light detector) is composed of nerve cells that connect to the rest of the brain. Areas of the brain that process visual input are functionally linked to areas of the brain that control attention, such as the prefrontal cortex. So there really is a strong anatomical connection between visual focus and attention. Your brain is "hardwired" to attend to aspects of the environment that your eyes focus on.

This type of visual tracking predates the evolution of humans and is widespread in the animal kingdom. Imagine a deer being approached by a predatory saber-toothed tiger. As soon as the deer sees the tiger, the deer's attention should be locked on finding a way to escape from that tiger. If it is able to do this, it will live longer than a deer that gets distracted by a distant palm tree waving in the breeze. As in other animals, the human brain is wired at a very basic level to attend to visual cues and focus on the most vitally important aspects of them. That said, for humans, sight is a more strongly reinforcing sense than it is for most other animals. So whenever your child looks at something, he instantly adds the first ingredient for successful concentration to it. When his eyes are directed at something, it is a reflection of his brain's judgment that something there is important, and at the same time, the act of looking at something increases his brain's power to concentrate in that direction.

Some studies have shown more fragmented and disconnected visual attention in people with ADHD. For example, a technology called *functional magnetic resonance imaging* (fMRI) shows which areas of the brain are actively being used in a human being. Studies using fMRI have suggested that children with ADHD have more frequent brain activities in multiple sensory-related areas of the brain (even during resting periods) than non-ADHD children. This supports the theory that ADHD brains prefer immediate and frequent changes in the sensory environment and resist a resting or steady state; these ADHD brains are wired to seek new stimulation constantly. ADHDers may benefit from training to develop and "refine" their visual processing. In other words, to develop the ability to concentrate, people with ADHD need to train their visual focus. Two common strategies to do this are visual tracking and the visualization of achievements.

Visual Tracking

Visual tracking is actively focusing on the object or task in front of your eyes. A frequently noted physical sign of ADHD is "darting of the eyes":

While a child with ADHD is talking or performing some other task, his eyes wander all around the room instead of maintaining eye contact with his audience or remaining focused on what he is doing. This shows that even as a person with ADHD is talking (or is supposed to be listening), his brain is searching for something else to keep him interested. In other words, the brains of people with ADHD get "bored" with what they themselves are saying before they are even done saying it! It is not hard to understand how this sort of transient and "overly speedy" change in attention can lead to a failure in successful follow-through. Additionally, this sign of ADHD can be very off-putting to other people in a social setting, because it suggests (correctly) a lack of focus that can be interpreted (incorrectly) as disrespect; this can lead to a lot of misunderstandings. A foundational strategy for the success of your child with ADHD is to teach the important lesson that listening *and* talking are properly done by fully engaging *both* the ears and the eyes.

Conversation is not the only task in which children with ADHD have trouble focusing their eyes. If your child learns to consciously focus his eyes on the most important aspect of his primary task, he will learn to focus his thoughts on the same thing. The eyes often "tell" the brain what is most important to focus on, rather than the other way around.

Most people find that working on a task is best done in a place that is free of visual distractions, such as pictures on the wall or random items piled up waiting for attention. Other people in the environment can also divert your child's attention from completing the task at hand. All this is more troubling for ADHDers than for the average person. For example, when taking tests, many students with ADHD become visually distracted by other test takers around them. Watching other students get up, perhaps finishing earlier, sets off a train of distracting thoughts in the ADHDer's mind. Once derailed in this manner, it is harder for the ADHDer to get his thoughts back on track and complete his test.

How can your child overcome these challenges? The answer is for him to train to focus his eyes in order to increase, rather than decrease, his ability to attend to the task at hand. Top athletes practice how to do this constantly: They train themselves to consciously make use of visual focus to *improve* their performance. A professional sprinter coming down the home stretch never drops his eyes; he keeps his head up and focuses his eyes intensely on the finish line. A basketball player who wants to perfect his free throws trains his eyes to focus steadily on the rim as he shoots. A professional tennis player trains his eyes to focus on the ball as it travels all the way to the strings of his racket.

So when your child is trying to accomplish a task, tell him to do what athletes do: "Focus your eyes!" If you catch him looking around the room when he should be reading, tell him to put his eyes back on his page. See if he can recognize the wisdom in deactivating his electronic devices so they are not constantly lighting up. He needs to put away that phone! He should not think he can concentrate on work, TV, and his smartphone simultaneously. By focusing his eyes, he is using the power of his visual system to activate the attention centers in his brain. Visual distractions will make it even harder for him to pay attention to what he needs to accomplish—and that's the last thing any person with ADHD needs.

Coaching Corner

If you want your child to do something, "eyes on me" or "look at me" should be the first instruction you give him. You will then have your child's attention and the instructions that come next have a better chance of being followed. By training his eyes to maintain focus on just one person or on the most important task at hand, your child is simultaneously training his brain to concentrate on achieving his goals.

Many companies are developing video training programs to try to improve attention. These often involve visual tracking, and their aim is to strengthen the user's ability to visually focus on one item of his choosing. Your child may be able to achieve similar results using a simple clock, as demonstrated in Exercise 6.1 on page 105.

There are two types of visual focus an athlete uses for success. The first is cognitive vision, or what can be called "thinking vision," and the second is peripheral vision, or "survival vision." Thinking vision is what you use when reading or looking intently at something. Survival vision is what you use when you react to something out of the corner of your eyes. For example, while sitting on the couch reading a book (using thinking vision), someone comes in the room and, from the side, throws a pillow at your head. When it enters your field of vision, you instinctively raise your arms defensively and move your head out of the way of the object.

EXERCISE 6.1

THE CLOCKWORK MIND

Daryl, age nine, came to Peter's dojo by referral from a school counselor. Daryl was diagnosed at an early age with autism. His attention span and ability to focus his eyes on one thing at a time was so limited that he had to have an assistant by his side to keep him on task at school. Daryl's parents were told that martial arts training had been successful in improving attention spans. Part of Daryl's martial arts training focused on accepting personal ownership of his ability to focus his eyes on one task at a time. To do this, an exercise called the "clockwork mind" was used. The exercise is designed to improve attention span and memory.

TOOL REQUIRED: An analog clock with a second hand.

INSTRUCTIONS FOR YOUR CHILD: While watching the second hand on the clock revolve, beginning at the 12, clap your hands each time the second hand reaches a new number. The goal is to continuously follow the second hand around the clock with your eyes for increasing periods of time. If your eyes lose focus and miss a number, start over again and wait for the second hand to return to the 12. When you wish to increase difficulty, do the activity for longer periods of time (two to three minutes) or create a variety of physical cues to denote each new number (clapping for the first number, snapping for the second, whistling for the third, etc.).

Utilizing both types of visual focus is necessary during a task such as driving a car. If you were to drive a car with *all* of your vision focused on the license plate of the car in front of you (using only your thinking vision), it would not take very long to get into a collision. In contrast, good drivers have learned to also take in the "big picture" (i.e., use survival vision) while driving, passively taking note of different aspects of the road and other cars, lights, and traffic patterns. It is because of the attention required while engaging both these types of vision that a driver will often remember the way to a new destination easily after driving it only once—whereas a passenger in the same car, whose attention was not fully engaged in this way, will not know the way if asked to repeat it. The ability to engage both types of vision simultaneously and to move one's conscious attention seamlessly between these two types of vision makes driving safe. It's important for your child to be in control of what his eyes (and brain!) see. Your child can practice switching between thinking vision and survival vision in Exercise 6.2 below.

EXERCISE 6.2

SOFT EYES

This exercise helps your child consciously control the kind of vision he is using, which controls how he focuses his eyes.

INSTRUCTIONS FOR YOUR CHILD

1. First, use your thinking vision: Find a spot directly in front of you and use your eyes to make a laser, "locked-on-target"-type of focus on it.

2. Keep the same visual focus, but start allowing more surroundings to enter into your perception by taking in a bigger picture. Imagine standing at the foot of a mountain and looking at a particular tree, then softening your gaze so you can take in the entire view without losing your ability to see that tree.

Shifting from "thinking" to "survival" vision with soft eyes creates a sense of tranquility. As part of the exercise, tell your child to alternate back and forth between these two types of vision to strengthen the bond between his vision and his physical state of being.

Visualization

Visualization is more than just picturing your actions as if watching them on TV: It includes re-creating the feelings, reactions, thoughts, sights, and sounds associated with those actions. When your ADHD child specifically visualizes himself completing a task *well*—instead of simply picturing the task in an abstract way—he becomes an active participant in creating success for himself. Professional athletes such as Tiger Woods and Michael Jordan have used visualization techniques to improve their games. They don't just train their physical eyes to focus; they train their "mind's eye" to focus as well. When an athlete visualizes shooting successful free throws in basketball or serving up an ace in tennis, he stimulates connections between his mind, body, and spirit that facilitate actual performance of that skill in a real situation.

The more vivid and true to life the visualization, the more powerful the effect. For example, a classic study by psychologist Alan Richardson tested three groups of athletes. One group physically practiced shooting free throws every day for twenty days, and another group spent the same amount of time mentally rehearsing the free throws. A third group only physically practiced for two of the twenty days. The group that did the mental imagery improved nearly as much as the group that physically practiced every day (and both groups improved far more than the group that practiced for two days). Similar studies have reproduced this effect in other sports, such as golf, where the test subjects visualized putting. These studies show that the brain does not differentiate as much as one would think between something it vividly imagines doing and something that is actually experienced.

> ### Coaching Corner
>
> *When your child visualizes himself achieving his goal, he can also create many different paths to take to that goal. If his first path to the goal does not work out in real life, he can bounce back and try a different method. Acting and living as though his goal has already been accomplished gives your child that extra motivation to really succeed, because he has visualized how great he felt upon completing the goal.*

Your child can use this technique not only to visualize himself performing a physical task, but also to visualize himself achieving his goals. If he sets a goal to keep his desk clean, ask him to repeatedly visualize in his mind's eye a sparkling, organized desk (or at least the top of it). Visualization can be an especially powerful technique to use just before starting a task that requires sustained attention. Before sitting down to do his homework, or to take a test in class, ask your child to envision a situation where he has successfully completed something, or won something. What a great feeling that was! In Exercise 6.3 on page 108, have him visualize that situation first, actively decide that he wants to experience that feeling again, and *then* set down to work.

EXERCISE 6.3

VISUALIZATION OF YOUR CHILD'S GOAL

In a quiet moment, ask your child to think about one of his goals. Have him vividly picture all the details; visualize it from every angle, with any associated sounds or smells. He should picture every step he would have to take until his goal is achieved. Hopefully, this "picture in his mind" will help him achieve the goal.

Below are some examples of questions he can ask himself:

- *Where would I be when I accomplished my goal?*
- *Who would be around me?*
- *What would it sound like?*
- *Who would be with me?*
- *How will I feel when I get it done?*

FOCUS YOUR MIND

To focus your mind means to think *only* about what you are doing. Holding the mind on your present action can be likened to holding a fixed physical position, like a low squat. As explained in the previous chapter, the mind corresponds to the cognitive part of the self. When trained properly, the mind has the power to tune out distractions, even in your child with ADHD.

Focusing your child's mind is the second ingredient in concentration. If his eyes are focused but his mind is not, it is essentially just daydreaming! The opposite of daydreaming is a state of mindfulness where both your child's eyes *and* his thoughts are engaged and focused on the present task.

The concept of blocking extraneous thoughts from current action is easier said than done for most people—and is a core issue for ADHDers—but it is a skill that can be trained. The sections below offer some training techniques designed to accomplish this.

Interval Training Techniques

Mikey was the second-grade class clown. He was goodhearted and well-intentioned, but he just could not sit still for more than thirty seconds to do math. When he did sit down, he rushed through his work, making every silly mistake possible. He often didn't even copy the math problem correctly from the book when he was doing homework, and half the time, he would add when the problem involved subtraction. Not surprisingly, he flunked most of his math quizzes and was sent for remedial math instruction. Mikey labeled himself "dumb at math." He didn't want to do any math, and one page of math problems looked like an impossible task to him. However, with training, he learned to focus on one problem at a time and to take a quick break when he was done with each one. That lengthened to doing a few problems at a time before he relaxed. As he learned to focus and keep from making silly mistakes, he found that he was actually quite good at math, with a knack for coming up with novel ways to solve problems.

Many athletes use a technique called interval training to build up cardiovascular stamina and power. In this technique, high-intensity bursts of exercise are alternated with lower-intensity periods of recovery. This essentially means working in short, but effective, bursts within a specific time period. Beginners often believe interval training is a method meant to increase physical capacity or ability; such people focus solely on the high-work period and may "zone out" during the lower-intensity "rest" intervals. Coaches and athletes who are more experienced understand that the low-intensity periods are just as important as the high-intensity periods. In almost any physical competition, there will be periods of intense drive and periods of recovery. In a team game like basketball or hockey, athletes are almost constantly being rotated in and out to sustain the level of intensity that is required for the whole game. In a single-person sport like tennis, the players will sit during the changeover. During these times, rest is important not only for the athletes to physically recover from the intense effort they have been giving, but also to keep their focus fresh for the next interval. The low-intensity period gives the athletes a chance to clear their heads. Additionally, it is often a time where they establish goals they would like to accomplish during the next part of play, which keeps goals immediate and relevant.

To use another example, golf players don't maintain the same intensity of mental focus throughout a long game; they focus on one hole at a time, taking mental breaks in between. There are even rules built into golf that help players achieve the necessary mental focus on each hole. For example, each player is accompanied by a caddie, who reminds the player of what to do between holes and between swings. This helps the golf players focus their minds very intensely when it is their turn to swing, and permits their minds to recover between holes. The low-intensity periods are there in part to train the athlete's mind to maintain focus while his fatigued body is recovering from a period of intense physical activity.

The same training concept can be applied to children who are working to improve their mental focus. Instead of always working in a "half-on" position, this concept teaches your child the difference between "on" and "off"—and gets him to practice "on." However, while it is great for him to be focused on a task, knowing how (and when) to relax and then regain focus is of great value, both socially and competitively. Asking your child to be totally focused *all the time* is neither realistic nor desirable—picture someone you may know who is always "too intense" or "on." Your child can practice this mental "interval training" technique in Exercise 6.4.

EXERCISE 6.4

THE TIMER TECHNIQUE

Maybe your child can concentrate for only two minutes before losing focus. Take a timer, set it for two minutes, and then start by asking your child to focus his mind as hard as he can on his task. Then, take one minute to rest or goof around. But use a timer, so that the "relax" minute is truly a minute. Start with two minutes on, one minute off. Be sure that his two minutes of work represents the most dedicated work of his life! The goal is to dedicate *all* 120 seconds to the concentration period. After your child demonstrates that he can focus his mind for two minutes, seek to expand to three minutes (or more) of 100-percent focused work!

During your child's rest minute, you may want to think of some - thing physical to do with him. Remember, physical activity releases endorphins and stimulates a change or variety in thinking and breathing, which helps the brain focus. You have only a minute of downtime to work with, so do something quick: jumping jacks, bouncing on a small trampoline, lifting some hand weights, or perhaps a few sit-ups or push-ups. If these don't work, a walk to the window may clear your child's mind and allow him to get some fresh air.

As he is trying to train his mind to focus in other areas, ask your child with ADHD to think specifically of times and activities in which he *already* does this well—whether it is video games, sports, or attempts to impress a potential girlfriend. Ask him to replicate that same level of mental focus for the task at hand. Think of this as "mental cross training." Muscles become conditioned by the workloads they repeatedly perform. Your child's brain can be conditioned in the same way.

Your child may never get past focusing his mind for a few minutes at a time. Or, you might find that he can concentrate for a few minutes on one type of activity, but an hour on a different type of activity. Although interval training involves some "down time," don't be discouraged—he will find that he gets more done this way, and in a shorter total period of time. He will be less anxious about doing work if he knows it is only for two minutes at a time; he will be less likely to procrastinate because it will seem more doable.

Mindfulness

Mindfulness training—also thought of as learning to "be present in the now"—rose in popularity during the 1960s in the United States, along with Buddhism and other forms of meditation. The traditional Buddhist concept of "mindfulness" is meant to apply to all aspects of life. Mindfulness means to be fully aware of the present experience of your whole self: heart and mind united in body. For example, mindfulness encompasses techniques that train the mind to focus on breathing (uniting the mind with the body). Mindfulness training involves paying full attention to the thoughts, feelings, and sensations that you are experiencing in the moment. Once made habit, mindfulness eliminates stress, anxiety, and self-doubt, as worry about the future slips away and challenges from the past are not revisited.

Mindfulness training can be applied in sports: An athlete performing his best isn't planning for the future or thinking about the past. His moves are all in the present. Athletes often train to focus on their breathing—this is not merely to make sure they have enough oxygen to physically perform at a high level, it also automatically focuses their minds and grounds them in the present. Stu Mittleman, world-record setter for the 1,000-mile run and the author of *Slow Burn*, said, "Your breath is the glue that connects the mind and the body." Breathing attaches the outside world to the inside world and provides the body with a natural rhythm.

Neurofeedback: A New Technique

One cutting-edge technology that some children with ADHD are finding helpful is neurofeedback. Neurofeedback is a technique in which your child's brain waves are monitored by electrodes that feed into a computer that then gives him visual feedback, rewarding him when he is able to maintain calm and focus. It can be expensive and hard to access, but there are a number of studies that show it to be effective.

Whether or not neurofeedback itself is obtainable for you and your child (for many people it probably isn't a realistic option), the basic principle behind it—training in mindfulness—is perfectly free and available to all. Your child doesn't really need electrodes and a high-tech computer set-up to train in increasing mindfulness; people in many cultures have been doing this for thousands of years without the assistance of high-tech bells and whistles.

This concept can be applied to ADHD. When your child's mind loses focus and disconnects from his body, conscious breathing can reunite the two. Children with ADHD often feel "out of sync," like the world is moving too slowly for them. Therefore, part of your child's training is to teach his mind to sync up with the rest of the world—to get in touch with the present moment. Many children with ADHD bounce from past to future and never (or only briefly) think in the present moment. They worry about starting their task (future) and think about the fact that they didn't get everything done yesterday (past). They worry about the consequences of not getting things done or about doing them well (future). They get angry that they were assigned the task in the first place (past), or fret that they have already done things just like this before (past again). They complain that the work is so boring (comparison with past work), while asking why they should have to do it again (future). Instead of all these concerns about past and future, your child

> **Coaching Corner**
> Breathing connects a person's inner rhythm to the external environment. Training in conscious breathing focuses the mind and grounds it in the present.

must focus on what he is doing in the *present moment* in order to concentrate on successfully attaining his goals.

As an example of a boy who is not thinking in the present moment in class, consider the words of Robert, age ten:

> **What I think about during class:**
> *What I'll do when I get home*
> *What I want be doing right now*
> *How much time I have left in class*
> *Scenarios, such as what I would do if an earthquake happened*
> *What I will be doing in the future*
> *Do I have any appointments?*

Exercise 6.5 below and Exercise 6.6 on page 114 promote mindfulness and the feeling of "being here now" by teaching your child breathing and focusing techniques. The mindfulness gained in these exercises trains your child to fully concentrate on his chosen tasks. They put your child in control of his own mind. These exercises are excellent techniques that can be done before school or work. Your child will start the day in a calmer frame of mind, ready to focus.

EXERCISE 6.5

BREATH PUSH-UPS

This is a three-step breathing exercise that will help your child center and reconnect the mind and body.

STEP 1:   Take one abdominal breath in through the nostrils (one part).

STEP 2:   Hold breath for four parts.

STEP 3:   Exhale breath out of the mouth for two parts.

Example
Begin by breathing in while clapping four times. Hold the breath without changing rhythm and clap sixteen times, then breathe out while clapping eight times. This is one cycle; work up to the point where you can complete ten cycles back to back without a break.

EXERCISE 6.6

A MIND OF PAPER

Have your child begin by sitting still in silence (eyes open or closed) and picturing a completely blank piece of plain white paper. He should first visualize this piece of white paper with edges and a size. He should then gradually increase the size of the paper until it is so large he cannot see the edges, and then he should hold this plain white image in his mind. When thoughts begin to interrupt his focus, he should allow them to fade away like clouds passing by in the background.

Eliminating Mental Distractions

Besides your child's internal thoughts about the past and the future, his most common distractions are most likely from electronics. Many children try to accomplish work on the computer while numerous other programs, like Facebook and Instagram, are open. Text messages constantly interrupt many teens and distract them from what should be their focus. Some children leave the TV on when they're trying to work. Most people feel they can handle this and that they are effectively "multitasking." Scientific studies have shown that this is actually an example of the mind's great facility for self-deception. An actual comparison of performance when multitasking versus when focused on a single task will invariably show that we do better when we are focused on one thing at a time; we all tend to believe we multitask better than we actually can.

Your brain can't actually perform two tasks at once. Instead, it switches between tasks. Research has shown that people who multitask actually take about twice as much time to complete the different tasks than they would if they had stuck with one task at a time. Nearly everyone who multitasks is less efficient than he would be if he did one thing at a time. This makes perfect sense: Because it takes time to refocus whenever the brain switches tasks, and because of mistakes that slip "under the radar" as the brain switches back and forth, it takes significantly longer to complete two tasks "at once" than to complete one task at a time. Each task is also more error-prone when multitasking.

It has been suggested that people who habitually multitask may become increasingly worse at focusing over time. According to this theory, as a result of habitual multitasking, the brain may lose the ability to prioritize and focus, and instead become more distractible. This may be a contributor to the rise of the diagnosis of ADHD in our increasingly high-paced, information-laden society. In any case, multitasking is not beneficial for children who are already having challenges maintaining their mental focus. In the words of John, age fifteen: "I will start to get dressed then find myself on the Internet. I will put one shoe on, then realize it is time for breakfast, go into the kitchen, and find myself still with only one shoe on."

It is hard to escape electronic distractions, especially since there is a genuine need for most of us to use computers at work or in school. However, just as it is ridiculous to try to lose weight with cookies scattered around the house, it is also ridiculous to think your child can concentrate on his work if there are electronic distractions tempting him everywhere within the same space.

Technology that Helps

Although technology can contribute to distracting your child's mind, it can be used to reduce mental distractions as well. There are a number of programs and apps that have been designed to help block electronic distractions. These include (among many others):

- "SelfControl"—This allows you to block certain websites for a set period of time. You can't password yourself back into the website.

- "AutoHideDesktopIcons" or "Camouflage"—These allow you to keep one app in the foreground of your computer, hiding other apps (although you can switch from one to the other easily).

- "StayFocusd"—This app limits your ability to visit your "temptation websites" to a set period of time each day.

See "Tips for Parents of ADHD Children: Home" (page 75) for additional resources.

Cultivate Habits that Improve Attention

The way that popular TV shows, movies, and pop music *become* popular is by being very *sensorially stimulating* (i.e., instantly entertaining or gratifying) without requiring much internal mental work (i.e., attention, concentration, mental processing power). In this way they reach the maximum number of minds as quickly as possible. One way to counteract this is to get your child to cultivate interests that do not fall into the category of "popular media."

If your child likes games, consider games that strengthen his attention span rather than breaking it down. There are many traditional games that can do this. For example, a child who usually plays video games can try the game of chess. A chess player must build up his ability to maintain attention over a long period of time. This is necessary to become good at chess, as a good player learns to recognize patterns on the board and design a series of moves (and consider his opponent's possible responses) that will get him to checkmate.

If your child is a music lover, cultivate an appreciation for classical music instead of (or in addition to) modern popular music. Most popular songs are, at most, a few minutes long and repeat a very brief melody and chorus several times. They contain short, repetitive, and simple elements in order to be maximally "catchy"—in other words, they are designed to be easy to remember and easy to dance to, but their patterns and meanings are not designed to command a lot of focused attention. In contrast, traditional classical music contains complex melodies, rhythms, and orchestration that are multilayered and interwoven. These typically play for long durations. To appreciate even part of a single movement in a symphony, your child must train his attention to keep track of melody, tempo, instrumentation, musical key, and more over prolonged periods of time.

Finally, consider some bonding experiences that can encourage attentiveness. Going on outings with your child and having conversations with him about the things you see will help his social development and will strengthen your relationship with him over time. Take some time away from the television or movie theater and spend it instead at the local art museum. As with the chess and classical music examples, it is probably obvious to you that it takes more "work" (and, yes, training!) to appreciate paintings and sculptures compared with watching a favorite TV show or a blockbuster movie—but, of course, that is precisely the point of this exercise. Just like any muscle in your child's body, his attention span will only grow "stronger" through repetitive exercise; that is what training is. The more he trains, the easier it will become, and as it grows easier, he may discover that he actually enjoys these activities after all!

The deck of cards in modern culture is heavily stacked against a child with ADHD—but that doesn't mean it is impossible to build up his attention span. You can help your child do so, and you can even have fun and connect with him at the same time, simply by taking his current interests and refining them. This has other benefits as well, such as increasing his appreciation for world culture and what it has to offer him for the full enjoyment of his life!

FOCUS YOUR BODY

To keep his actions constructive, your child must control his body. His body is the strongest connection his mind and spirit have to the present world. The mind and spirit can jump around from past to present to future; the body, however, exists and moves only in the present. We can't physically move in the future, and we can't physically move in the past. We all can *anticipate* movement in the future and *remember* movements of the past, but our actual ability to move exists only in the present moment. So being connected to (fully aware and in control of) one's bodily movements requires the self to be present in the moment. This is why we say the body is the part of the self that anchors the other parts (the mind and the spirit) to the present.

Some children with ADHD have a lot of physical energy. Their bodies are most comfortable in motion. They don't like to sit still and always seem to be fiddling with something, touching things. One word that is often used to describe them is "fidgety." (Remember, though, that your child doesn't need to be "hyperactive" in order to be diagnosed with ADHD. Some children have a hyperactive variant of ADHD, and some do not; a child can be distractible while he is moving, but a child can also be distractible when he is just sitting still.)

We view your child's physical energy and liveliness as good and positive forces. They're valuable! People pay a lot of money for caffeine and other stimulants to have more energy. The challenges arise from too much *unfocused* energy. In your child with ADHD, these challenges may include trouble with accomplishing responsibilities because he can't sit down long enough to complete tasks. Your child may have difficulty listening to and following instructions because he has to get up and walk around while people are talking to him. Even if he is able to pay attention, your child's fidgeting may make him appear nervous; this can be off-putting to other people around him. In general, other people may become annoyed (rightly or wrongly) from watching your child's constant movement. This is often the case in a school setting, where a teacher who is trying to control and instruct a class views any child who moves excessively as a liability.

The urge to move is natural in children with the hyperactive variant of ADHD. Obviously these children are not *trying* to be annoying or "bad." In fact, they may be trying hard *not* to move. Paradoxically, it takes a lot of energy for them to be still. For someone who is hyperactive, it feels awful to have to sit when his body wants to get up and move. It takes a lot of willpower to slow that body down; it takes energy that would be useful if it could be harnessed and directed to the task at hand. If your child is concentrating on limiting his movement, he's correspondingly not concentrating as much on the lesson or the work that needs to get done. Many children—especially young ones who have trouble seeing things from other points of view—have challenges with "self-control" because they do not understand why they have to be still.

Athletes face similar challenges in the sense that they also have to train themselves to move at the right speed and with the right timing. Often, athletes have to train themselves to move faster rather than slower, but the principle is the same. The idea is to train to perform the right moves when they are required. In almost every sport, an important saying is, "timing is everything." The following five techniques are designed to focus your child's body so that his timing syncs up with the present moment.

1. Add Exercise Before the Task

In general, we recommend some form of exercise for your child before any situation in which he has to sit still. This can be quick: just stretching and some light calisthenics before going to school, for example. Anything is better than nothing; your child does not need special clothes or a gym. Remember from Chapter 5 that exercise is a natural "focuser" because of the chemical changes in the brain that it generates. (See page 93.)

2. Assume a "Ready" Posture

Getting ready to complete a task should involve a special posture that signifies a preparedness to work. Athletes often position their bodies in a way that imbues their first step with energy. Think of a sprinter about to run; he does not just lollygag around before the gun goes off. Think of a baseball player about to take a swing. He does not just hang around home plate, waiting for a pitch to come his way; he raises his bat and keeps his eyes on the pitcher. Think of the center about to hike a football, or a ballet dancer getting her body into position on stage just before the curtain goes up.

When your child needs to work, he must put his body in a posture that signals: "Let's start, and do this with energy." Your child's physical movements mirror his personality. Tell your child that no one in the universe can control his body besides him; therefore, his body tells other people about him. If he wants to be the best student in the room, tell him to sit like the best student in the room, rather than all slouched over. If he wants to be efficient, he needs to walk with purpose and energy like an efficient person. "Body language" speaks to the world around you. Focusing your body is moving the right way at the right time for the right reason; it is a form of communication between yourself and others, in every waking moment.

If your child is an athlete, consider having him assume the "starting" posture for his sport, and then move to do his work. For example, if he is a tennis player, have him first put his body in the same position he would use to serve on the court. Then, sit down to do his work. This may seem silly, but he is sending his body an important message: It's time to get ready, get set—go! In time, your child will be able to drop the starting posture and create the same "ready" state by mentally rehearsing it. (See "Visualization" on page 106). Some children can benefit from changing into their team uniforms before sitting down to work, because the action of putting on their athletic uniform makes them feel more focused.

Your child doesn't have to view himself as a sportsperson to use this technique. We gave the example above of a ballet dancer getting ready before the curtain rises—if your child likes to dance and is used to starting *"en Pointe,"* that works! And if your child doesn't dance or do anything physical, but simply likes music, that can work too: He can briefly play, sing, or hum his favorite song before getting down to work, so long as he uses it as a means to focus his body. In Exercise 6.7 on page 120, your child can practice adapting a positive posture.

EXERCISE 6.7

POWER POSTURE

Have your child emphatically say the word "yes." Have him say it again, now with twice the emotion. Have him yell it louder. . . . then again, even LOUDER. With increasing volume, intensity, and emotion, ask him to yell "YES" in different tones—angry, scared, or sad. Finally, have him YELL "YES" out in a *celebratory* tone— as if he just won a major prize or the lottery.

Next, ask him to notice: What did his body say when he yelled "YES!"? What body language (specifically, what gestures or postures) accompanied his celebration at the end? These are his physical triggers for feeling positive. For some children, it's a fist pump; for others, it might be clasping their hands together and shaking. Your child can use these celebratory gestures as "ready postures" in the future.

Experiencing victories—not only emotionally, but also physically— can help guide your child in creating a personal power posture. This is a way for your child to connect his body and spirit. Even if your child feels disempowered in the moment, adopting his "power posture" will communicate a message of positivity to everybody else in his world. More importantly, it will communicate a message of confidence that will help him rise to the next challenge and continue to perform at a high level.

3. Add a Harmless, Non-distracting Activity to the Task

Squeezing a ball or squeezing your legs are excellent outlets for physical activity while remaining seated and focused. Some people place a band around the legs of the chair their child sits in so the child can kick at it. The catch here is that you should be thoughtful about what a "non-distracting" activity is. People around your child will get annoyed if he sits in a test room tapping his pencil against the desk or kicking the side of his chair noisily. Work with your child to find a way that he can harmlessly burn some of his energy in these situations without distracting himself *or* annoying those around him.

4. Add a New Habit to Overcome the Challenge

Some movements are done unintentionally, out of habit. For example, if your favorite food is lying out on the counter, you will most likely move toward it and eat it, even if you are not hungry. A number of psychological studies have shown how important environmental cues are in triggering habits. For example, if it's a person's habit to eat when he watches TV, then looking at the TV will often trigger an impulse to get something to eat, even if he is not hungry. So if his goal is to eat less, he will have a higher chance of success if he eliminates the cue (TV=food). To do this, he might have to start eating in a different room from the TV.

Sometimes, to accomplish a goal, it's best to alter routine—to do something different and create variety. If your child fidgets a lot at his desk (and it interferes with his work), what can he do differently? Have him try standing instead of sitting. Try switching chairs. If he can't sit through a movie, try having him sit in a place other than his "usual seat" in the theater. If your child's habit is to rush out of the room once he's done with his task, leaving his items scattered, ask him to try using his left hand to gather his things, rather than his right (reverse if he is left-handed). Changing up his usual habits will help eliminate cues that lead to unwanted behavior.

5. Slow Down and Think about Each Movement

An athlete who needs to train in a particular skill will often be coached in the mechanics of the skill by rehearsing at slower speeds. Only once the moves have become second nature—that is, burned into "muscle memory"—will the coach or trainer encourage the athlete to add speed and power. The "slowing it down" part is key for your child with ADHD, just as it is for an athlete learning a new technical skill. Going slowly keeps unneeded and undirected movement to a minimum. In other words, it refines and focuses the movement.

You can help your child train himself to focus his movements using a "think fast, move slow" mindset. Physical movements of your child's body can then become an anchor for bringing your child's mind and spirit into focus during the present task. In Exercise 6.8 on page 122, your child can place a focus on his body language.

As an example of how to implement these five body-focusing strategies in ADHD, consider the case of Sally, a teenager with ADHD who

EXERCISE 6.8

MUTED TV

Much of what we "say" is actually communicated via body language, but sometimes we're not aware of what our body language is saying. One quick exercise to train your child to keep his body congruent with what he is working to accomplish is to have him envision a camera filming what he is currently doing (or you can actually take a video of him). He should imagine that he's watching himself on TV with the volume on mute. What do his actions say? What message does his body language, including his posture, convey? Communication, even among humans who love to talk, is actually heavily weighted toward nonverbal signals.

runs around her house every morning while getting ready to leave, then rushes out at the last moment without thinking about whether she has everything she needs for the day. She is frustrated because she often forgets to bring her homework to school, even though she did it the night before. This is something she wants to change.

Our first strategy is to implement regular physical exercise (Strategy 1). Sally might decide to do fifty jumping jacks every day before she leaves the house in the morning to center her focus and release extra energy. That might take her about a minute, so even though she always feels like she's running late and has no time, she can admit that a minute of jumping jacks is something she has the time to do.

Our next strategy is to add some variety to Sally's routine. Sally might decide to leave the house using a side door, rather than the front door. Because she is doing something a little differently that deviates from her routine, the effect will be to slow her down. This alone will improve her chances of thinking about her departure long enough to remember to go over what she needs to take with her (Strategy 5).

More importantly, this affords Sally with the opportunity to use Strategy 4 (create a new, more constructive habit). Now that she's doing something different in her routine and has slowed down a bit, she can train herself to use exiting through the side door as a new cue to pause and check her bag to see if she has brought all her homework for the day.

Not all strategies will work in every case. Different strategies work for different children in different circumstances; experiment to find a routine that will effectively slow your child down and allow him to focus. In Exercise 6.9, you and your child can brainstorm new techniques and how to apply them to your child's particular situations.

EXERCISE 6.9

THE MENTAL PAUSE BUTTON

Have your child think about one area in which his hyperactivity or impulsiveness is a challenge for him. What can he do to make his movements more deliberate? Write down some plans using a separate piece of paper. To start, use some (you don't have to use all) of the five strategies to improve the results:

1. Exercise before the task

2. Come up with a "ready posture"

3. Think of a non-distracting activity

4. Create a new habit

5. Slow down and think!

FOCUS YOUR SPIRIT

As discussed in Chapter 5, "spirit" is the immeasurable part of the self (for some people it can have religious connotations—for others, it doesn't). Your child's spirit is his *will* to train and to succeed. It's the emotional, from-the-gut motivation, the part of the self that makes him do better than the mind thought he could. Your child's spirit also needs some focusing at times!

There are different types of spirits, which we will simplify here by focusing on two types: "Happy-go-lucky" and "Eeyore" (named after the character in *Winnie the Pooh* who perpetually has a raincloud over his head). Of course, these are not mutually exclusive and most people, including children with ADHD, have a little of each spirit type at different times and in different situations.

People with happy-go-lucky spirits go from whatever makes them happy to whatever makes them happier, ignoring pesky details like deadlines or being on time. This is a precious and endearing aspect of many personalities, and one that is beneficial in many ways. Notably, children who are happy-go-lucky are, by definition, not worriers. They tend to be joyful and to find delight in many activities. However, happy-go-lucky spirits are not without challenges when demands are placed on them. They often lack the motivation to do what they don't like because their nature is to do what makes themselves happy. Thus, they find it challenging to focus on what authority figures want them to do. For people with happy-go-lucky spirits, life would be fine if they could just do what pleases them, but that is not always the way life works out. Unfortunately, even if your child starts out happy-go-lucky in life, he could become depressed and discouraged if his ADHD creates extra challenges for him or diminishes his success.

Refer back to Chapters 2 and 3 on goal-setting to help your happy-go-lucky child think about reasons to make improvements and achievable ways to get there. This may encourage him to stick with a goal and care more about the outcome.

If an athlete's mindset toward his skills is "all is well" when it isn't, he is less likely to work on his skills and more likely to lose in competition. One function of a coach is to do a reality check on an athlete's performance and tell him objectively where he still needs to train. Similarly, an ADHDer who tends to be overly optimistic may need advice from somebody with a clearer view of his situation to tell him where he still needs work. (More information about coaching can be found in Chapter 9.)

Annabeth, age sixteen, was definitely happy-go-lucky. Nothing bothered her! She did note that she wasn't doing well in school, that she always lost her things (she was on her tenth cellphone), and her friends always told her that she never paid attention to what they were saying. But she dismissed it all with a giggle: "That's just me!" She had a winning, sweet smile, and was so good-natured about everything that parents, teachers, and friends made excuses for her. Year after year the same patterns remained. But at age sixteen, her parents realized that she was going to college soon and they would not be able to help her as much. A teacher sat her down at school and had a serious discussion with her about how she could do better. She began a concerted effort to make some changes at school.

In the opposite corner is the Eeyore spirit, named after the cynical and grumbling donkey in *Winnie the Pooh*. Eeyore spirits tend to think, "Why should I have to go through school or work? It's just not that meaningful to me." An ADHDer with an Eeyore spirit is likely to grouse about all the work he has to do and all the demands placed on him that separate him from what he would like to do. Eeyores also tend to compare themselves negatively to others (e.g., "She has it so much easier than me.") This is similar to an athlete who feels like he's being punished in training: "Why should I put in all these long hours doing the same drill again and again?" "Why can't I eat a Twinkie once in a while, instead of always eating these low-fat protein nuggets?"

> **Coaching Corner**
> *Your child's spirit is his unique gift to everyone around him. He contributes his one-of-a-kind outlook! But sometimes his spirit will need refocusing so he can become a more positive person. If he feeds positivity with his faith in his ability to look for the positives, then negative thinking will starve to death.*

Unfortunately, the human brain in general is prewired to focus on negatives (this is called the "negativity bias" in cognitive psychology). This means that a negative remark is innately more significant to most people's brains than a positive remark. You have probably noticed that if somebody insults you, you are much more likely to register that and to take it to heart (and even ruminate on it) than if somebody compliments you (which will probably make you feel good in the moment, but may have a much more short-term effect). It's important to know that the human mind has this innate bias, and so unless that "negativity bias" is corrected by training in a counteracting habit of thought, it may lead you (or your child) to see the world in a more negative light than it truly is. In other words, "seeing the glass half-empty" is actually a natural tendency in nearly everybody that needs to be overcome, or "unlearned," as we mature. This is another place where you as a parent can help your child grow in a positive way.

One simple yet effective way to combat the negativity bias is the "three-for-one" technique. If you catch your child making a negative statement (e.g., "I had the worst day!") ask him to think of three positive statements about the same thing ("Well, I did laugh at that joke in gym class," "Somebody complimented me," "I got that project done"). This three-for-one thinking is how your child can convert (with training and time) from a "glass half-empty" kind of person into a "glass 100 percent full" person (50 percent water, 50 percent air!). Your child can practice this technique in Exercise 6.10 below. The long-term goal is for this pattern of thought to become reinforced—for this positive brain circuit to become stronger than the one that is driving the negativity bias. Think of the Positive Cycle of Success versus the Negative Cycle of Failure in Chapter 3, both of which strengthen with "exercise."

EXERCISE 6.10

THE GLASS IS 100 PERCENT FULL

On another sheet of paper, have your child write down at least three good things that happened to him today.

Another effective way to reverse the Eeyore spirit is to train in gratitude. Gratitude is an immensely powerful outlook that lifts the spirit and provides inspirational drive. Norman Vincent Peale wrote, "The more you practice the art of thankfulness, the more you have to be thankful for. This, of course, is a fact. Thankfulness does tend to reproduce in kind. The attitude of gratitude revitalizes the entire mental process by activating all other attitudes, thus stimulating creativity." To paraphrase Peale, one of our own favorite mantras is, "Gratitude is the attitude!" What we mean by this is that when your child's mind adopts the mindset of gratitude (by reminding himself of everything positive in

Coaching Corner

Adopting an attitude of gratitude will help your child become a happier person who can more easily recover from disappointments and let go of resentment and anger. Practicing gratitude will also increase his motivation to improve himself in order to act positively toward others. Gratitude is the most powerful positive emotion. Cultivated daily, it grows in its ability to overpower negative, or "stinking," thinking.

his life), his spirit naturally aligns into a posture that is ready to act on the world positively. This is a way for your child to align his mind and his spirit so that these two parts of himself are ready to move forward and take action. Reminding himself of all the positives in his life (see Exercise 6.11 below) will give your child the strength and inspiration to keep going. Fear, doubt, frustration, anger, hopelessness, and other negative emotions are all neutralized by the attitude of gratitude.

There are really no "have to's" in life. We all make choices about what we do or don't do—even though it sometimes feels as if we have no choice. If your child really doesn't want to participate in school, nobody can *make* him learn anything. Similarly, nobody can make a person with ADHD improve himself, get better grades, or become more organized. In the end, it is the ADHDer who must make these choices. When gratitude is present, resentment and selfishness fall away. Ask

EXERCISE 6.11

ATTITUDE OF GRATITUDE

Questions are an excellent tool for directing the focus of our minds. Asking the right questions can lead us to cultivate an attitude of gratitude that is present even on the toughest of days. Gratitude leads to a feeling of abundance, which in turn leads to giving. It reminds you of how much you have and how much you can do with what you have. When gratitude muscles are conditioned, they will be able to withstand setbacks and temporary defeats.

Help your child answer the following questions on a separate piece of paper:

1. What are five things I am thankful for?

2. What are four things I am most excited about today?

3. What are three things I love?

4. What are two situations that make me smile and laugh?

5. What am I giving to others today? What am I giving to myself?

your child to think about the tasks he has to do today. Is everybody in the world able to do them, or are there some people who don't have the opportunity? If he can think about why he is fortunate to be able to do the tasks that challenge him, they will seem less like tasks and more like rewards. The difference is all in his attitude. If he can start thinking about that project he has to complete as something he is lucky to have the brains or the opportunity in life to do, it becomes less of a "have to" and more of a "get to" situation. That alone is extremely empowering!

SUMMARY

In this chapter, we discussed how to help train your child to focus his eyes, mind, body, and spirit. Athletic champions describe this state of perfect focus as being "in the zone." This state continues to be a key ingredient in outstanding performances. We have gone over techniques to help your child slow down and pay attention to what is happening in the present moment around him. The training techniques that we presented will take time to become automatic in your child, but it's never too early to start implementing them. Once attained, they are skills that can help him for the rest of his life. As with any skill, your child will need to work hard to internalize them—but once he becomes aware of what he can accomplish by achieving this level of focus and has been rewarded for it a few times, he will begin to do so more and more naturally out of his own desire to be successful and to have a positive impact on the world around him.

In the next chapter, we will discuss strategies your child can use when working with groups or teams of people who may not understand the way his mind works.

7

T.E.A.M.

Together Everybody Achieves More

"Coming together is a beginning. Keeping together is progress.
Working together is success."

—HENRY FORD

As a parent, you have a role to play in helping your child understand the wisdom of working with others to overcome obstacles created by ADHD. However, young people often want to make changes on their own. For example, if you try to help your child organize her room, she may say to you, "I'll just do it, it'll be okay"—while you fear that without help, she will slip back into a well-worn behavior of leaving papers and clothes everywhere. In part, this difference in perspective is a consequence of a disparity in your ages and experiences. People who have accumulated more experience come to realize that it is often in their self-interest to seek help from those around them. A strong belief that one can accomplish significant goals entirely on her own is often a byproduct of youthful inexperience. How can you help your child see the benefit of working with others?

In this chapter, we will describe four principles that successful teams use. Your child can apply these in the classroom, at home, or wherever else they are necessary to lift her performance. This will require that she begin to think of herself as part of a team. The idea behind this chapter is to identify the "team" that surrounds your child, even if she is not on an official sports or academic team. As described in the next paragraphs, the groups that we are talking about here can be classmates, family members, or even your child's "competition." ADHDers can take the spirit of teamwork and competition and apply it to their own situations, harnessing the power of *everybody* around them to keep themselves accountable for consistently improving their own performance.

DEFINING A TEAM

Ask your child to consider that she has friends, family, and others around her who could be of help. Remind your child that athletes work in teams to lift individual performance as well as to bolster the overall outcome for the group. A great athletic team is a synergistic team: Individual members come together to create something greater than the sum of the parts—certainly something far greater than any one person could accomplish on her own.

Even athletes in individual (non-team) sports don't compete entirely by themselves. The whole basis of sport is to compete against others. Without competition there would be no tournaments, no championships, and no medals or trophies. Sometimes a rivalry—which means that there is another person out there working hard for the same goal—can motivate an athlete to do her very best. Think about athletes getting pumped up for the "big game": They go out on the field giving it their all!

As discussed by Stephen Covey in his best-selling book, *The Seven Habits of Highly Effective People,* we start out as dependent individuals who grow to become independent—and with further personal growth, we become *inter*dependent with others. Interdependence means that all members of a group are dependent on each other, in an equal fashion. Independence is egocentric: The focus is on "what I can do by myself, for myself." Interdependence requires additional maturity because it involves the ability to see beyond your own self and your own needs, and to empathize with and trust other people. When your child moves to interdependence, her ability to "play to win" (as discussed in Chapter 2) skyrockets as people on her team lift her to higher levels of performance.

The concept of "teamwork" can apply to working in a formal team (e.g., a group of people working together on the same project), in which the members need to cooperate with each other in order to get a specific task accomplished. "Teamwork" can also mean working individually in a common situation (e.g., individual students in the same classroom who share similar but separate goals). Even if their personal goals differ, the students in this classroom are part of the same group. The classroom works as a "team" in the sense that we mean it: It is a team of people in the same situation together. It is also a team in the sense that students will help each other out (for example, if one student forgets to bring her calculator, another student might offer to share). Your child can even view her "competitors" in the classroom—maybe they are high-achieving friends or siblings—as a part of her team to the extent that they inspire her to achieve at a higher level.

In this "team," every "player" (classmate) cooperates to create an environment that is conducive to learning for everybody. This includes behavior such as sitting in the assigned seat on time, paying attention, listening to others when it is their turn to talk, working quietly on an assigned project, and listening to the teacher and doing what she says. These behaviors are enforced in preschool and kindergarten, and are often automatic by the time a child is in elementary school. However, kids with ADHD (especially the hyperactive variant) have particular challenges with this behavior; by the time they get to elementary school, they are already behind other members of their "team" (classmates) in knowing how to "play" (behave in the classroom). These children may have challenges participating as a "classroom team member," and this leads to increasing frustration as they progress in school and as performance expectations continue to rise. (For tips on dealing with more specific issues in school, such as taking tests, see "Tips for Parents of ADHD Children: School" on page 169.)

Point out to your child with ADHD that the classroom is a "team" just like any sports team, and that the rules of the classroom are like the rules in her favorite sport (such as rules governing "offsides," "personal fouls," or how and when a player can kick or throw the ball). As on a sports team, the "rules" (stated and unstated) in a classroom are there so that all members of the "classroom team" can work together effectively and contribute to win. For some children with ADHD, this sports team analogy can help them understand why it is important for them to train and master the "rules of the game" in the classroom just like on the playing field.

To help your child remember the benefits of working with a team, ask her to memorize a commonly-used acronym for T.E.A.M.: **T**ogether **E**verybody **A**chieves **M**ore. The idea of T.E.A.M. is for your child to learn how to use *everybody* available around her as a source of inspiration to generate higher achievement for herself. Your child's classmates, her sports team, the groups in her extracurricular activities, coaches, teachers, friends, and rivals are all a part of her team.

How can your child combine her own strengths with those of the people around her to create better personal performance? Now that we've defined what we mean by a "team," we next describe four strategies that will empower your child to propel her own best performance in every situation.

TEAM STRATEGY 1.
UNITE THE MIND, BODY, AND SPIRIT OF THE TEAM

Remember from Chapter 5 that athletes (and ADHDers) are most successful when their mind, body, and spirit come together to work toward and achieve their goal. Recall that "mind" in this model refers to the cognitive aspect of the self; it is the intelligent, premeditated planning part of who we are. "Body" refers to the physical aspect of the self and to keeping that part healthy and in shape to perform at peak levels. "Spirit" refers to the immeasurable, from-the-gut, transcendent aspect of the self that serves as a source of inspiration and motivation, even when it seems impossible or illogical to go on.

From individual athletes come the team, and so an athletic team has its own mind, body, and spirit. For an athletic team to be successful, the mind, body, and spirit of each individual player must be united not only within the individual athlete, but also with the mind, body, and spirit of the team as a whole. This is one reason why many

> ### Coaching Corner
> *In this chapter, we are looking at the mind, body, and spirit again, but applied to a group situation. Because your child will frequently operate in group situations, it is key for her to learn how to create and maintain a positive team spirit. You'll see the importance as you read on!*

athletes on teams not only practice together, but socialize off the field as well—it's all about building up the collective mind, body, and spirit.

Along these lines, the three main ingredients for optimal performance by both the individual and the team are to:

1. Be *mentally* clear on the goal.

2. Be *physically* prepared to attain the goal.

3. Be *spiritually* motivated to achieve the goal.

The Mind of the Team

The mind of the individual affects the mind of the team, and vice versa. A sports team functions best when every player works toward the same goal. Similarly, a team will not function well if some members try to move the team in different directions. That's the difference between a line dance where everybody has prepared and agreed on what the moves are, versus one where a few dancers have not prepared, don't know what they are supposed to do, or have decided to just throw in some personal moves of their own.

Dr. Shad Helmstetter asserts in his best-selling book, *What to Say When You Talk to Yourself*, that "seventy-seven percent of everything we think is negative, counterproductive, and works against us." Phrases like "I can't," "I'm not good enough," or "I'm too lazy" cloud our thinking too often. If individual team members have not spent the time needed to positively program their thinking (remember the "attitude of gratitude" that we discussed in Chapter 6), then that 77 percent negativity will work not only against themselves, but also against everybody else on the team. Under the influence of these few, the team will be divided and move in different directions.

> ### *Coaching Corner*
> *Your child will benefit when she views everyone around her—whether they were assigned to help her or not—as members of her "team." Whether she considers others around her "allies" or "opponents," they are all members of her team in that they can help create conditions that will allow her to achieve her best.*

Whether the team is a family unit, a group of friends, the students in a classroom, or a formal team assigned to work together to achieve a specific task, there will always be both individual and team goals. Nevertheless, a team will produce a winning performance when every individual is accountable for her own winning performance. Unified energies create a cohesive, strong result. The team—and the individuals within—will then be able to "play to win," as discussed in Chapter 2.

For example:

- The team of sixth-graders assigned to complete a project together might share a goal of getting an "A."

- The team of kids working beside each other in band class might share a goal of producing great music.

- The team of friends in high school all might share a goal of getting good scores on their SATs.

However, some people within each of these teams might have personal goals that interfere with or detract from the team goal:

- Some children on the sixth-grade team may decide that their goal is to get the project done as quickly as possible, regardless of their grade.

- Some children in the band may have a personal goal of making the learning experience as fun as possible, while ignoring the more technical aspects of making music.

- Some of the individuals on the team of high school students preparing for the SAT may decide that their goal is to get a *higher* score than their friends.

The examples we gave above, and your child's answers from Exercise 7.1 on page 135, should make it clear that anybody can choose to contribute to or detract from team goals for a variety of personal motives—but ADHDers may have some special challenges in this regard. An ADHDer may sometimes diverge from the team goal because of a loss of focus: Either she is drifting to another task because of inattentiveness, or her impulsivity drives her to do something else. She may find the pace of the team to be too slow. If this is the case, the ADHDer can use the "mind" of the team to help her refocus and get back on track. This requires accepting the pitfalls of ADHD and using that self-awareness to request the team's assistance. What do we mean by this? If your child knows that she has a tendency to wander off track or to procrasti-

EXERCISE 7.1

PLAYING TO WIN AS PART OF A TEAM

Instructions for your child:

Part A (Playing to win on a team): On a separate piece of paper, write down the teams that you have been a part of. Now, try to think of a situation where you contributed to the team's success in a specific way. List the team, the situation, and how your contribution helped lead to the win. Think of at least three separate examples. What did you enjoy about helping the team win? Is this a feeling you wish to repeat?

Part B (Choosing not to play or playing just for fun on a team): Now think of a team (your family, classroom, sports team, extracurricular club) that you've personally been a part of in a situation where you did *not* contribute to the team's success. Maybe you chose to goof off when others were counting on you; maybe you didn't follow the rules, or became emotional and walked away. On your paper, list the team, the situation, and how your behavior undercut the team. Think of at least three separate examples. How might these situations have turned out differently if you had been helping the team win?

nate, she should ask someone on the team who is good at sticking to a schedule (or at staying "on point") to check in with her regularly to remind her about the goals and reorient her toward the deadlines ahead. Younger children may be reoriented by the teacher who is supervising the group, and you as a parent may facilitate that by talking to both parties. The point is that your child should feel comfortable asking those around her for help. Using the team analogy helps remind your child that every player on the team needs help from other team members or from the coach (the teacher) for the whole team to succeed. The whole team benefits when this happens effectively. Be encouraging in your approach. Everyone has a role they can play.

In the beginning of this chapter we mentioned interdependence, meaning mutual dependence. What is in it for the team member who is helping the ADHDer? For one thing, that person is then helping the *whole* team stay focused by helping a person who might otherwise disrupt the team's mindset. This maximizes the chance for the ADHDer to make her special contribution to the team—maybe it's her speed or creativity—which will improve the whole team's level of success.

As we discussed in earlier chapters, it is important for ADHDers not to substitute other people's goals for their own—but they do have to "buy in" to the goals of the team. The goal that the team is trying to reach must be relevant to your child with ADHD. If the goal of the group is not important to the ADHDer (e.g., the goal of the group is to get an "A" on the project, but your child's priority is to get it done quickly), your child will inevitably lose interest. A corollary to this is that the ADHDer can maintain momentum more easily if she can define a part of the project that is personally important to her. For example, the final grade might not be important to her—but if she can "own" the part of the project that she *does* find interesting (e.g., making the graphics) she may find herself doing a great job and contributing something important to the group goal anyway. This can generate praise and social reward from the team, which may mean more to your child than the "A" grade that means more to a different team member. Whatever the personal motivation for your child, achieving this type of success contributes directly to a Positive Cycle of Success (refer back to Chapter 4) and encourages your child to use the same strategies to make similar contributions in future team situations.

Tips for your child to contribute to the team mind

- An individual can use the strengths of the "team mindset" to compensate for her own weaknesses—and in turn, can contribute her strengths back to the team.

- The child with ADHD should actively request help from other team members as needed to remind her to maintain her focus and "keep her eyes on the ball."

- The child with ADHD must "buy in" to team goals, or else identify a personal goal that aligns with the team's overall goal.

The Body of the Team

In Chapter 5, we defined the body as the physical basis of the self and described how to keep it prepared to perform optimally, including getting proper sleep, nutrition, and exercise. In this chapter, we are discussing the body of the team, and this means something a little different. Of course, individuals ideally should make sure that their bodies are well-rested, well-fed, and physically trained or prepared to complete the task at hand.

But when we say "body" in the team context, we mean the structure of the team and how to make it conducive to achievement for a team member with ADHD. The way the team is structured is particularly important. The team will be most successful when each member, including any with ADHD, has a well-defined role that plays to her strengths. John Wooden, the famous UCLA basketball coach, was a disciplined observer: He would watch his players shooting in practice and keep careful notes on where on the court they made the greatest percentage of their shots. He then designed plays with each player's individual shooting strengths in mind, and instructed each player to shoot from a certain location.

An approach like this is especially important for your child with ADHD. The tendency in ADHD is to get a new idea (the ball) quickly, and then run with it without a well-defined plan. It is important that a child with ADHD knows not only what her own individual strengths are, but also how they align with the team's strengths, weaknesses, and goals. If your child is clear on what she is supposed to do to contribute to the team and when she has to do it, she will focus on reaching that goal for the benefit of everybody on the team.

> *Jackie, age twelve, was having trouble doing long-term projects in social studies. Although she loved the subject and wanted to do well, she never knew where to start. Her partners would divide up the work and assign things for her to do that she did not want to do. She would put these tasks off and then do a poor job at the last minute, angering her partners, who then called her flaky and irresponsible. The teacher responded by spending a few minutes at the beginning of each project coaching whatever group Jackie was in, to subtly ensure that Jackie had a well-defined responsibility that played to her strengths (such as drawing the map), as well as a clear timeline of when she needed to be done.*

The teacher in the example above did it right: She identified Jackie's strengths, and encouraged her and her team to use those strengths constructively. Then she gave Jackie clear and time-structured directions, such as were discussed in the "Take Action" section in Chapter 4. "Take Action" applies to team settings, too. For example, in a classroom team, your child with ADHD should be around the more focused and diligent children so that their diligence will be "contagious" and help direct her.

Tips for your child to contribute to the team "body":

- Each team member should have clear roles and responsibilities. Defining these is especially helpful to any member with ADHD.

- The roles should be aligned with the personal goals/strength of the ADHDer. (See also "The Mind of the Team" section above.)

- The ADHDer should work closely with team members who are naturally more focused.

- The team environment should be designed in a way that optimizes attention, focuses on task and on timeline, and minimizes distractions.

The Spirit of the Team

The spirit of the team is a product of the spirit of each individual. Remember from Chapter 5 that an individual's spirit is enhanced when working with others to serve a larger purpose. Morale, which is an outgrowth of spirit, has a profound effect on team success and cohesion. And more than either "mind" or "body," spirit is highly contagious. A child with ADHD can often help bring energy to the team spirit, but must understand that, good or bad, her spirit affects those around her. If an individual team member brings her "stink face" to the group, then the entire team is going to feel stinky! Conversely, if each team member brings her positive energy to the group, then the entire team is going to feel joyous. Ask your child which team ("stinky" or "joyous") she would rather be a part of, and on which she would perform at her best. Advise her to always do her part by bringing the appropriate personal spirit. In turn, your child will benefit from the energy and focus of other team members to keep her on track when she doesn't feel like working or gets distracted and loses focus.

For some, the point of competition is to beat other players or the opposing team. But just because one team wins doesn't mean that everybody else has to lose. For example, scientists competing to make a discovery may spur each other to work harder and be more creative

—ultimately accelerating the finding of a discovery that benefits everybody. It is the same in every human endeavor—competition can be a very healthy and positive force for progress. It is our belief that the most effective teams are those in which each individual member is united with other members to accomplish a goal that includes the betterment of all—and healthy competition can motivate everybody to work harder to cross the finish line.

It is important to emphasize the great heights that your child and her team can achieve by working together with the proper team spirit. Just as a rising tide lifts all boats, on a team with this type of cooperative spirit, everybody on the team wins because everybody puts out her own best performance. In fact, the word "competition" derives from two Latin roots: *com*, a prefix which means "with" or "together," and *petere*, which means "to seek." So "competition" literally means "to seek with others" —striving for a goal *with* other people. Rather than necessitating "win-lose," competition can be a powerful mechanism to create a "win-win" situation that is transformative for each competitor. How does this happen? "Defeat" becomes irrelevant when the overall "victory" is the maximization of contribution, leading to the betterment of each competitor.

The feeling of connection within a team is contagious and raises the game of each team member to the highest level. Connecting to others can make anybody feel that they serve a larger purpose. This bolsters self-esteem as well as individual achievement. To make an analogy, although each finger of the hand has a different role and can act independently when necessary, it is only when the fingers work together that the full capacity of the hand emerges.

Tips for your child to contribute to the team spirit:

- Bring your energy and "joyous face" (not your "stinky face") to boost team spirit.

- Remember that nobody else has to lose in order for you to win.

- The goal of competition is to maximize your (and your competitors') potential to succeed and contribute.

- Use competition as a way to connect with your team members, so that each member wins both by putting out her own best performance and by growing closer to the group.

TEAM STRATEGY 2.
BELIEVE THAT YOU CAN ADD SUCCESS TO THE TEAM

Children with ADHD often come to feel deficient compared to their peers. They may have a past history of not performing well and being blamed for it (whether by others or themselves), or they may have gotten into trouble for impulsively blurting things out or acting in a way that detracted from the team spirit or the team goals. Poor self-esteem can lead to a child with ADHD feeling that she doesn't have much to contribute to a team. This, of course, is a self-fulfilling prophecy—if your child believes she has nothing to contribute, she won't even try to contribute, and so her belief comes true.

An ADHDer can be told that she's doing fine, but unless she really believes in herself, it will be hard for her to contribute to the team's success. She needs to really experience true success. But how does a child come to believe she can be successful if she has a long streak of challenges behind her?

Children with ADHD often feel that many tasks are harder for them to accomplish than for other people, and that may be true. However, it's what the ADHDer tells herself after such a comparison that can make all the difference. Does your child tell herself: "Everybody is better than me, I might as well quit!"? You will recall from the game matrix in Chapter 2 that this is the option of "choosing not to play." It is the product of defeatist thinking.

Instead, your child must learn to focus on her effort and what she *can* contribute. *Everybody* has something that she can contribute to team success. A winning team is created from the unique talents, strengths, and weaknesses of indi-

> **Coaching Corner**
> *Tell your child: You ARE enough. All you need is already within you. Feed your faith in yourself, and self-doubt will fade away!*

vidual team members and how the team as a whole responds to those individual differences. If everybody on the team supports and contributes to the team goal, the team itself will be strong regardless of individual team member weaknesses. A team can weaken to a degree because of an individual's skill weaknesses, but it plunges if one or more of the team members are in a "choose not to play" mode.

Go through Chapter 2 again and explain to your child that when she contributes whatever she can to the team goal, she is "playing to win."

Coaching Corner

In Chapter 1, we mentioned Thom Hartmann's idea that ADHD isn't so much a "disorder" as it is a distinct way of processing information. Humans are social creatures that have always lived in teams (think of families, tribes, or nations) in which individuals contribute specialized skills (hunters, gatherers, inventors, healers, and so on) that lead to success of the team as a whole. Your child with ADHD is a unique contributor to her team; if she can appreciate and work to maximize the unique contribution she makes, other team members will come to appreciate it as well.

Nobody but your child can contribute something that reflects her personality. Not everybody has equal or natural skills for a particular task. But everybody has the capacity to work hard and to try her best. Your child with ADHD may have more to contribute to the team than she realizes. She can brainstorm some contribuitions in Exercise 7.2 below. Her contribution may not be immediately obvious or get a lot of attention, but it may be critical to the team's success just the same.

EXERCISE 7.2

ADDING YOUR CHILD'S INGREDIENT TO GROUP SUCCESS: THE *CAN* EXERCISE

Instructions for your child:
Think of two situations where you might work in a team. Ask yourself: "How *can* I improve the experience?" "What small changes *can* I make today that will help the team?" Fill in the answers to the following on another sheet of paper.

Team situation 1
My contribution:
What can I do to maximize my contribution?

Team situation 2
My contribution:
What can I do to maximize my contribution?

TEAM STRATEGY 3.
COMPETE FOR THE RIGHT REASONS

As discussed throughout this book, many people (with and without ADHD) compete for the wrong reasons, whether as part of a team or individually. They may be trying to outdo other people. They may be trying to fulfill other people's expectations. When your child competes for the wrong reasons, difficulties will arise, regardless of her ADHD diagnosis or anything else.

Fear Is a Poor Motivator

Often, a fear of failure is the root motivation for competing. Some people believe that they must excel so that other people do not get ahead. This is the "play not to lose" option of the game matrix discussed in Chapter 2. In the long run, it is certainly not an ideal way to achieve success or personal satisfaction in life.

Some children and their parents fear that if the child isn't an academic superstar, she will be a total failure. This kind of "black-and-white" thinking recognizes only absolutes, rather than all the shades of gray in between. Thoughts like these create a false dichotomy, as comically stated in the movie *Talladega Nights:* "If you ain't first, you're last!" But, of course, in most cases that's simply not true; there are many times and occasions where it's okay not to be first, and certainly there are many situations where there are alternatives other than "first" or "last." More importantly, in life there are countless ways to be successful, and many of the most successful people in business, politics, community, etc., were actually pretty mediocre in school.

Competing out of a fear of failure has long-term downsides. Your child's body responds to fear with a "fight-or-flight reaction." There is a structure in the brain called the *amygdala*, whose job it is to process fear. The amygdala takes the sensation of fear and turns it into the physiologic changes that we all associate with fear: The body releases chemicals (such as adrenaline) that cause the heart to race, the eyes to dilate, and the muscles to tighten and "get ready." This system is hugely important in an evolutionary sense. In laboratory settings in which their amygdalae have been removed, experimental animals lose their natural fear of predators. Animals in the wild without a functioning amygdala clearly could not survive for very long.

However, if the "fear" reactions instigated by the amygdala are repeated too often over time, another part of your child's brain, the *hippocampus,* can shrink. The hippocampus is very important for learning, memory, and rational thought. The negative connection between the amygdala and the hippocampus helps to explain why it is difficult for somebody to objectively evaluate a situation when she is really worried. Fear distorts reality; you probably remember a time when you were very afraid, and details of your situation took on an inflated importance. After you had calmed down, you may have said to yourself, "What was I so scared of?" and were amazed at how important the little details seemed at the time.

When under chronic stress, the amygdala undergoes changes that make people more susceptible to stress and fear. The result is that it takes less of a stimulus for the person to feel "stressed out." Over prolonged periods of time, the capacity for rational thought diminishes, and the tendency to become hopeless and depressed increases. In other words, over time the "thinking" (can do) part of the brain can be subdued by the "shrinking" (don't try) part of the brain. When people are affected by this, their ability to positively cope with life's challenges, let alone to excel, is poor.

To summarize, competing out of a fear of failure does not truly optimize performance for your child in the short term, and over the long term it is likely to create a negative, unhappy adult. If your child's chief motivation to perform is because she is afraid to fail, she isn't really performing at her best. The stress engendered by this type of competition over time is likely to lead to other troubles in her life, including low motivation and depressed mood.

Ambivalence Prevents Achievement

As you may recall from Chapter 2, ambivalence is having two strong, conflicting feelings about something and is a common obstacle for children with ADHD. An ADHDer with ambivalence may feel "stuck" and unable to move forward when trying to reach a goal. This can be exacerbated when the child's goals are different from the goals that others want her to accomplish. For example, parents sometimes push their child in directions the child doesn't really want to go.

Consider the case of Tara, age sixteen, who was pushed into taking Advanced Placement (AP) classes in some subjects because her parents and college counselor thought it would "look good to college admissions officers." The problem was that although Tara agreed that taking the

classes would look good, inwardly she did not want to *be* in those classes—
and so she did not *do* well in them. This is a form of passive-aggressive
sabotage that occurs when the spirit's goals conflict with those of the
mind and body. (See Chapter 2 regarding the trouble with ambivalence.)

The ambivalence illustrated by Tara's poor AP class performance
could happen with any child, but it is a particularly common trap in children with ADHD. The personal interest that an ADHDer holds in pursuing a goal impacts her ability to perform, because her ability to sustain
attention to the goal is affected. As emphasized in Chapter 2, an ADHDer
is unlikely to accomplish a goal (particularly a challenging goal) simply
because she is expected to do so; she must "own the goal" (this is
reviewed in Exercise 7.3 on page 145). She must be motivated from
within in order to keep her "eye on the ball."

Coaching Corner

*Evaluating your child's motivations is crucial for success—but it is also
important for you as a parent to examine your own motivations for
helping your child and where they are coming from. One of the most
common situations we see is that the parent is fearful that the child
won't "be successful," as defined by the parent. So the tendency is to
"push, push, push." Stress is created when the child resists pushing.*

Competing out of joy or out of passion for the task and for its outcome (i.e., competing not merely to "win," but because the task itself or
what it creates is personally important) is a far more effective way to
optimize performance, and is also personally beneficial over the long-
term. When mice in laboratory experiments live in environments
enriched with activities and objects that stimulate them and keep them
happy, important areas of their brains literally grow in response. The
hippocampus, the brain region that shrinks under conditions of chronic
stress, grows new neurons when the brain is stimulated in this way. This
is not just true of laboratory mice: Recent research shows that children
who grow up in enriched environments similarly have larger hippocampal sizes as adults. When your child's goals are her own, and working to
accomplish them gives her a sense of joy rather than a sense of fear, she
will grow and become stronger from them—in mind, body, *and* spirit.

EXERCISE 7.3

OWNING THE GOAL, REVIEW

Instructions for you and your child:

- Review the "S.M.A.R.T." goals your child wrote down for Chapter 3, Exercise 3.2 (page 54).

- Have your child re-write each goal from Exercise 3.2 on a separate piece of paper. Now leave the room (the parent should not be present while the child does the next step).

- Have your child, on her own, write down next to each goal a rating on a scale of 1–10 for how much she personally *feels* this goal is important to her for the *right* reasons. Does she want to pursue this goal because it is personally important to her to achieve, or is she pursuing it for other reasons? (e.g., To please someone else? Because she is afraid of what others might think if she doesn't succeed at it?)

- When you return to the room, discuss her ratings in a non-confrontational manner. It may be helpful for a neutral third party to be present!

TEAM STRATEGY 4.
HAVE A SENSE OF HUMOR!

Sometimes, the other members of the team "get it" and understand what they have to do, but your child, for whatever reason, makes mistakes. Maybe it's just an "off day," but things are not going well for your child. What can you tell her to do? She can cry, or get angry—but where will that get her? Instead, ask her to try having a sense of humor about the situation.

We all experience challenges, and one helpful way to face them is with a sense of humor. Laughter releases endorphins that improve your child's mood and make her feel relaxed. Humor connects people, and as discussed above, "competition" and working with a team are all about connecting people. Having a sense of humor is a great way to dispel tension and deal with frustration, because it can improve your child's ability to come up with creative ideas to move out of a bad situation.

Laughing about challenges is more productive than crying and being angry about them. Sadness tends to diminish the motivation to change and fix things because sadness is often linked with hopelessness. Rather than motivating someone to act, sadness is more likely to lead to a state of inactivity. Sadness also tends to be alienating. While some people around your child will be sympathetic, others will be frustrated with her—frequent moaning and complaining often puts other people off.

Anger is also not constructive. When your child becomes angry, she will have difficulty processing information (thus the expression, "She was so angry she couldn't see straight"). This relates to what we discussed in the section "Fear Is a Poor Motivator" (page 142): The amygdala can impair the function of the hippocampus (and other brain regions). In simplified terms, angry people are driven by their amygdalae and operate on an emotional level rather than on an intellectual level. When your child is angry, people around her will have a hard time communicating with her, both because she is off-putting and because even if they do try to communicate, her brain is not in a state to receive new information. An angry child (or adult) is apt to immediately reject any new information offered to her.

Coaching Corner

Appropriate laughter—particularly the ability to laugh at oneself— is a powerful mechanism to defuse tension, increase flexible thinking, and "hit the reset button" in the face of a challenge or setback. Laughter keeps things in perspective and reduces anxiety. If you can say: "It's only one test! You'll get 'em next time" with a smile on your face, that helps put a "C" in perspective. It is important to distinguish this, however, from inappropriate laughter that puts down other individuals, the team, or the goal.

If your child can instead generate a sense of humor in a challenging situation, she will unwind, regain control, and connect with teammates in a positive way. She will be more open to finding her way out of problems—that is, she will be more likely to search for and find a creative solution, and people around her will also be more inclined to help her find it. Your child will be able to relax and share her thoughts with team members, and she will be better able to hear the ideas of others and use them constructively. This promotes discussions and connections between team members, which build up team spirit.

Of course, inappropriate laughter is not what we are advocating. The idea is not to make fun of others, or to diminish the seriousness of a team project or goal. Being the "class clown" can be disruptive for other team members. With inappropriate laughter, others will not connect with your child in a positive way. In Exercise 7.4 below, your child and some classmates or friends can bond as a group through a humorous activity.

EXERCISE 7.4

L.O.L. WITH A TEAM

Ever notice that when you walk into a room of people laughing, you end up laughing too? Joy can spread! This is an exercise that can be used if your child is working with a partner or group. You may want to share it with her teacher for group projects in class. You and your child can do it together if you are getting on each other's nerves. This exercise is simple; all it requires is the floor and the word "ha."

One person will lie on the floor on their back. Then have your child rest her head on that person's stomach. If there are more people, follow this pattern with every person putting her head on someone's stomach. Be creative! Two people can lie on one stomach, the group can make zig zags or circle patterns. . . . just be creative and playful. Once everyone is lying down, the only instruction is for each person to say the word "HA" as loud as she can to get the other person's head to bob up and down. This promotes laughter and bonding among the group.

SUMMARY

This chapter reviewed the synergistic effects of working within a group. ADHDers have to learn how to reap the benefits of working with a group so that "team" truly does mean that Together Everybody Achieves More. The four principles we discussed in this chapter are: The mind, body, and spirit of each individual member affects the group; your child should engage in competition for the right reasons (not out of fear of failure or to please someone else); the child needs to believe that she can add success to the group; and having a sense of humor about challenges is important to the team's morale.

Should all else fail, your child can still contribute to the team through a willingness to work. Pat Riley, coach of the Los Angeles Lakers basketball team during some of their best years, called the desire to work "your hardest hustle." Riley kept track of each of his player's "hustle" statistics (like going after a loose ball) to reinforce how important this quality is. Look for and praise hustle when you see it—your child with ADHD can be proud of this ability and bring that energy to any team situation. Strong hustle often precedes a standout performance.

In the next chapter, we will examine setbacks and obstacles that are commonly faced on the way to achieving goals. We will discuss some strategies that you and your ADHD child can use if she feels like giving up.

8

Failure Is Temporary, Defeat Is a Choice

"There are no secrets to success. It is the result of preparation, hard work, and learning from failure."

—COLIN POWELL

Every ADHDer is going to have times when he feels like things aren't going well. He may feel he is in a "hole" and have a hard time pulling out of it. When ADHDers face the same obstacles over and over again, many start to view failure as something that "just always happens." People with ADHD may start to see failure as something they are destined for. This provokes a lot of anxiety about doing anything, which contributes to the Negative Cycle of Failure. The temptation for many children in this situation is to give up and say things like, "I knew it wouldn't work," "I'm just cursed," or "I'm not meant to do this, I shouldn't have even tried." Even worse, maybe a failure prompts your child to say, "I won't try anything this hard again. I'll only do things I know I can do." Children may label themselves as lazy. Self-identifying as lazy will give them an "out" from changing anything, since they believe lazy people are incapable of working hard. These defeatist ways of thinking can lead to depression, which can make ADHD even harder to manage and diminishes motivation.

On the other side, complacence can play a role in accepting failure. Many children are subconsciously happy with what they had been doing, even if it has caused them challenges. It's easier to stick with what they know than to make a change; giving up is often the easiest road to take. Those who never had a strong belief in their success use failure to validate their fears.

It's not always going to work out. There will be times when all your child's plans and hard work fall through. As the saying goes, "Sometimes you're the dog, and sometimes you're the hydrant." Like a boxer who has been knocked down, the challenge is to get back up. If your child feels like he's been punched in the face for eight rounds, his nose has been broken for three, and his lungs are burning trying to get some air, it will be virtually *impossible* for him to have an objective opinion about how the fight is going. How does he get up when he's been so beaten down?

> ### Coaching Corner
> *All children will suffer setbacks and even failure. It's how they respond to these challenges that will make all the difference in their progress. This chapter will help your child grow stronger and more motivated to keep going in the face of setbacks!*

This chapter will offer six constructive techniques you can use to help your child with ADHD keep going when he feels like he is failing.

PARENT STRATEGY 1.
USE THE RIGHT WORDS

The words your child uses can frame how he thinks about his setbacks. Attitude is everything: We *create* meaning out of our circumstances through the words we use to describe them. Zig Ziglar (author and motivational speaker) stated, "Your attitude, not your aptitude, will determine your altitude."

Sometimes your child can't control events in his life, and setbacks will happen. It is understandable to feel disappointed and frustrated when challenges occur. But then what? We all experience failure once in a while, but being *defeated* by failure is the real challenge. So the question is: What does your child say to himself to process his feelings after a setback and get back on the right (winning) track?

What your child says to himself after a defeat affects how he thinks about it and how he acts in consequence. One trap he may fall into is to say, "I'm not good at . . ." He tried something, it didn't work, and so "I'm not good at it" becomes the easy explanation. Why is that explanation easy? Because it explains a failure as "not my fault": It's not your child's "fault" if he's just not naturally good at something, right? This reasoning prevents any need to try again. If your child is "just not good" at something, why should he even *try* to succeed at it?

But there is one word that transforms the statement, "I'm not good at . . ." This word is *yet*. When "yet" is placed at the end of a statement, it turns a negative into a positive: "I'm not good at _____ *yet*." Your child can practice saying this in Exercise 8.1 below.

You can think of "yet" as encompassing the concepts of Yes, Energy, and Time. By saying "yet," your child is also saying *yes*, he wants to keep trying. "Yes" is a success word, and one success creates further successes (remember the Positive Cycle of Success from Chapter 3). "Energy" is important because your child must be willing to create and harness his energy and effort to reach his goal. "Time" is important for several reasons: The "failure" is now in the past. In the present, your child is deciding that his future is open for success to happen—"I'm not good at _____ yet, but I'm going to keep trying and get better at it over time."

When "YET" is used in this way, it contains within it both the understanding that your child has the ability to change, and a *commitment* that he is going to put in the energy to change. Saying "yet" is recognition that the current setback is just one bump in the road. The road to success is still there, and your child still has every intention of taking it. Your child can think of "yet" as an antidote word. Antidote words can have a powerful ability to heal. "Yet" transforms a negative personal identity statement into a positive promise. Saying "yet" acknowledges that with continued effort, things can get better in the future.

EXERCISE 8.1

THREE LETTERS THAT TRANSFORM SENTENCES: YET

Ask your child to think of three times that he recently said "I'm not good at . . ." Write those down on a separate piece of paper. Then, have him re-write the sentences, adding the word "YET" at the end of each one.

Notice and appreciate how this word transforms each sentence. (This technique also works for "I can't do . . .")

Another example of an antidote word is "challenge." We recommend relabeling "problems" that your child may encounter as "challenges." It makes a huge difference to say "My challenges include. . . ." instead of the negative statement "I have a problem with. . . ." Saying that something is a problem can be paralyzing. A problem is ongoing and has no solution. If your child has a problem, it is *his*; he now possesses a flaw and it becomes a part of who he is. In contrast, the word "challenge" implies a task that can definitely be overcome with effort. A challenge exists externally, not internally like a problem does. Problems are stumbling blocks that can only trip you up, not make you better, whereas "challenges" are opportunities for personal growth disguised as obstacles to success.

Your child might face difficulties when it comes to overcoming new challenges and may say something like, "This is too hard." Repeatedly saying "It's so hard" ignites feelings of sadness and low self-worth. It also mentally reinforces the idea that accomplishing the task is going to require a huge effort. To reverse this thinking, ask your child to add a

> ### Coaching Corner
>
> *Getting in the habit of using "antidote words" like "yet" and "challenge" (in place of "problem") is a powerful way for your child to transform his mode of thinking from negative and paralyzed to positive and proactive. Try to think of some more antidote words to replace negative phrases. Amazing attitudes can be formed— it's easier than it may seem!*

positive verb or phrase on to the end of the "It's so hard" statement. Verbs are action words, so adding one to a negative statement can transform it into an opportunity—into something that can be done. "It's so hard" becomes: "I'm *training* so hard *to accomplish this task*" or "It's so hard *to focus on finishing my homework on time*." Simply adding these verbs and action phrases is a way for your child to remind himself that he is taking positive actions to resolve a difficult situation. Or, if he is not taking action *yet*, then adding these words forces him to think of what he *can* do to fix the situation. If an athlete says, "I can't jump this hurdle"—he won't. But if he says, "I can't jump this hurdle yet," he will get ready to try. Reframing the situation in a positive way helps your child want to try harder and also gets him personally invested in the outcome. This increases his focus naturally. Your child can practice reframing his situations in Exercise 8.2.

EXERCISE 8.2

TRANSFORMING "IT'S SO HARD" STATEMENTS INTO "CAN DO" STATEMENTS USING ACTION WORDS

Ask your child to think of three times that he recently said something was "too hard" or "so difficult." Write those down on a sheet of paper. Then, have him transform these sentences by changing them into phrases that describe ways he can work to solve the difficulty.

Examples

- *"It's so hard* to get an A in Spanish" becomes "I'm *studying hard* to get an A in Spanish."

- *"It's too hard* to do this math problem" becomes "I need to *think* hard to *solve* this math problem."

Write these antidote phrases down on the paper.

PARENT STRATEGY 2.
SUCCESS = EFFORT X TIME

It may be cliché to say, "Change takes time," but it is the truth neverthe-less. As the title of this strategy tells you, success is achieved by multi-plying effort by time. The significance of this equation is that a larger amount of effort and time equals a bigger success. If either effort or time is zero, success will also be zero. But as we discussed in Chapter 3, you and your child may frequently hear the media message that you can be successful in no time and without any real effort, such as by winning the lottery or getting "discovered" by someone famous. Truthfully, the odds of success happening to your child in this way are extremely low.

Expecting change to come immediately can contribute to a feeling of failure. Kids often perceive a temporary setback as a permanent failure, and their parents may make the related mistake of believing that a tem-porary setback shows that what they are doing to help their child "isn't working." In doing so, both kids and parents lose the perspective of time. Much like training a body, it takes time to discipline a mind. You as a parent are trying to change years of your child's doing things in a certain way (in some cases, ten or more years), and it is therefore unrea-sonable to expect changes instantly.

In contrast to this modern myth of easy, instant success, the ancient Greeks and Romans emphasized the story of Hercules, the half-god son of Zeus. Even though he was born great, Hercules still had to go through several "Herculean" labors over *time* in order to succeed. (One of the stories about Hercules' determination is told on page 155.)

Another prominent historic figure who emphasized the importance of persistence was U.S. President Calvin Coolidge: "Nothing in the world can take the place of persistence. Talent will not; nothing is more common than unsuccessful men with talent. Genius will not; unrewarded genius is almost a proverb. Education will not; the world is full of educated derelicts. Persistence and determination alone are omnipotent. The slogan 'press on' has solved and always will solve the problems of the human race."

> ### Coaching Corner
> *If a picture is worth 1,000 words, an action is worth 1,000 pictures! Tell your child to act today.*

Persistence means continuing to strive over time until a goal is reached. For an ADHDer, moving on to a new idea or to a new thought at the first setback is likely to feel more natural than persistence, a quality which he may find challenging to put into practice. But without persistence, a setback becomes an ending rather than just a bump on the road to success. An ADHDer with persistence and passion for a goal will have a totally different outcome than one who quits at the first setback.

To achieve persistence, your child must come to accept that mistakes and failures are part of the road to success. Unless your child is willing to make mistakes, he is probably not playing to win. If he is playing to avoid mistakes, he is not putting his all into what he is doing—he is "playing not to lose." He may be playing not to lose because he is *afraid* to make mistakes. Dr. Carol Dweck writes about the different ways people respond to mistakes in her book *Mindset: The New Psychology of Success.* There are those who feel that mistakes are an opportunity for personal growth—that mistakes are a natural and useful part of learning. Then there are those who feel that mistakes reveal inadequacy. To this group of people, mistakes mean that they are not smart or talented, so they try to avoid making them. Over time, those who accept that mistakes are opportunities to learn and grow outperform those who believe that mistakes reveal their personal shortcomings.

Overcoming challenges requires effort, risk, and a willingness to make mistakes. Without effort, there is no reward. If something is too easy, then getting better at it is not exciting. Overcoming a true challenge is *fun* because it requires personal growth and development. Success will then give your child great personal satisfaction because he will know his endeavors are what led to success. He will find that if he sticks with and overcomes one challenge, he will have the confidence to apply that determination to other aspects of life, and more great things will come his way.

Sure, there will be some things that he finds he *can't* do. If your child's challenge to himself is to play basketball as well as Kobe Bryant, or to swim as fast as Michael Phelps, he is (probably) not going to get there. Remind your child that taking smaller steps and setting realistic challenges are important to building up confidence: Improve footwork in soccer. Improve lap time in swimming by ten seconds. He must seek out opportunities to achieve *his own* personal best, not someone else's. This is important because it builds the Positive Cycle of Success that we discussed in Chapter 3. It also improves his hope that he will one day reach his "big time" goal.

Hercules: A Story of Persistence

Here is one of the myths of Hercules, meant to epitomize the merit of taking the hard "high" road instead of the easy "low" road. This version originates from the Greek Sophist Prodicus of Keos and dates to approximately 400 BC:

Hercules meets two women at a crossroads. These women are personifications of Virtue (who is often depicted in classical paintings as modestly and simply dressed) and Vice (who is often depicted as stripped to the waist or dressed "over the top"). They both advise Hercules to follow the road they show him. Virtue points toward a rocky and steep road. This will be a difficult road to follow; it will take a lot of commitment, persistence, and discipline. Vice points toward a more pleasant, attractive road. Hercules can take this easy, flat road, on which he can have a lot of fun, right now (i.e., instant gratification). However, it will eventually lead him to ruin. In contrast, if he takes the challenging road, he will earn a beautiful but distant future. Hercules the hero chooses the high, difficult road to long-term success that Virtue shows him.

People who have high hopes set more goals and are less likely to get derailed in their pursuits. Instead of looking at challenges as insurmountable "problems," hopeful people are more likely to think flexibly of plans to rise above or to go around challenges. High-hope people also understand the difference between being weary *in* a challenge, and being weary *of* a challenge. Overcoming each challenge reinforces a person's high-hope thinking. High-hope people are more likely to ask for help, which reinforces the bonds between themselves and those around them. These relationships help keep them from quitting, as their associates root them on and care about the outcome. In contrast, low-hope people get stressed out, don't think of ways to overcome challenges, don't ask for help, don't attend to building relationships that could help them, and quit. Exercise 8.3 on page 157 encourages positivity.

Consider the Japanese proverb "Nanakorobi yaoki," which means "fall seven times and stand up eight." No matter how many times your child falls down, he must get up and try again. The idea is to always keep fighting and never give up. Milton Glaser, the iconic American graphic designer, said, "The real issue is not talent as an independent element, but talent in relationship to will, desire, and persistence. Talent without these things vanishes and even modest talent with those characteristics grows." This quote reiterates what we noted earlier about the significance of saying, "I'm not good at . . .*yet*." Talent is secondary to determination. If your child stands back up and tries harder every time he "falls," or is defeated, eventually he will no longer fall down.

Psychologist Dr. Angela Duckworth similarly emphasizes "grit," a personality trait related to persistence. According to the Duckworth Lab's website, "Grit is the tendency to sustain interest in and effort toward very long-term goals." Duckworth "scores" a person's grit; a higher "grit score" appears to be one of the most important factors— even more important than a person's intelligence—for predicting success. Think about how your child would rate in terms of "grittiness."

PARENT STRATEGY 3.
GO FOR INTERNAL SATISFACTION INSTEAD OF EXTERNAL REWARD

Former UCLA basketball coach John Wooden said, "Success is peace of mind, which is a direct result of self-satisfaction in knowing you did your best to become the best you are capable of becoming." In other

EXERCISE 8.3

PREEMPTING NEGATIVITY WITH POSITIVITY

Try to envision a challenge that is coming up for your child. Is it going to be a hard math test? A difficult piano performance? An oral report or other public speaking challenge? Whatever the challenge, have your child visualize how he might feel during the test if he believes he is failing it. He can use the visualization strategies in Chapter 6 to help him envision what it would feel like to be hopeless during the test.

Now, think of some positive statements your child can say to himself to get going again. Here are some examples, borrowed from Dr. Shad Helmstetter:

- I am positive. I am confident. I radiate good things. Every day in lots of ways, I get better and better.

- I am intelligent. My mind is quick and alert and clever and fun. I think good thoughts, and my mind makes things work right for me.

- I am interested in many things. I appreciate all the blessings I have, and the things that I learn, and all the things I will learn today and tomorrow and forever—just as long as I am.

What will your child say to himself to get him through the challenge of feeling hopeless?

words, if your child measures success by how much effort he puts out, then the focus of his goal becomes to give his best effort. If he gives it his all, he will *always* be successful. He *can* control the effort he puts out, even if he can't control external aspects of the situation, such as whether or not someone gives him a trophy for it.

Take an example from sports. An athlete can't control whether he is playing a more accomplished opponent, or how psyched up his opponent is coming into the game. He can't control whether the referee makes good calls or bad. He can't control environmental factors, such as the temperature. He *can* control his own physical conditioning before the game. He *can* control whether he plays the best he can that day. When you define "success" in this way, the scoreboard doesn't tell the whole story; it is up to the athlete to determine if he has been successful or not.

This is true not only in sports. A student can't control how hard a test is, or whether a teacher is grading fairly—but he can control whether he prepares well for the test. If your child has done his best and put out his best effort, he may or may not achieve external success, but he can feel successful internally.

Extrinsic rewards can be motivating, but intrinsic rewards directly build a personal creed of doing your best no matter the situation. At the West Point United States Military Academy, first-year cadets, or "plebes," are allowed only four responses to questions from upperclass-

---

Process, Not Product

"Process, not product" is a key tenet in martial arts training. It emphasizes that the journey toward a goal, and what you learn during it, is more important than the end result. There is a famous parable from Eastern philosophy that illustrates this principle:

There's a young apprentice wishing to be the best swordsman in all the land. He's heard of a Master Teacher who lives in the mountains. The young apprentice decides to make the all-day trek into the mountains to find the Master and ask if he will accept him as a student.

The apprentice happens upon an ancient monastery high in the mountains. He knocks on the door only to be greeted by the old Master he was seeking. After the apprentice pleads for admittance, the Master finally addresses the student, saying, "Come in; if I am to be your teacher, we must first have tea."

Excitedly, the young student rushes into the doorway. While the two walk across the courtyard inside for tea, the student attempts to impress the Master by bragging about his skills.

The two are seated at the table for barely a minute when the young student asks, "Master, you are the greatest swordsman in all the land: You are a legend. How long will it take

men. They may say: "Yes, Sir (or Ma'am)," "No, Sir," "Sir I do not understand," or "No excuse, Sir." For example, if asked by an upperclassman, "Mister, do you think those boots are polished?" the plebe will automatically want to offer an explanation of extenuating circumstances that led to the scuffed boots, such as, "Sir, while lining up in formation another cadet bumped into me." But because the plebe is restricted to the four possible replies, the only answer is "No, Sir."

This practice has many purposes. It instills in the cadet that he can't rely on external recognition for his efforts, because (rightly or wrongly) that may not occur. He also can't rely on using external factors as excuses for failure. Instead, the one thing he can control is doing everything within his power to meet a goal, and then he can (and must) accept the

me, as your capable student, to become a Master Swordsman too?"

The Master replies, "It will take you five years."

Shocked, the impatient young apprentice exclaims, "Five years?! What if I practice all day in between your teaching me, how long will it take then?"

The Master replies, "Then it will take you ten years."

"Ten years?!" the student says. "What if I move in with you, become your live-in student, and for all day and night dedicate myself to studying and constantly practicing? How long will it take then?"

"If you do all that, then it will take you twenty years to become a Master Swordsman."

Totally confused, the young student then asks, "Master, I don't understand. Every time I said I would do more to become a master in less time you told me it would take even longer to achieve, but why?"

Calmly sipping his tea, the Master nods, puts the tea cup down, and takes a breath. He looks the young apprentice in the eyes and says, "When you are so focused having one eye on your destination, it leaves only HALF of you to focus on the journey, and it will therefore take you twice as long to reach where you want to go."

consequences of whatever happens next. He may have to learn to live with injustice sometimes, because that is a part of reality. (Note that learning to live with injustice in the moment is not the same as accepting it as the way things have to be in the future.)

Perhaps your child did not achieve the goal that was set; maybe that was his fault, and maybe it was not. Or, perhaps he did achieve the goal that was set, but became frustrated when that one success did not lead to external recognition or to further success and happiness. Focusing on the journey, rather than the destination, yields satisfaction, growth, and long-term development regardless of these factors. One way to think about this is that a goal is merely a way for your child to expand his horizons. The goal itself is not the true objective—instead goals are merely a tool, with personal development being the *true* objective.

Another way to look at this is that the planning and work that goes into achieving a goal are important if they teach your child a process that he can apply to other goals in life. Consider again the multiple small Positive Cycles of Success depicted in Figure 3.5. Once your child has the process down, he can go from one success to the next, reaching for bigger and bigger goals as he builds momentum. For example, although your son's stated goal may be to "get all A's this semester," the semester eventually will end, and so that particular goal will be reached (or not). But if he designs and executes a plan that gives him confidence in his ability to work hard, to study effectively, and to solve challenges as they arise, he can translate the process to other settings (later semesters or new work environments) with justifiable pride.

> ### Coaching Corner
> *This strategy of focusing on internal satisfaction will enable your child to feel good about the effort he gives. Then, if he has a setback, he won't fall apart about it because he knows he gave it his best effort. What happens to your child is not as important as what happens in your child.*

We have all heard the old saying, "Give a man a fish, and feed him for a day; teach a man to fish, and feed him for the rest of his life." By the same token, a student benefits only a little by learning one fact, but will enjoy a successful future if he can internalize the learning process, applying that learned model to any endeavor he chooses. If you teach your child to pursue excellence, you are building character that he can take into any situation. An external victory won't mean much if your child ends up saying, "I wish I had done more." However, if your child knows that he has done all he can do in order to make something happen he will feel like a winner even if it doesn't work out. In Exercise 8.4 below, your child can think about all that he is capable of doing.

To quote NBA coach Pat Riley, "When you know you've given all that you've got, there's no pressure, no shame, and therefore no consequences if you lose. . . . There's always a challenge to give your best. . . . You have to take your opportunity to rise above any excuses or mediocrity in that situation and let people know that you are significant and you do matter. What you do does matter. You have a mission, as much as any athlete."

EXERCISE 8.4

WHAT *CAN* YOU CONTROL?

This exercise is about redefining goals. Many of your child's goals concern external factors, but an often overlooked component is the internal process that goes into achieving these goals.

Here are some examples of external goals and the internal processes behind them:

EXTERNAL GOAL		INTERNAL PROCESS
I am going to get all A's	→	I am going to study for every test
My coach is going to put me in as a starter	→	I am going to listen to and implement what coach says during practice
I am going to win the tournament	→	I am going to practice my routine every morning
My group's project is going to be the best	→	I am going to work on my part every afternoon

What are your child's goals? How can he restate them so they focus on a process that is under his control? What will give him the internal satisfaction of knowing he did what he could? Have him consider these questions as he writes down his external goals and the internal processes behind them on a sheet of paper.

PARENT STRATEGY 4.
STAND LIKE A WINNER: OWN YOUR MOVEMENTS

Recall Chapter 6, where we discussed "Focus your body" as one of the four keys to optimal performance. Focusing your body is also a key to persistence in the face of a temporary setback. Just as your child's posture prepares him to perform optimally—and communicates with his mind, spirit, and with other people his intent to do so—it also communicates that he is not to be deterred by a temporary setback. In this section, we remind you to help your child use the power of body language as a tool to overcome setbacks. If your child's body language is positive, it will help him come out of the "hole" he is in.

> ### Coaching Corner
>
> *Just as the focus of your child's eyes helps tell his brain what to pay attention to, his posture helps tell his brain what his attitude is. This may seem counterintuitive (most people assume that communication between brain and body flows only in the other direction), but it is true: People who smile not only look happy, they feel happy; people who sit up straight and assume an active physical posture not only appear to be more interested, they actually feel more interested. They can more easily pay attention to what is happening around them.*

Actress Mae West famously said, "I speak two languages, Body and English." Body language is universally understood. If your child's body is poised negatively, he is communicating to himself and to others that he is defeated. That is, if your child's eye contact is poor, if his back is slouched, or if he walks as though he's being dragged somewhere to get his teeth pulled, he's communicating that he is having a hard time thinking positively about the situation. So if your child finds himself "down," remind him to check his body language. A lot of body language is processed at the subconscious level. What is your child's body language saying? Is it pulling him up? Or is it bringing him down? Coach your child to stand like a winner, even when he is struggling. A student with his head down on his desk will do worse than a student (with the same talent and preparation) who sits up straight and looks like he is engaged in the class.

By changing simple physical habits, your child can change old patterns of behavior. For example, in the movie *Dead Poets Society*, the English teacher (played by Robin Williams) instructs his students to stand on their desks to create a new perspective from which to view the world, thereby creating a breakthrough in their understanding. Your child can think of similar changes in Exercise 8.5 below.

When your child is "down," laughing and smiling can help improve his mood. Most people assume that you can laugh or smile only when you're *already* happy. In truth, laughing and smiling can actually *make* you happier. Laughing and smiling are primitive means of communication; they are among the first purposeful activities babies make. Laughing and smiling make you feel good in many ways: These actions relax your muscles and boost your immune system. They trigger the release of dopamine and endorphins, chemicals that affect your brain in a way that makes you feel joyful. Laughter gets your heart beating and your blood flowing. Additionally, as we discussed in Chapter 7, laughter promotes the bonds between your child and those surrounding him. Having a sense of humor defuses tension and promotes constructive efforts.

As mentioned in Chapter 6, our brains tend to overvalue negative criticism and to fear risk and mistakes. Because of these inborn tendencies, most people make decisions based on fear. In other words, the human brain comes programmed to "play not to lose" (play to avoid

---

EXERCISE 8.5

WORK LIKE A WINNER!

Does your child look like a great student when he is working on homework? Or does he sprawl over his bed as if he were on vacation? When your child is waiting to bat, is he watching the game and cheering on his teammates, or is he hunched over on the bench and playing games on his phone?

Take a photo of your child when he physically looks unfocused. Compare it to a photo you take when he is "in the zone." Show both photos to your child. Ask your child: What physical stances can he use to make him feel like a winner? Encourage him to assume this stance whenever success is the goal.

failure). The good news is that humans also come with a built-in work-around: laughter. Laughter is an instinct that helps us loosen our inhibitions, take social situations and our social standing less seriously, and thereby helps rid the body and the brain of this prewired fear of failure. So when your child is feeling inhibited and afraid of failing, encourage him to smile and to laugh (so long as it is not inappropriate to the situation). By assuming an "I'm being positive" posture, he will move toward happier emotions and "playing to win." It is no coincidence that "emotion" and "motivation" share a Latin root, *emovere,* meaning "to move." To summarize this strategy: Your child's body movements, posture, and facial expressions affect his psychology. Motion affects his emotion: If he changes the way he's moving, he will also change the way he is feeling.

PARENT STRATEGY 5.
DITCH THE GOAL OR CHANGE THE PLAN

Failing to achieve a goal that your child had previously set is also an opportunity for him to reevaluate whether or not it's the right goal. It's important to teach your child to use "flexible thinking." Sometimes the goal—or the plan to achieve the goal—*does* need to be adjusted if it is not working out. Although we certainly don't recommend "giving up"(or "choosing not to play") as a general approach to challenges, it is important to balance persistence in the face of a setback with a thoughtful evaluation of what went wrong, and consideration of whether the goal is still the right goal and worth going for again. Taking a breather, or trying something else for a while, makes sense sometimes.

Sometimes the wrong goal was set to begin with. The initial goal may have been too ambitious—e.g., saying "I want to play basketball as well as Kobe Bryant" or "I will only be satisfied with 100 percent on the test" instead of "I want to improve my free throw percentage in basketball" or "I want to finish a test without making silly mistakes." If the goal is too lofty, success will be elusive—and your child will not be able to celebrate. If perfection is the goal instead of progress, your child will remain unsatisfied because perfection is an unattainable ideal.

The economic concept of "sunk costs" can apply here. A sunk cost is a payment that cannot be recovered. Individuals sometimes continue pursuing what they have invested in (even if it is obvious that they will suffer further economic loss) because to change their path means to discard all the effort they've already placed into that strategy. As we've mentioned, the human brain is wired to avoid change and to avoid losing. Rationally, people should not make decisions about what to do in the future based on prior costs. Those costs are in the past, and can't be changed; the decision about what to do next should be based on what could happen in the future. However, people often do make emotional decisions based on what they have already "sunk" into a project. The humorist Will Rogers wrote, "If you find yourself in a hole, stop digging." Part of the reason why this is such a funny and enduring quip is because as obvious as it sounds, it is often difficult to do in practice. In short, it is very challenging to give up on a deeply held "core" belief, value, or task that you've already put effort into, but it may be the best thing to do to improve the future.

If your child keeps failing to reach his goal, is his heart fully in it? It may be worth examining his motivations for reaching the goal. Is he doing it for himself, or is he trying to fulfill another person's wish for him? Remember from Chapter 2: He has to be committed to his *own* goal.

Sometimes people confuse the "plan" with the "goal." In the quest to fulfill and stick to the plan, they may lose sight of the goal that led to the plan in the first place. As we stated earlier in the chapter, the process (the plan) is important—and, in some sense, is more important than the goal itself. However, if the process was designed to achieve a goal that your child later decides is the wrong goal for him, then the process may need to change too.

This classic mistake is illustrated in the book-turned-movie *The Bridge on the River Kwai.* In it, the British Colonel Nicholson, a prisoner of war in a Japanese work camp, implements a plan to show up his Japanese captors and simultaneously demonstrate the spirit of his British men and the capability of his POW officer corps. He engages his men in building an amazing bridge for the Japanese, but in his zeal he forgets that his overall goal should not be to complete the building of a strong bridge, but to defeat the enemy by allowing that bridge to be blown to smithereens by British agents. In the end, he realizes that his goal was wrong and changes it, blowing up the bridge himself.

The goal is the outcome your child is committed to achieving; the plan is the tool he uses to achieve the desired outcome. Sometimes the goal is the right goal, but the plan isn't the right plan. Both goals and plans should be reviewed regularly, especially if there is a setback—either the goal or the plan to achieve it can always be changed.

Recall the concept of kaizen from Chapter 4. Kaizen is the method applied in many businesses to make small, meaningful improvements in productivity. As the first step in kaizen, it's important to have a plan that is easily visualized or written down, so that it has the potential to be reviewed and improved. If your child finds that some aspect of his plan to achieve a goal isn't working well for him, but he wants to keep his goal, he can tweak the plan. He can practice this method in Exercise 8.6 on pae 167. Using kaizen means that a plan can be improved incrementally until it is successful. The goal doesn't need to be scrapped just because a plan doesn't produce success right away.

If your child is going to scrap the goal or the plan, it's important to make sure he doesn't decide to do this based on a negative mindset (e.g., when he is tired or discouraged). Tell your child to remember: What you do when you are working to keep your head above water is what defines you. Try to make sure he is evaluating the goal or plan on its merits rather than basing his evaluations on moment-to-moment feelings.

6. CONSIDER A COACH

Every professional athlete has a coach who he turns to for mentorship and advice. An athlete who has just been defeated must have a professional with experience in his sport to provide perspective on his performance. Likewise, your ADHD child might benefit from the assistance of a coach who can guide him toward his goals. An experienced coach knows when it is time to consider changing an athlete's goal or the plan to get

> **Coaching Corner**
> The decision to change the goal or the plan should not be based on emotions—it should be a carefully considered decision. How can your child know when to persist, versus when to make a change? This is a time when Strategy #6—having an objective outside advisor (coach)—can be extremely useful to your child with ADHD.

there; an experienced coach also knows when to get an athlete's head *back* in the fight, and how to get him *back* on the plan when he feels like giving up. An ADHD coach can do the same for your child.

EXERCISE 8.6

IT'S A CINCH BY THE INCH AND HARD BY THE YARD

Kaizen (little improvements over time) creates success. Rather than looking to create 100 percent improvement, your child should seek to improve by one percent and then repeat it many times.

Review a time where your child had a plan to do something and the plan didn't work out, so he gave up. Think about what could have happened if he had modified the goal or plan instead of giving up on it entirely. On a separate piece of paper, have him write down his goal, the plan that didn't work, the reason why the plan didn't work, and a small change he can make in the plan.

Example

- **Goal:** I want to keep track of all my homework every day.

- **Plan that didn't work out:** I am going to write everything due in my planner (color-coded).

- **Reason(s) for failure:** Plan failed because I never took the planner out of my backpack and I didn't have enough colored pencils and pens (color coding was too ambitious).

- **Kaizen:** I am going to attach the planner to the outside of the backpack so it will be easier for me to find and remember to write in it. I don't have to color-code the assignments; just writing them down each day is enough to keep track of them.

There are many reasons why athletes who are supposed to do well sometimes don't. Some are sidelined for physical reasons, such as injury. Some unexpectedly fumble because of a mental holdup, such as insecurity, fear, or overconfidence. Some get distracted by what coach Pat Riley called "peripheral opponents." These are external distractions, such as other people's expectations of the athlete; comments on his performance; or trivial tasks and errands that can eat up an athlete's time, distracting him from his goal.

That's one reason why it's so vital for your child to have a coach in his corner. (See Chapter 9 for advice on selecting or being a coach.) Many of the challenges that athletes face can also be applied to your child with ADHD. Just as a coach can help an athlete identify and overcome these obstacles, an ADHD coach can objectively help your child identify where the roadblocks are in his life. The coach can then help him train to overcome these challenges.

SUMMARY

As author James Michener said, "Character consists of what you do on the third and fourth tries." Success is going to reflect repeated effort by your child with ADHD. In this chapter we discussed six strategies to deal with the inevitable setbacks that ADHDers will face. These strategies are to practice positive self-talk (such as saying "I can't do this *yet*" instead of "I can't do this"); remembering that success is the product of energy and time; relying on internal satisfaction instead of external rewards as motivation; using body language to lift performance; and remembering that goals and plans can be scrapped or modified and should be reexamined periodically.

These five strategies can be reinforced with the sixth strategy: Utilizing an ADHD coach. In the next chapter, we go into this strategy in depth. We discuss both how to be an ADHD coach and tips for selecting somebody else.

TIPS FOR PARENTS OF ADHD CHILDREN
AT SCHOOL

You and your child have read about how your child can use his eyes, mind, body, and spirit to concentrate. You have also read about how to utilize the "team" of people around your child to help him recognize his strengths, as well as strategies for him to use to overcome setbacks. These are important concepts that your child should keep in mind when he feels frustrated at school. When challenges arise—whether they are in behavior, following instructions, or taking tests—the following tips are worth keeping in mind. These tips can be shown to your child's teacher and school officials; this is especially helpful if they do not have a lot of experience teaching children with ADHD. When your child can expect consistent guidelines to be placed on him at home and at school, it can improve his behavior in the classroom as well as his performance on tests and assignments.

CLASS STRUCTURE

- Your child should be seated in a quiet place to complete tasks; e.g., priority seating at the front of the class, near kids who tend to be quiet.

- Physical activity can be interspersed with classroom assignments. This can be as simple as having your child pass out assignments or run papers over to the principal's office. Jumping jacks or other activities that are aerobic and don't require equipment can be helpful as movement breaks. Allow your child to stand if needed while working.

- Attaching a band around the bottom of your child's chair that he can kick will allow him to release some energy unobtrusively. Having something quiet to fidget with, such as a stress ball, can help your child keep his hands to himself.

- Ask the teacher if it is possible to schedule the more academically challenging subjects in the morning hours, leaving the more active, nonacademic subjects (PE, art, music) for later in the day.

- Look for ways for your child to be a leader in class, or to get positive reinforcement in a public way.

- Encourage your child to engage with other students through exercises that promote bonding.

- Make sure lines of communication are open between the teacher and your child. Your child may get stressed in class at times and it would be greatly beneficial if he feels there are opportunities to discuss his feelings with the teacher.

- The teacher must recognize that your child is a "whole person." Make sure the teacher knows about areas outside school in which your child excels and has success.

- Your child will do best with teachers who are clear-cut and organized in their presentation of materials. It is helpful if teachers are able to provide written outlines when needed. Teachers need to be structured, but not too strict or disciplinary.

- The teacher should check with your child before he goes home to make sure he has the proper materials and has correctly recorded assignments.

- An interactive and experiential learning classroom environment is generally best.

- Your child should be allowed to ask for clarifications and to have directions repeated without being ridiculed.

- Keep oral instructions concise.

- Give assignments both orally and in written form.

- Present assignments neatly and clearly with a minimum of clutter.

EXTRACURRICULAR ACTIVITIES

- Get your child involved with activities in which he can feel successful.

- Martial arts is a great activity for kids with ADHD because it teaches discipline, bolsters self-esteem, and releases energy.

- Every child is different—consider whether he would perform better with a team or in an individual sport or activity.

GIVING INSTRUCTIONS

- Try to make sure child's attention is "on" when you or his teachers give instructions. Try not to repeat yourself. Give the instructions once, looking right into your child's eyes.

- Ask your child to "listen with his eyes." Ask him to stop periodically to think about where his eyes are and if he is using them to attend to what is being said.

- Provide cues prior to important announcements and keep the information short and to the point.

- Avoid giving multiple instructions for different tasks, and avoid giving instructions too rapidly—this can be overwhelming.

- Make sure your child understands the instructions before doing the work.

- Ask your child to explain in his own words what he is supposed to do.

MATH

- Check online for games that help reinforce math facts; there are quite a few (for example, www.ABCya.com, www.mathplayground.com). Older children can use flash cards to help drill math facts.

- The use of a calculator and open book tests allow children to progress without being overwhelmed by having to memorize.

- Use graph paper to line up equations, especially with multiplication or long division.

- Cook! Recipes often use fractions in very practical, easy-to-understand ways.

READING

- To keep your child's mind from drifting, ask him to make reading as active an activity as possible. Take notes and highlight. Post-it notes can be helpful.

- Try to relate what your child is reading to personal experience.

- Reading a summary of the literature before reading the book can be helpful.

- Ask your child to remind himself of what the main idea of the chapter is as he is reading it.

- Kurzweil software (www.kurzweiledu.com) provides some helpful aids for reading difficulties.

- If reading difficulties are persistent, consider getting psychological testing for reading processing difficulties.

SCHOOL STRUCTURE

- Some children need special accommodations to help them be successful in a school setting. Some teachers give the accommodations informally; however, you may need to ask your school to set up a 504 plan or an Individualized Education Program (IEP). These programs ensure that a child with a learning disability can access services (or even specialized instruction) that allow him to succeed. The National Center for Learning Disabilities Website is an excellent resource for this (www.ncld.org).

TEST PREPARATION

- Tell your child to begin studying well ahead of time; the best way to remember something is to repeat it over several days.

- Use study checklists to organize time before exams.

- For test preparation, reading notes and textbook chapters over is very inefficient for most people.

- Interactive preparation such as making flashcards or taking practice tests can be more helpful.

- Organize information actively into graphs, charts, pictures, timelines, etc. Make mnemonics. Mnemonics are memory devices that involve creating an easy-to-remember phrase using the first letters of the words or information that need to be memorized. (There are a number of books on this.)

- Some children are very anxious about taking tests. They may benefit from intervention from a therapist. Generally, relaxation strategies (such as deep breathing or visualization) can be helpful. Activities that build self-confidence (martial arts, drama classes, other sports, etc.) can be helpful as well.

TESTING ACCOMMODATIONS

- ADHD children may need to take tests in a separate room free from distractions (a "least distractible" environment).

- Children with ADHD may need time and a half, double, or unlimited time whenever possible, both on school and standardized tests. For kids in high school, accommodations are available for the SAT and ACT, but requirements for accommodations need to be looked into well in advance (at least two months) of taking the tests.

- For children who have trouble writing, circling answers in the test booklet rather than filling in bubbles is helpful; using a computer for writing essays may be beneficial.

- As needed, provide clarification of directions and questions.

WRITING

- For trouble with the physical act of writing, consider programs such as Handwriting without Tears (www.hwtears.com), and/or working with an occupational therapist to find the best kind of pencil or pens. Try to have your child learn to type as quickly as possible. There are a variety of typing programs available, such as Type to Learn.

- Dictation programs, such as Dragon Speaks, are improving and becoming very useful. These programs transcribe the user's speech into written text.

- Children who have trouble writing should make notes on provided outline forms. Children can also use the "buddy" system and get a copy of their peer's notes.

- Consider a digital pen (such as the LiveScribe Pulse Smartpen), which turns handwritten information into stored digital data.

- Templates for how to approach written language tasks can be helpful (such as how to write a persuasive essay, creative story, etc.). Inspiration software is designed for the purpose of improving organization and written composition skills (www.inspiration.com).

- Written assignments should be done on the computer with the use of a spell check program, and should be untimed. There is an iPhone/iPad app called Typ-O, which is helpful for spelling.

9

Picking the
Perfect Coach

Janey, nine years old, often rushed through her work, especially writing. In contrast, she put a lot of time, attention, and detail into her art projects. With writing, she had developed a self-image (and a reputation) as some-one destined to write the least amount possible. In art, she had developed precisely the opposite self-image and reputation, as someone who always did excellent and detailed work. Her ADHD coach pointed out to her that she did have the ability to do careful and thoughtful work, as displayed in her art projects, and she could apply this same ability to her writing. Janey was totally surprised, but once this insight was made, she was able to start bringing "Art Janey" to writing. From then on, she put much more effort into fully answering questions in a considered, thorough manner.

ADHD coaching is a recent concept, introduced in 1994 in Edward Hallowell and John Ratey's book *Driven to Distraction*. ADHD coaches differ from psychiatrists or psychologists in that coaches do not prescribe medication, do not necessarily have a professional degree, and are not legally required to be certified (as with life coaching, ADHD coaching is self-regulated). However, as with a psychiatrist or psychologist treating ADHD, the goal of an ADHD coach is to teach her clients strategies and skills to manage ADHD.

Every competitive sports team has a coach to guide and inspire the players. A coach helps an athlete set appropriate goals and develop a training program to achieve them; keeps an athlete on track and develops the athlete's skills; helps the athlete overcome challenges and frustrations; and establishes an emotional bond with the athlete and uses it so that the athlete believes in herself and feels confident in her growing abilities. An athlete feels empowered and performs better with the support of a good coach.

Likewise, a coach who specializes in ADHD can help her clients reach their goals. The ADHD Coaches Organization (ACO) defines ADHD coaching as a "supportive, collaborative, goal-oriented process" that combines life coaching, skills coaching, and education. An ADHD coach could be someone your child looks up to, such as a teacher or tutor, a family friend, an athletic coach, or a church official; or, she can be a professional who may hold a certification in ADHD coaching. (See Resources for a list of organizations that might help you find a professional coach in your area.)

In this chapter, you will learn how to find the right coach for your child—someone who, like an athletic coach, will bond with your child and help her through the rough spots, give her techniques to improve her behavior, and provide an unprejudiced view of how she is doing. An ideal coach will be accessible—someone who takes the time to get to know the child she is coaching. A coach also needs to be affordable financially. That said, although having Mom or Dad do the coaching may seem like the easiest and least expensive option, the emotional bonds between a child and a parent may be more of an obstacle than a benefit to proper ADHD coaching.

WHY SHOULD YOUR CHILD HAVE A COACH?

It may seem like your child is doing fine: Whenever you ask if she needs help with her homework or help reaching one of her goals, she says, "No, I can do it" or a vague, "It's okay, I'm working on it." However, for many children, it's hard to ask for and accept help. In doing so, they have to admit they don't have it all together. Some of the same people who ask for help in one aspect of their lives (athletics, for example) reject the idea of doing so in other aspects of life. ADHDers will often need help from others—but it may be difficult for them to ask for the help they need, in part because their ADHD may be frustrating to themselves and to others. In contrast, athletes have a different mindset: Seeking help is expected of athletes (more so than it is for other people), partially because coaching is so built in to athletic culture.

A serious athlete plays to win, and all serious athletes have coaches to help them. Having a coach turns someone who says, "I like to play basketball" into a person who says, "I *am* a basketball player." Saying "I am a basketball player" (whether you are a professional or not) implies that playing basketball competitively is a part of your identity. Your goal is to play your best and win games. In contrast, the statement "I like to play basketball" implies that just shooting the ball around is something you enjoy doing once in a while. You can remove "basketball" from the phrase altogether to get the simple but powerful statement, "I am a player"—meaning that you are somebody who is mentally, physically, and spiritually playing the game (whatever the "game" may be) to win. A coach contributes to establishing this identity in many ways. Athletes frequently come to view their coach as a "father figure" or "mother figure." Athletes accept that they will have to be corrected; this is a structured part of sports.

There are many reasons why ADHDers, on the other hand, tend not to ask for help. Some ADHDers have poor self-esteem, and in order to ask for help, your child needs to feel that she is *worthy* of help. Your child may feel that other people can do the work with no problem—and she does not want to feel different from others. Other children with ADHD feel that they are not the problem—the problem lies with all the demands put on them by others, and so they think the solution to their challenges in life is to avoid those people and situations (parents, teachers, the work itself, etc.). This is the pitfall of externalization that we discussed in Chapter 2.

Also, unfortunately, many ADHDers have irritated those nearest and dearest to them—family and friends with whom they interact daily. So, they don't know who to turn to instead. ADHDers can be misperceived as lazy, due to procrastination. They tend to run late because they may not get organized until the last minute, or because they have a hard time estimating how long a task will take. They have a tendency to lose things. They may give the appearance of not listening well. These issues, especially when repeated over time, can annoy and alienate the very people who would otherwise be in the best position to help.

Children with ADHD are prone to being oppositional; they tend to say "no" often and impulsively, without thinking things through. They frequently argue with the same people who are trying to help them. These are isolating traits which make it much harder to ask for help.

Of course, not every child with ADHD will have all (and some may not have any) of these tendencies. However, to the extent that they are present, these tendencies complicate the relationship between the child with ADHD and the people with whom they interact on a daily basis. Tell your child not to view herself as a failure who needs a whole personality transplant, but advise her to ask for help to identify the skills she needs to improve. One such skill may be organization. Another may be time management. Possibly it's finishing projects, or double-checking her work. If you and your child are having trouble identifying the skills she wants to start with, take another look at the goal-setting strategies in Chapter 3.

Albert Einstein defined insanity as "doing the same thing over and over again and expecting different results." You will see many people who do the same thing over and over again in their daily lives, and yet are perplexed about why things don't improve for them. Left to themselves, most people repeat the same behaviors, don't change their habits, and don't fundamentally alter how they react to situations. Albert Einstein also said, "The significant problems we face cannot be solved at the same level of thinking we were at when we created them." In other words, nobody (your child included) can move forward without growth. A coach will help your child learn to do things differently, and that is how outcomes change.

A coach can help your child grow by providing an objective, outside perspective about where to make the most productive changes. Ideally, it is best to find a coach before your child finds herself in "crisis mode" from ADHD and starts feeling extremely overwhelmed. Many people only ask for help once things around them have already collapsed and they start to feel hopeless. Then the coach has the added challenge of overcoming that hopelessness, in addition to instilling the training designed to maximize performance. If possible, it is better to get help before your child hits rock bottom.

Let's slightly adapt the Positive Cycle of Success and the Negative Cycle of Failure from Chapter 3 to better illustrate the effects that a coach can have on your child's success. (See Figures 9.1 and 9.2.)

Having your ADHD child and a coach start with small attainable goals will build up your child's self-esteem. It will also build up her confidence in her coach and make her more likely to confide in the coach when she is having trouble with a task. The coach can then offer helpful

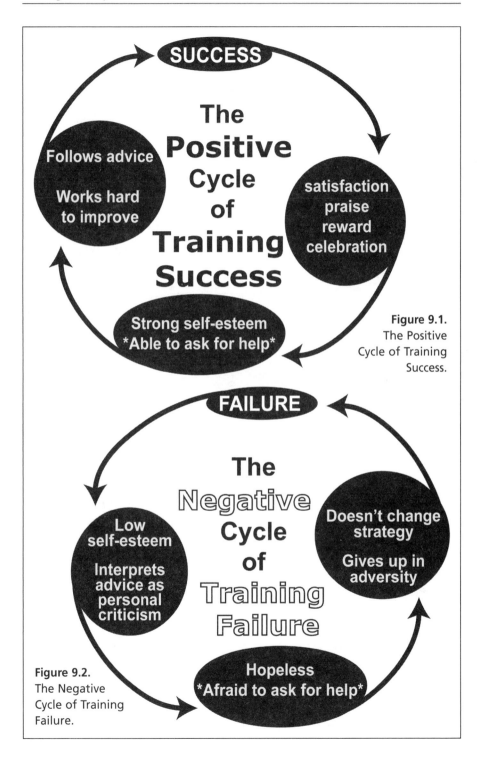

Figure 9.1. The Positive Cycle of Training Success.

Figure 9.2. The Negative Cycle of Training Failure.

advice and strategies to further your child's progress, and your child can start working toward bigger and bigger goals.

You, as the parent, know your child best and may want to take on the role of coach yourself. In the following section, we will talk about how to *be* a great coach. What strategies are important for coaching ADHDers? This information can also be shown to anybody who is in a position to help a child with ADHD—whether it is another parent, a teacher or tutor, a therapist, or an official, hired coach. If you'd like information about what to look for in an outside coach, turn to page 195.

Coaching Corner

Helping a child with ADHD set and attain S.M.A.R.T. goals (Chapter 3) is part of coaching because each cycle of successful goal achievement contributes to the trainee's self-esteem and confidence. This strengthens the bond between the trainee and the coach, making it easier for the trainee to seek out further assistance and accept critical feedback from her coach. Looking at the size of your child's challenges isn't productive. Looking at the size of your child's potential is!

SO YOU WANT TO BE A GREAT COACH:
FIVE BASIC PRINCIPLES FOR COACHING ADHDERS

As a coach, how much should you push somebody who has ADHD? In other words, how much troublesome behavior should you excuse because of ADHD? The answer is that you should push past where the ADHDer has been. That is, if the child has a certain problematic behavior, the idea is to improve upon that behavior. Your ADHD child may eventually get to the point where she has *no* problematic behavior at all, but first she has to be coached into *less* problematic behavior. You must look at the goals you and your trainee have identified, evaluate where your trainee stands in relation to them, and push toward these goals. A necessary key to personal growth is to be pushed out of our comfort zones. However, we don't want your child to enter the "shock zone," where she feels overwhelmed by the amount of change. In the shock zone, your child loses the ability to improve and instead may completely shut down. The idea, then, is to push your child out of her comfort zone but not into the shock zone. Where is this correct zone? If the amount of discomfort can be managed through positive self-talk or praise from the coach, then it's probably the right amount of pushing. Stay positive! A coach who is continually looking for strengths to praise will have a different perspective on what behaviors she can accept, what she can let go, and what to focus on, compared with a coach who always looks for weaknesses.

The question that inevitably follows is, "How much should I punish somebody who has ADHD?" A positive-leaning coach will focus on positive reinforcement of good behaviors (progress toward the goal) rather than on punishment of bad behaviors for missing a target. We believe that positive coaching is the most effective way to raise the game of whomever you are coaching. That doesn't mean the coach will never give criticism. However, the majority of the feedback the coach gives to your ADHDer should be positive.

There is a difference between influence and authority in constructive coaching. A coach inspires and influences through personal example and praising the behaviors and traits she wishes to see in her trainee. In contrast, a coach who uses authority ("do it because I'm the coach and I tell you to") does not create long-term changes. Using influence and inspiration instead of authority also has a positive effect on the internal locus of control; when the trainee is in charge of herself, she is inspired to better herself.

If you are a parent, you may or may not want to be a coach, and the ADHDer may want or need you in a different role. To best help your child, your key role may be to give unconditional acceptance and emotional support. In that case, it may be better to hire a different coach (information about picking an outside coach will be provided later in this chapter). There are still ways you can help your child in her everyday life (see "Tips for Parents of ADHD Children: Home" on page 75).

It is often difficult for a parent to also play the role of coach due to the lifelong bond between parents and children. It may be easier for you to let your child's missteps slide in order to avoid hurting her feelings or to prevent a meltdown. Providing feedback and guidance may be difficult; a parent and child can easily become flustered or frustrated by each other, and what was supposed to be a learning moment can turn into a yelling match. Reactions and feelings about the child's progress are more intense and emotional when a parent is the one who directly takes on the role of ADHD coach.

Consider the relationship between you and your child. Ask yourself these three questions: Can I be objective? Can I see the positives in the ADHDer? Can I give constructive criticism when needed? If you feel that you are ready and able to do these things, you might be a good coach for her. If not, think about the following strategies as you are evaluating different coaches for your child. Whether it is you or someone else who becomes the ADHD coach for your child, these coaching strategies are key to making the relationship work between the coach and the ADHD child.

COACHING STRATEGY 1.
PUT THE ADHDer IN THE DRIVER'S SEAT

Remember from previous chapters that there is only one person who can set goals for herself—and that is the trainee. If you set goals for your trainee, you can coach all you want, but until she owns the goals and decides for herself that she wants to achieve them, she won't really move toward them. Your best results will come from a trainee who is self-motivated. Your job is to help the ADHDer start and maintain the Positive Cycle of Success.

If a person does not want to change anything about herself or her life, no amount of coaching is going to help. You can coach until you are blue in the face, but until a trainee is ready to accept your advice, you will just be a frustrated, blue-faced coach. Sometimes, the reflexive answer to "What do you want to change?" is "Nothing." However, in our experience we have found that with a little more questioning, ADHDers will stop, think, and find something that they want to do differently. You may find that they have some great ideas about ways you can help them that you hadn't thought of yourself.

If an ADHD child takes some initiative in deciding the next steps, she will have a greater stake in the outcome, will be more likely to stick with the training program, and will be successful. ADHD children— who often are told what to do, regardless of whether or not they want to do it—will find it a wonderful change to be listened to by someone in a position of power (their coach), instead of always being the listener. To gain trust, you will have to learn how to listen to your trainee without judgment.

Talking to the ADHDer about what she needs to accomplish will also help form a positive, useful emotional bond between the two of you. You can use the coach's assessment questionnaire below as a starting point for communication. Your trainee will find it liberating to be able to express her needs. On your side, you will understand the person you are

The Coach's Assessment Questionnaire

Here are some suggested questions to ask the ADHDer you're trying to help:

Goals

- What are the main objectives that you want to accomplish in the next three months through coaching?
- What is your desired outcome in the long term through coaching?
- Do you have a vision of who you want to be? If so, what is it?

Your Life

- Where are you the most focused? When are you at your best?
- What have been your three greatest accomplishments in life so far?
- What is the hardest thing you have had to overcome? What did you do to overcome this?

Coaching You

- What would you expect or like me, as your coach, to do if you fall behind on your goals or objectives?
- What shouldn't I do? What types of approaches will discourage you or lower your motivation?

Of course, you may have to rephrase things to some degree and direct the conversation more with younger ADHD children, but you will be surprised at how even young children are able to participate in such an exchange.

coaching much better. You will learn what is important to her, and what will motivate her best. You will also learn what turns your trainee off.

When you give your trainee the freedom to tell you what she wants—or doesn't want—from you, this forces the lines of communication wide open. It will connect the two of you and turn you into a team. You will be the coach and guide your trainee to the finish line, but you will work together to get there. It's the difference between being on a tandem bike where the ADHDer either isn't pedaling or is actively braking—versus being on a bike where both of you are pedaling and accelerating toward the finish line.

COACHING STRATEGY 2.
HELP THE ADHDer SEE THE POSITIVES

Parents and teachers need to see the positives in the ADHD child. The child with ADHD may have been frequently exposed to other people's criticisms: "You're disorganized," "You're too slow," "You never listen." People remember negatives easily, especially if they hear them over and over, and these statements become incorporated into their self-image. By the time they ask for help, they are often the ones making the negative statements: "I'm disorganized," "I'm slow," "I'm stupid."

> **Coaching Corner**
> Giving your child a say in the direction she wants to go will automatically increase her attention to her goal.

Help the ADHDer avoid negative statements; focus instead on "What can you improve?" and "What do you want your goal to be now?" It's the coach's job to pull the trainee away from the reflex of using her past challenges as excuses. For example, if someone views herself as lazy, she will not work hard because she will think, "I've always been lazy, that's just who I am." The coach needs to help the trainee tap into her strengths to sustain her energy and self-esteem. Positive coaching requires a centered and thoughtful approach that, when consistently applied, will lead to more efficient and effective performances.

It's important not to view the behaviors associated with ADHD in an overly negative light. "Filled with energy" could be a positively-viewed trait, but instead is often cast as "hyperactive" or "out of control." People with ADHD are often very creative, and in part it may be their lack of impulse control that makes them so. You can't fully unleash your creativity if you are always tamping yourself down. Poor impulse control can be a significant and dangerous challenge (think about someone who has poor impulse control while driving, biking, or skiing), but it can also lead to great things. People who constantly "put things together" in ways different from people with "straight" brains arrive at novel solutions that can move society forward.

DESCRIPTIONS OF ADHD VIEWED POSITIVELY

ADHD Traits Viewed Negatively	ADHD Traits Viewed Positively
Hyperactive	Energetic
Impulsive	Comes up with great ideas quickly
Talkative	Social, friendly, quick-witted
Being the "class clown"	Funny, has a good sense of humor
Hurrying through tasks	Efficient
Distractible	Interested by many different things
Daydreamer	Creative, big thinker
Doesn't follow directions	Independent

It is of the utmost importance to maintain a positive outlook when dealing with ADHD. With a positive outlook, people are better at accurately assessing themselves and their situation. They are better at seeing "the big picture." Without a positive outlook, people are unable to access their own strengths—and then where are they? Nowhere!

Hope is key to having a positive outlook, and people who are hopeful are better able to overcome obstacles and think of new strategies that might work when the old strategies fail.

We all need to switch strategies now and then. As a coach, it is your job to help someone get back up when they fall. *Flexible thinking* is a psychological concept that describes the ability to shift strategy. For example, imagine that you want to go to the movies while your child wants to go out for frozen yogurt. A child who doesn't have flexible thinking will fixate on saying, "But I want to go to get yogurt." Somebody who is able to think flexibly can come up with a solution: "Let's get yogurt first, and if we have time we can go to the movies," or "Let's watch a movie on TV and eat ice cream from the freezer." Coach the ADHDer to be able to find alternatives like these. People who are able to come up with such alternatives will become more hopeful because they will realize that they don't have to give up entirely when one option doesn't work.

People who are hopeful also believe in themselves; it is hard to be hopeful if you don't believe you can do something. Not only are hopeful people good at thinking that they *can* do things, they are also good at thinking of *different ways* to do it. Conversely, someone who has lost confidence in her ability to do something won't think very much about *how* to do it. ADHDers may have lost belief in themselves by the time they need coaching. Thus, a coach needs to train the ADHDer to reverse this mindset of hopelessness.

A coach can do this by being complimentary—but wait, doesn't a coach need to be corrective? Actually, it's important to be both. There are times when you should give positive statements and times when you need to go critical. To reiterate, a positive statement is supportive: "You're doing great" or "I am impressed with what you just did." A critical statement gives room for improvement: "That wasn't so good," "You made a lot of careless mistakes that time."

There is actually some data on the optimal balance—how often to go positive and how often to go critical. The ratio of positive to critical statements needed for optimal performance has been studied by several groups of researchers. A balance of three positive statements for every critical statement (a three-to-one ratio) gets the best performance out of most people being coached. These positive statements can be given over time, or all together (for example: "Sandy, I love how you stood tall and confident walking up for your presentation, but try to keep better eye contact with your audience next time. Then we'll see that confidence and your presentation will really shine!") Within this ratio, people who are being coached seem to bounce back quickly from criticism, and not have it negatively affect self-esteem. Trainees in this situation can absorb criticism and use it to do better, rather than to crumple.

Too much criticism can be counter-productive; too much positivity can fail to elicit the desired change. If the ratio is too low—that is, if there are not enough positive statements to balance out the critiques—the critical statements become less effective at changing behavior.

Interestingly, trainees also don't do as well if the ratio of positive to critical feedback is too high (i.e., there is a lot of positive feedback and little or no criticism). If the ratio is higher than the optimal three-to-one, the person being coached doesn't absorb the positive support as well, and the behavior doesn't improve as much. The trainee may not believe the coach's positive statements as much if they are not mixed with a bit of "reality talk." Another way to think about this is that the trainee may not feel she has "earned" the positive feedback if there isn't a (properly measured) dose of criticism to accompany it.

Data from the Gallup Organization backs up the need for positive reinforcement: In a workplace environment, managers get much more out of their employees if they focus on the employees' strengths. If your manager ignores you, the chance of your actively disengaging (becoming uninvolved with your work) is 40 percent. If your manager is critical—if he focuses on your weaknesses—your chance of actively disengaging is 22 percent. However, if a manager focuses on your strengths, you have a very low chance of becoming disengaged—only 1 percent.

> **Coaching Corner**
>
> *Effective coaches pay attention to delivering the appropriate balance of positive versus critical feedback to their trainees. Positive feedback should outweigh criticism; most trainees respond best when three positive comments are given for every one critical comment.*

Unfortunately, schools are not often designed to play to an ADHDers' strengths. For example, a child with ADHD whose strength is sociability is discouraged from being sociable in school, because the typical model is to work alone; sociability is viewed as distracting. A child who has a tendency to forget details will be penalized for this, rather than being encouraged to ask someone who is compulsively good at details to give her reminders and keep her on track. Keeping up with routine paperwork feels like special punishment for ADHDers, but it is important in many schools. Given a structure that showcases their weaknesses and does not demonstrate their strengths, it is no wonder that ADHDers often feel that they have the deck stacked against them in a traditional school setting.

COACHING STRATEGY 3.
CREATE AN EMOTIONAL BOND

The coach needs to be able to create an emotional bond with the person she is coaching. This is essential to communication. If we don't care about who is talking, we are not likely to listen to what she says. This is true in any field. For example, political candidates try hard to appear likeable and caring, so that their constituents will be sympathetic to their message. We all have had teachers whom we adored—and therefore, we worked hard to excel in their classes. Without an emotional bond, the person being coached will not take to heart what the coach is saying. To be a great coach, you need to know how to bond with the person you are coaching—even if she frustrates you sometimes. However, the coach must not become too enmeshed.

The coach has to remember that coaching is not simply about telling somebody what to do. President Dwight D. Eisenhower said, "You do not lead by hitting people over the head. That's assault—not leadership." All people with ADHD have already been told what to do a million times. It's not a matter of getting the information to them, but of finding a way to make it possible for them to actually do what they need to do. The strategy is not "Me vs. You," which creates conflict.

The strategy needs to be "Me *and* you *for* you." You, as a coach, are trying to help someone in her struggle against parts of herself that sabotage success. You are trying to team up with a person's best instincts against her worst instincts. Given that your goal is to help her, it is most helpful to be a partner rather than to be in an adversarial position with your trainee.

Former UCLA basketball coach John Wooden defined a coach as someone who can give correction without causing resentment. For most people, this is easier said than done—that's one reason why a good coach is so valuable. The skills to be a good coach rarely occur naturally; they must be learned. How do you correct without creating an adversary?

One effective way is to lead by example. The most effective coaches exemplify and personally demonstrate the techniques they are trying to teach people. If you want to coach someone to be honest, you need to be an honest person yourself—otherwise, why should anybody listen to you? Similarly, a disorganized coach telling somebody to be organized will be seen as hypocritical. In other words, "Do as I say, not as I do" is a terrible coaching strategy; "Believe me, because I'm living it myself," works better. Theodore Roosevelt once said, "People ask the difference between a leader and a boss. The leader leads, and the boss drives." Be a leader.

Another practice that successful coaches use is nonjudgmental redirection. A coach must be careful not to place value judgments based on behavior: "You're being good" or "You're being bad." To correct behavior, it's best to point out the specific, desired behavior and then to praise somebody for doing it right. Take the example of a kid running around the pool. Yelling, "Bad kid!" doesn't tell her how to walk safely. "Stop running" is an improvement on "Bad kid" in that it at least directs the child on what she should be doing instead. But "Walking feet, please" achieves the same thing—it tells the child the specific, correct thing to do, and at the same time is respectful of her and offers an opportunity for her to be praised: "Good job walking around the pool."

A coach is most valuable in helping an ADHDer see her potential for improvement and gain from defeat. It is said that from failure comes success, but it is frequently difficult to understand and believe that when you feel like a failure. When people fail, they have a hard time seeing past it and lose faith in themselves. The coach who believes in the ADHDer when the ADHDer lacks belief in herself will be best able to help the ADHDer get through the rough spots. Timing is essential, and the coach must be attuned to when the trainee is in a "high" mode and when she is in a "low" mode. Is she seeing things from the perspective of a confident person, or from the perspective of a person with low self-esteem? The coach must be able to help the trainee view challenges in a new way, especially when the trainee is at a low point.

During times of personal struggle, children with ADHD can lean on the emotional bond they have made with their coach. That bond will be strengthened if the coach can contribute something positive. Nobody needs a companion in defeat who makes them feel even more defeated. When a coach helps a struggling ADHDer feel more successful, she is both using and strengthening the emotional bond between them.

An athlete who can't perform at the top of her game becomes frustrated, which often leads to discouragement, which depresses motivation. Likewise, a child who isn't fulfilling her potential because of ADHD is going to feel frustrated, leading to lack of motivation. To escape a low-motivation state, a coach will need to empathize with and neutralize this frustration.

Feeling overwhelmed and not knowing what to do about it is like being in a hole. Climbing out of a hole that you've gotten yourself into is almost never done in a single jump. It is done step by step, climbing out bit by bit. A coach can help empower an ADHDer by pointing out small improvements that she can make and reminding the trainee that exit from the hole is possible. Each of the next steps will be a step in the right direction. The trainee needs to feel emotionally bonded to the coach so that she can listen to advice and use it to find a way out of emotional darkness.

Coaching Corner

Good coaches know how to create and maintain the most effective emotional distance from the trainee. As with giving positive and critical feedback, a key concept is balance: A strong emotional bond gives the coach leverage to help the trainee, but the coach must also keep a part of herself separate. The coach must maintain an independent emotional "center of gravity" so that she is available to support the trainee when the trainee is struggling.

However, too much emotional bonding can be detrimental instead of beneficial. A coach must not become so emotionally intertwined that she can't be objective. If a coach is too emotionally entangled, the coach may have difficulty correcting mistakes made by the person with ADHD. The coach who is too "wrapped up" and takes her trainee's challenges on as her own may feel that if the trainee fails, she (the coach) is also a failure. The coach and the trainee will then feel that they are pushing each other's buttons all the time.

The first rule of lifeguarding is: You can't save somebody else if you're drowning yourself. A coach must keep a part of herself apart from her trainee at all times—if she becomes too enmeshed and intertwined, they will succumb to failure together. By standing a bit apart, the coach will be able to pull the trainee up when she needs it without being overbearing.

COACHING STRATEGY 4.
INTRODUCE CHANGES WHEN THE ADHDer IS RECEPTIVE

Often, an ADHD coach is asked to step in to coach a person who is resentful, angry, and not in any mood to take advice. This is often the case when the ADHDer is a child whose parent is making her get help. How does a coach approach such a person and get her to become more receptive to advice?

One strategy is to try to coach someone right after she has exercised. Exercise can make people less angry and more receptive to outside influences. If you are looking to challenge old beliefs or ways of thinking, the best time to do this is when the trainee is physically depleted and extra energy has gone from her body. When a physical breaking point is reached, the door to the mind opens.

This is illustrated in the 2004 movie *Miracle,* a film about Herb Brooks coaching the USA Olympic hockey team in 1980. In one scene, each highly talented player insists on grandstanding and playing for his own benefit instead of for the team. After they lose a big game due to this lack of focus and teamwork, Brooks keeps the athletes on the ice, repeatedly having them skate full sprints for hours. He keeps this up until they are so fatigued that each member of the team drops their individual egos in exchange for a team identity as a whole comprised of different parts.

Billy Blanks, founder of Tae Bo® Fitness and world-renowned karate champion, has taught this lesson many times: If you can get a diverse set of people to perform a workout that is *so* tough that they become physically exhausted, they will come together and realize how alike they are, instead of focusing on their differences. Peter Johnson, one of our authors, has observed this tendency numerous times while coaching at his dojo. After a tough training session, people have a way of opening their ears to hear things from a fresh perspective.

> ### Coaching Corner
> *When we are in a good mood, stress is low and rational thinking is high. So try to get your child to do something rational and productive when she is in a good mood!*

Perhaps your ADHDer, however, does not exercise. She may be more receptive to improvements immediately after doing some other absorbing activity, preferably something that she loves: painting, playing music, building something—anything that makes her feel successful. Note the reasons why she loves her activity of choice and think about how you can translate those preferences to the activities she has been putting off.

A coach should not just walk away from an ADHDer who has low (or no) motivation, but should realize that the child may not be ready to listen to all the great ideas on how to fix her life. Sometimes lack of motivation comes from depression, and sometimes it stems from hopelessness, which is related. A depressed person tends to hold the view that things won't get better. A hopeless person may not be clinically depressed, but may lack motivation because she doesn't know what to attack first. In both cases, the trainee winds up feeling that her efforts don't make a difference.

As a coach, when you attempt to help an ADHD trainee who is depressed or hopeless, or who doesn't see a need to make changes, you must plan on introducing any changes very slowly. That may not be your style. You may be a "big plans" kind of coach, but you have to adjust your process to "coach small." Ask the trainee where she would like to start, and think of the smallest forward step she can take and actually achieve. Then celebrate when she does, before setting the next goal.

For example, one technique (similar to the timer technique introduced in Chapter 6) to get your trainee with ADHD to lengthen her attention span is to use a stopwatch and have her work hard for a very short period of time, concentrating the whole time. Maybe your trainee can only manage one minute of sustained attention. Start there, and celebrate it once it's achieved. The next challenge will be two minutes. The more victories that pile up, the less hopeless the ADHDer will feel over her inattentive tendencies. She will become more attuned to victories and success over what she can change, rather than to hopelessness over what she can't.

> *Sammy, age eight, would not focus on his math homework. What should have taken fifteen minutes would take him an hour. Naturally, he started to hate math, and the emotional breakdowns engendered by math homework would take up even more time. He used the stopwatch technique and saw that in just two minutes, he could finish three problems. He finished the assignment in ten two-minute sessions. With proper reinforcement and continued training from his coach, he became an excellent math student: He established and built upon a Positive Cycle of Success.*

COACHING STRATEGY 5.
STRUCTURE THE ENVIRONMENT

A coach can help her trainee by structuring the ADHDer's environment. A structured environment is based upon regularity; routines are expected, known to all, and maintained. This will help the ADHDer shape behavior, because she will know what to expect and what is expected from her. A structured environment tells someone, "This is what is going to happen here." In contrast, a free-form environment leaves ADHDers at the mercy of their impulses; for example, they may procrastinate more because without a schedule, it is easy for them to say, "I'll have plenty of time to do this later." Children with ADHD can often function reasonably well at school, but when left to do homework on their own at their own pace, with many distractions surrounding them, their performance deteriorates.

A karate dojo (school) is an example of a structured and disciplined environment. Instructors and students all put on a uniform, take off their shoes, and bow before class starts. Lines are formed for drills. There is a warm up, then class. Then, everyone takes another bow before leaving. One purpose of this structure is to use group behavior to increase the probability that a desired individual behavior will occur. The karate student knows how to behave (and is more likely to maintain that behavior) because everybody in class is behaving similarly. Robert Cialdini, psychologist and author, uses the term *social proof* to illustrate that people will do things they see other people doing. Using "social proof" as a way of influencing individual behavior, instead of trying to impose a standard without structure, is a proactive, positive way of reinforcing changes in behavior.

The idea, then, is to develop routines that will help a trainee achieve desired behaviors automatically, without having to rely only on willpower. The more somebody has to rely solely on her willpower, the harder it is to maintain a desired behavior. Remember the cookie example from Chapter 6: If you want to lose weight, but have cookies all around, you have to rely on willpower to not eat them. Most of us are not very successful in the face of that constant temptation. However, if you develop a routine in the store that takes you away from the cookie aisle so that you don't buy the cookies in the first place, you won't have to rely on willpower to not eat them at home.

Your trainee may say, "But I like cookies!" (Or Facebook, or video games, or whatever is distracting her.) It's important to point out that these things naturally grab her attention and make it much harder for her to focus on what she needs to do. Having those activities available suck attention away from the more mundane tasks that are not as fascinating to her brain. Time-consuming computer games are designed and marketed by experts to suck players in and keep them there. A great deal of neuroscience goes into making video games as tempting as possible, but this kind of neuroscience works *against* the ADHDer (unlike the neuroscience behind this book!). So, these types of diversions should never be used for "breaks," although they can possibly be used as a reward at the end of the day when work is completed or on days when no work is required. The message to your trainee can be: It's okay to do these fun activities—but do them in a way so that they don't compete for your attention and prevent you from achieving your desired goals.

Remind your ADHDer that she does not need help being distracted. In short: Advise her to turn the cell phone off. Work in a room without a TV. Block the tempting portions of the Internet when working on the computer. Structure the environment so these distractions do not appear.

Environmental triggers can be helpful as well as harmful. A coach can help by trying to structure the environment with triggers that lead to desired behaviors. One example of this might be to post a calendar on the wall that shows how much time is left until a due date. Another might be to write the afternoon's schedule on a white board. Or, the coach can show the ADHDer how to pack up her backpack so she is most likely to turn something in (for example, flagging homework that has to be turned in with Post-it notes). The idea is to make good habits more likely to occur, rather than less likely.

In addition to structuring the environment, structuring time is important. ADHDers often do best working in small chunks of time, as intensely as possible. They also tend to have a hard time transitioning from activity to activity; once they get into one activity, it's hard for them to leave it for the next. Structuring the environment to emphasize time cues can therefore be helpful. A coach can help her trainee make a schedule. Note that this doesn't mean "the coach makes a schedule for the ADHDer." Instead, the coach *guides* the ADHDer into making a realistic schedule. This schedule should incorporate "fun" or "relaxation" times as well as "work" times. The schedule should be posted or otherwise easily accessible so that the ADHDer will be able to see clearly what she is expected to do at all times.

This chapter so far has discussed coaching *principles*. For specific recommendations that coaches can make for ADHDers, look at the exercises presented throughout earlier chapters as well as the "Tips for Parents of ADHD Children" sections on pages 75 and 169. The next section of this chapter focuses on the criteria you should look for when hiring an independent ADHD coach.

PICKING THE PERFECT COACH

As we have discussed, ADHD can be irritating for the child who has ADHD as well as for the people around her. Although teachers and parents are in a good position to help, they may not be the *best* people to help—and in some cases, because of a long history of emotional exchanges, they may be the worst. In these cases, an ADHDer needs to find someone else to coach her.

Coaching Corner

If your child knows she is the one who is supposed to be doing her homework, and you do it for her, you are giving her the message that she doesn't have the ability to do it. This also tells her (falsely) that her homework is not her responsibility. She will lose self-respect. In the long term, this is not a winning strategy.

Children with ADHD are often frustrated with their parents. Parents are often frustrated with their ADHD child because they feel the child is challenging their authority, or is "not trying hard enough." A child with ADHD can often feel isolated and become very sensitive to criticism. Instead of listening to feedback, she may ignore it, become depressed by it, get defensive, or become angry at the person who gives it. Many times parents find it easier to just do the ADHDer's task themselves, rather than coach her through it.

For example, many parents will help their child (even an older child) get dressed in the morning, instead of going through the conflict of trying to make the child focus on dressing herself. While this saves time and helps a child with ADHD get through her morning routine, it does not give the child the independence or motivation to dress herself.

In another example, parents who are afraid of their child getting bad grades will do some of the homework themselves, or organize their child's notebooks for her. These actions may seem helpful, but they are detrimental to the child's learning process.

It can also be tempting for parents to expect less than they should from their child with ADHD. Subconsciously or overtly, parents may express a statement like "She can't do such-and-such because of her ADHD." Nobody benefits from hearing that she can't do something. It is helpful for parents to *understand* ADHD and the challenges it creates for their child. But it is *not* helpful for them to think or say, "She has ADHD, so she shouldn't try this," or "I'll just do it for her." Parents may also feel that they have failed in their parenting because their child is not succeeding as they want.

If you would like to hire an outside coach, you can ask your child's doctor for a referral. You can also search for a coach by using your local chapter of Children and Adults with Attention Deficit/Hyperactivity Disorder (CHADD) or a website such as ADHDCoachInstitute.org or ADHDCoaches.org.

Coaching can be done by a psychologist, psychiatrist, or other therapist, such as a licensed Marriage and Family Therapist (MFT) or a Licensed Clinical Social Worker (LCSW). There are also ADHD coaches who do not have a degree but who may be excellent; they may also be less costly, especially if mental health benefits are not included under your health insurance plan. Costs vary depending on the coach and on your insurance.

Some coaches require a commitment of at least one session a week for three months, to ensure that the patient is making steady progress and internalizing the new management strategies. Remember that coaching is not a process that necessarily leads to "instant" results. Success must be measured over time. Take time before choosing the coach to talk with her and understand her philosophy as best as you can. Even just talking with the potential coach will tell you a lot about her. Although this is basic, look for a coach who returns phone calls in a timely manner. If this isn't happening when you are setting up the initial appointment, it will not happen during the course of the therapy. Try to find a coach who can fit into your child's schedule so that your child will not have to give up a cherished activity to see the coach. You might start with a long list of coaches, but the latter two issues can help narrow the list down very quickly.

Sometimes the ADHDer herself can be helpful in selecting the right coach. Your child may have feelings about whether or not she can work with a particular coach. This is not meant to be a replacement for doing your own due diligence as the parent, but it *is* a valuable marker in determining your child's ability to connect with a specific coach.

As coaching is a partnership, it is helpful to know ahead of time what specific issues you would like the coach to address with your child and what goals your child would like to accomplish. You can use Chapters 3 and 4 of this book to help refine these goals in preparation for meeting with a potential coach. While coaching may not work for every child, it can be highly effective for many others and push them in the direction of organization, self-regulation, and goal achievement.

As a parent, you may worry about trusting somebody else to work with your child. The following four tips for selecting a coach can reduce concerns and help you find somebody who will be effective.

TIP 1. Pick Somebody Who Is Caring but Objective

There is a difference between the emotional bond between a child and her parent and the bond between a child and her coach. How do athletes and coaches develop a good emotional bond, and how can that be applied to children with ADHD and *their* coaches? Feeling connected to one another is an important aspect of an emotional bond, as Dr. Edward Hallowell (a leading expert and author on ADHD) has said: "[Connectedness] is a sense of being a part of something larger than oneself. It is a sense of belonging, or a sense of accompaniment. . . . connectedness is my word for the force that urges us to ally, to affiliate, to enter into mutual relationships, to take strength and to grow through cooperative behavior."

Trust is another important building block to an emotional connection—but a coach also needs to be someone with objectivity. People who are easily angered or frustrated do not make objective coaches. An objective coach is both honest and empathic: A coach needs to genuinely want to help her trainee overcome personal challenges. Such a coach will make it a priority to get to know the strengths and weaknesses of the person with whom she is working. The coach should respond to the tougher aspects of ADHD by helping the trainee view her personal struggles more objectively as challenges, and then helping her strategize the most effective means to overcome those challenges.

In sports, an athlete has to learn to listen to what the coach is saying in terms of objective performance improvements, and get past feelings of "She thinks I'm not very good," or "I should already be a starter," or "I'm already doing that task well."

In other words, if the athlete is too tuned in to what the coach feels about her, or if she is focusing too much on the emotional relationship between the coach and herself, it can be detrimental to progress. For example, if the athlete is focusing on feeling underappreciated, she may not benefit from well-intentioned criticism or advice and instead see it as a personal attack.

Coaching Corner

In her biography My Fight/Your Fight, *Ronda Rousey, the female UFC mixed martial arts champion, describes finding the right coach as being like finding the right boyfriend. The analogy is apt: With the coach selection strategies described in this chapter, remember that finding the right coach for your child is a process—much like finding a partner in life—that may take more than one try before you arrive at the right match.*

To really understand what the coach is saying, the athlete has to listen in the moment and take the emotional content out. This requires trust. If an athlete trusts the coach and fully believes that the coach is looking for ways to improve her performance, she can more easily listen to the objective advice the coach is offering. Just as the focus between an athlete and her coach should be on what can be done specifically to help the athlete perform better, an ADHDer and her coach also must focus on specific performance targets. When a child with ADHD trusts her coach and also connects with her emotionally, the child will feel comfortable being honest and sharing her feelings about what they are working on. This is a crucial step in making improvements because the coach will both validate those feelings and give the trainee helpful advice. If the child feels her coach understands her and has her best interests at heart, she will be willing to try what the coach suggests.

But that is the first step; the coach also has to be able to deliver. If the coach promises improvements that can't or won't come true, trust can be lost. The coach does not have to be flawless in her help and predictions, but she has to be honest and knowledgeable enough to maintain trust.

The qualities of empathy and objectiveness can be hard to identify in the first meeting with a potential coaching candidate. It may be beneficial to "pre-screen" candidates by reading reviews by other parents who have worked with them, if these are available online. But in the end, the most important thing you can do is to meet with the coaching candidate and interview her one-on-one (not just over the phone). In assessing this interview, trust your own judgment: Specifically, how did the coach make you feel during the interview? Was she a good listener? Did she ask good questions and make accurate observations? Did she make *you* feel like she understood *you?* This is important because it is a safe bet that however the potential coach made you feel, she is going to make your child feel the same way.

TIP 2. Look for Someone Who Will Increase Your Child's Self-Esteem

Your child may be reluctant to work with a coach because she is afraid of being told what to do, or more precisely, of being told that what she is doing is wrong. In the past, other people may have given feedback to your child that was not helpful or welcome. The reluctance to obtain a coach is perfectly understandable in this context. And that is why it is critical that both you and your child realize that the coach you choose is not there to criticize, but rather to do the opposite. Any coach for ADHD must have a positive disposition and be prepared to give lots of positive feedback along the lines of: "I believe in you—you've got this one in the bag!" In fact, as explained earlier in this chapter, it is important that the coach for your child gives a lot more positive feedback than negative feedback.

Self-esteem refers to what a person thinks about herself. People who lack self-esteem feel pessimistic about their abilities. Self-esteem is a prerequisite for self-improvement—without a belief in yourself, why work on yourself? Norman Vincent Peale said, "When [people] believe in themselves, they have the first secret of success." If your child feels valuable and feels that she has something to contribute, she will interact with others much more constructively than if she feels that she doesn't offer value to a situation.

But self-esteem tends to suffer in ADHDers. From toddlerhood on, ADHDers tend to get in trouble in many different ways and more often than people without ADHD. As a young child, a person with ADHD may internalize a view of herself as a "bad child." As they grow, many ADHDers perceive themselves as "not smart" because of obstacles to academic success. Or, they may know they are smart but that they aren't achieving as much as some of their fellow students. This is frustrating and makes them feel that there is something wrong with them.

Once your child has poor self-esteem, it becomes a self-reinforcing situation. She starts to accept that she is somehow defective, and deals with the world on that basis. She doesn't expect much of herself, and accepts that other people must be right when they criticize her. This affects her ability to form and maintain healthy relationships as an adult, and she will be at higher risk for being unsuccessful in later years of school and in the workplace. Poor self-esteem is associated with a higher risk of physical illness, trouble with the law, and mood disorders such as depression.

Failures are inevitable, but it's what you do after them that counts. A good ADHD coach will emphasize that failure is something we all must pass through on our way to success. Professional basketball star Michael Jordan once noted, "I have missed more than 9,000 shots in my career. I have lost almost 300 games. Twenty-six times I have been entrusted to take the game winning shot. . . . and missed." He then made the point that without these failures, he would not have experienced success.

Self-esteem is built by continued perseverance toward a goal, despite challenges or temporary failures on the way to success. An effective ADHD coach understands that self-esteem is developed and created inside the child who is taught to see the positive lesson in a challenge. Vincent Van Gogh said, "If you hear a voice within you say 'you cannot paint,' then by all means paint, and that voice will be silenced." A coach can create the difference between someone who quits and someone who keeps going. A coach reminds your child of what she *can* do. A coach can help a child with ADHD move past setbacks. In helping to accomplish goals, the coach helps shift the Negative Cycle of Failure into the Positive Cycle of Success.

Traditionally, clinical psychology and psychiatry have focused on lists of symptoms and diagnoses: "This person has ADHD." "This person is depressed." "This person has anxiety." In contrast, positive psychology (the study of the strengths that enable people to succeed) focuses more on concepts such as, "This person is hopeful," "This person has perseverance," or "This person is creative." Positive emotions include joy, love, and hope.

Often, ADHDers fall into the trap of saying, "Because of my ADHD I can't _____." It's good for your child to understand how ADHD affects her thinking and gives her certain tendencies. But a good coach will point out that your child is not actually limited by ADHD. She will help your child use her strengths to compensate for her weaknesses, and help your child when she stumbles. With a positive and upbeat coach, your child can learn from mistakes instead of being defined by them.

When a child has access to her own positive emotions, it builds her up physically, emotionally, and mentally (see the chart on page 185 comparing the negative view of ADHD traits versus the positive view). Positive emotions have even been associated with improved immune function and less physical signs of stress, and may influence how long we live. Positive emotions often increase intuition, improve the ability to work with others, and let us see the "big picture." They increase cognitive flexibility—the ability to shift perspective—and speed.

Positive coaching is not as simple as saying only good things. A coach has to correct when necessary. However, the focus should be on the positive aspects.

Matthew, age twelve, was always making silly mistakes. He made so many of them that they caused him to constantly fail tests, particularly math tests. His coach helped him see that he was somebody who could persevere; the coach pointed out how Matthew kept trying. Matthew then was able to see himself as someone who perseveres and rededicated himself to checking his work. Eventually, he was able to catch his own mistakes regularly.

TIP 3. Find a Coach Who Does Not Have (Uncontrolled) ADHD

Sometimes, having a coach who also has ADHD is great. After all, fellow ADHDers understand what you and your child are going through. They "get it." They recognize your child's issues and know, from their own experience, what might work in certain situations. However, if the coach herself has not successfully dealt with her own ADHD issues, this could be detrimental. The most effective coaches lead by example: They live by what they are trying to teach you. A coach who, in essence, says, "Do what I say, but not what I do," will have a hard time impressing her recommendations on people who can see that the coach herself does not abide by them. ADHD children will have no trouble seeing the truth— that the coach can't do what she is asking the child to do. Ralph Waldo Emerson said, "What you do speaks so loud that I cannot hear what you say."

Given that ADHD has some genetic contribution as well as learned components, many children with ADHD have parents with ADHD (or similar traits). If these parents have successfully dealt with their own behavioral challenges, they can be very helpful coaches for their children. However, some parents have not coped well with ADHD themselves. If this is the case, it is a second reason (in addition to potential emotional conflict) why parents may not be the best coach for their own child. When today's parents were growing up, ADHD was not talked about as much or as openly as it is now. Therefore, many parents who had ADHD were not diagnosed as children. Instead of learning strategies that could have helped them, they may have heard a lot of criticism.

If parents have not effectively dealt with their own ADHD challenges, it can significantly affect how their children handle ADHD challenges. For example, let's take the issue of organization. David, a thirteen-year-old eighth-grader, had C's and D's in school—not because he

Coaching Corner
Your child's coach might have some suggestions for you to change your own behavior; try to listen and change what may be lifelong habits!

was truly a C or D student, or unmotivated, but because he had a ton of missing homework assignments which significantly lowered his grades. He did the assignments, but frequently lost them in his room and forgot to bring them to school.

His parents were frustrated with him because he kept losing his assignments. However, when they talked about strategies for organi zation, it became obvious that both parents were just as disorganized as he was. There were piles of papers lying all around the house. Nobody seemed able to throw junk mail away. His parents frequently had to look for their own keys, cell phones, and other necessary items, which made

David late to school. In short, it would have been incredible had David been anything but disorganized himself.

In this situation, David would be best served by a coach who is an organized person. That coach would be able to believably share tips and insights. In contrast, even if David's parents knew what to say to him in order to get him organized, it would be hard for him to buy into what they were saying and take them seriously given their own behavior and habits.

To find a coach, look for someone who has strengths that complement your child's weaknesses. If your child needs help with time management, find someone who habitually runs on time and can help your child adapt to run on time too. If your child needs someone to help her with procrastination, find someone who has mastered working with deadlines so that she can demonstrate different approaches to achieve this. If your child tends to only look at the "big picture," find someone who is detail-oriented to help your child pay attention to the details too. This may be something about a prospective coach that is only evident over time, as it may be hard to assess in the first few sessions. If you suspect that your coach might have ADHD herself (you might just ask her!), ask how she has dealt with her own challenges. How she responds to this question will tell you a lot about her, including her degree of insight into herself, her level of self-confidence, and her ability to objectively and compassionately help your child while leading by example.

TIP 4. Find a Coach Who Has a Greater Sense of Meaning and Purpose

A sports event is meaningful to watch because we see it on many levels. On one level, soccer is a bunch of people running around after a ball. When you think about it that way, who really cares about the outcome? However, the game becomes more interesting when you think about it as a competition between two teams that have trained to their fullest physically and mentally, and who now battle over the ball to score goals in pursuit of an ultimate team victory. Using the game to view the dynamics of teamwork, cooperation, and overcoming adversity is a great way to find inspiration and meaning in what could otherwise be seen as a fruitless activity.

When a team is fighting for a championship, the level of meaning increases: Now, we are watching two of the best teams in the league, country, or perhaps the whole world struggling to see who is going to be the *very* best. Only one can be number one! Each play takes on even greater significance. One mistake could make the difference between being the champions and being also-rans.

Many ADHDers have a hard time caring about certain aspects of their lives because they don't feel those parts are meaningful. For example, many students don't see the point in learning much of what they are taught in school (e.g., "Who cares about trigonometry?"). They may have a point; schools arguably have significant room for improvement when it comes to teaching subjects in an interesting, fresh, and relevant way.

As we discussed in Chapter 5, one way to take your child's life to a higher level is to infuse her goals with a greater purpose. Ask your child to forget, for a moment, *what* she is working on and whether she wants to be doing it. Focus instead on *how* she is working on it. For example, forget that it is trigonometry and that she might not be interested in trigonometry because she doesn't see its relevance to the rest of her life. Is she giving it her all because she wants to be the kind of person who does her best, no matter what? If she can look at it that way—as a personal achievement challenge—the fact that it is trigonometry is no longer a problem. It becomes a tool in her quest for excellence. By definition, when we transcend an activity, we bring a higher value and meaning to it that goes beyond the activity itself. As discussed in Chapter 5, this speaks directly to the "spirit" part of your child's self, allowing her to drive personal growth.

The best coaches will help your child find a sense of greater meaning and purpose in her training that speaks to her inner spirit, empowering her to use that part of herself to push for her highest goals. Finding a coach who inspires your child in this way will help her maintain a positive trajectory and facilitate subsequent feelings of happiness and self-worth.

To find a coach who has this inspiring quality, ask her how she generally approaches roadblocks when she coaches. Specifically, when the coach has encountered a trainee who resisted advice, what kind of motivational approaches did the coach take? More generally, talk to the coach and then trust your gut: The more you talk with a prospective coach, the more you will be able to feel for yourself what motivates her, and how encouraging and inspiring she is likely to be for your child.

SUMMARY

For your child to be the best that she can be, she will benefit from having a great ADHD coach. Often, the best coach for your child will not be her parent (although it might be in some cases). This chapter discussed five strategies to keep in mind should you take on the role of ADHD coach: Put the ADHDer in the driver's seat using the coach's assessment questionnaire; help the child see the positives in a situation; create a strong, but not overwhelming, emotional bond; suggest changes when the trainee is receptive; and help the ADHDer structure her environment.

Whether it is a parent or an outside person, a coach should have the following qualities: The ability to be objective, honest, and to connect to your child; the ability to increase your child's self-esteem; the ability to understand ADHD without having uncontrolled ADHD herself; and the ability to inspire and infuse a sense of greater meaning into your child's efforts to overcome ADHD.

Remember that finding a good coaching match for your child may take several tries and failed attempts. This truly is a "match-making process" where the personalized "fit" has to work in both directions. You can get advice from other parents in similar situations, but in the end, you have to do the homework yourself and interview coaches personally; a good coach for one child with ADHD may not be the best coach for another child with ADHD. By following these guidelines and using your own judgment and patience, you are ensuring that your child's coach will be an effective and trustworthy mentor.

While working with an ADHD coach is very effective for many people, for others, it is not enough. These children may benefit from medications that increase their tendency to focus automatically. In the next chapter, we will address the topic of medications, and when to consider using them to supplement the nonmedication strategies that are the main topic of this book.

10

The Prescription Decision

After Abby, age fourteen, started taking medications for her ADHD, she said: "It's going well. I really like it so far. It helps me focus. When I'm doing my work, it's really weird because I'm not distracted by anything else. I can do my homework now. It's not such a horrible thing to do it. I feel like doing more things. I actually cleaned my room without my mom asking me to."

Although the idea of taking medications for ADHD can be controversial, there is no doubt that medications *can* help people with ADHD. When—if at all—should you add medication to your approach to overcoming your child's ADHD?

Parents frequently come into Dr. Sarah Cheyette's pediatric neurology office seeking help with deciding whether to start medication and which medication to try. Her patients have found that when things go right with a medication, the upside can be enormous—a child who previously could not focus for more than a minute can suddenly accomplish tasks and concentrate. This can be an incredible, positive feeling for both the child and his parents, and can lead to better self-esteem and entirely new concepts of what is possible for the child.

However, there have also been times when things don't go as planned. There can be significant side effects, or the medication may not work well for a child. Patients may try a series of medications, hoping to find one that will work. If a child is experiencing other emotional or psychological issues (such as depression) that contribute to his challenge with focusing, ADHD medications may not address them or may even make them worse. Many parents and children feel that getting a diagnosis of ADHD in the first place means that they have failed in their responsibilities, and they may begin to rely on the medication too much.

We believe that there is great value in using non-medication techniques, such as the focusing strategies featured in this book. These strategies can help your child form and strengthen important connections in his brain through the repetition of good habits. As with any type of training, the more your child practices good habits, the easier and more natural they will become. If your child repeatedly trains hard in these mental exercises, his brain will become programmed to focus and work hard in other life tasks where the outcome really matters.

Medication can help your child focus more automatically. This can be really helpful when an ADHDer is so overwhelmed by his symptoms that he cannot use the tools in this book effectively. With this focus, he will be able to absorb the non-medication techniques in this book, learn and grow from them, and establish lasting change and progress. Eventually, once these techniques become deeply ingrained habits, it may or may not be necessary to stay on medication in order to remain successful.

The take-home point is that while medication can be helpful, it generally should not be relied on by itself. Without the insight and positive habits gained from the training strategies discussed in this book, ADHDers are less likely to navigate the inevitable rough patches in school and in life. Two of our authors are specialist physicians who have treated children and adults with ADHD: We know from direct experience that all medications have side effects. However, we have also personally witnessed many cases in which medication significantly improved an ADHDer's life. We believe that it is best for parents and children to be fully informed and to consider every tool available to help the situation. In this chapter, we discuss the side effects and benefits of medication, as well as the basic chemistry behind each type of available ADHD medication. This chapter will present the information you need to determine the best method of treatment for your child.

WHEN SHOULD YOU CONSIDER MEDICATION?

Unlike medications used to treat diseases such as high blood pressure or seizures, the medications used for ADHD are generally not about physical safety or choosing life versus death—unless your teenager with

ADHD can't focus well enough to drive safely, or your child with ADHD is so impulsive that it puts his body in danger (i.e., by jumping off a swing set). In some respects, this makes it harder to decide whether or not to use a medication. Since your child doesn't *have* to take medication, how do you decide if your child *should* take medication?

Some children are not going to thrive even with the strategies presented in this book, because their focus level is too low. Some children will also reject the behavioral help that you as a parent (or their teachers, tutors, or coaches) try to give them. A child may feel that he is being unfairly criticized and that people are picking on him—that the problem is not him, it's everybody else. If the behavioral strategies that have been already tried (e.g., rewards for good behavior and punishment for bad behavior) do not work, parents and children give up on behavioral strategies in general. There are not a lot of options left at this point. Some parents will enroll their child in a school oriented toward ADHD children or try a homeschooling option if their current school situation is unsuccessful. However, this is not an option for most families. In cases such as these, medication can help a child get and stay focused.

Here are some examples of children and teenagers weighing whether or not to take medication. Do any of these scenarios sound familiar?

Thomas was a nine-year-old in third grade who was doing "okay" in school. He was performing at grade level in all subjects. His intelligence testing indicated he could be doing better, but he frequently made silly mistakes on his assignments. At home, his mother had to fight with him to get him to do his homework. Even if she could get him to start it, he never completed it on his own unless she sat with him and constantly refocused him. He was always arguing with his parents and teachers, and comments on his report cards often were variations of "If he would just apply himself. . . . " His parents had taken him to a psychologist to see if he could become more motivated. They were paying out of pocket and not seeing any results. Neither threats nor rewards worked. They did not know what else to do.

Samantha was an eighth-grader whose parents had been working with her on focus and organization issues for years. She had improved a lot, but still had challenges. She was very impulsive and blurted things out a lot, and consequently had few friends. She forgot about her homework at times, although she meant to do it. Her parents still had to keep on top of which projects and assignments were due. She was an A- or B+ student most of the time because of her parents' help, but she could easily get all A's on her own if these challenges were overcome. She and her parents wanted medication for when she got to high school, since grades would count for a lot there. Her parents were also concerned about her eventually learning to drive if she were not medicated: "One unfocused or impulsive moment behind the wheel could be fatal."

Martin was seventeen and had significant challenges in school. While displaying flashes of brilliance, he almost never turned in his work, even if he had actually completed it. He spent a lot of time working on smartphone apps that he created and was trying to market. However, he was in danger of not graduating from high school because of poor grades. His opinion of his ADHD was: "I have a lot of energy and can be very driven in pursuit of a goal. I have a high-powered brain and I don't want to slow it down—what good is owning a sports car if you can only take it up to third gear?" He was at least partially open to medication because he wanted to graduate high school. While his parents had confidence that he was going to eventually be successful, they were very concerned about his being able to function on his own in college.

In the above scenarios, medication may be the "stepping stone" that enables each child to succeed. Medications for ADHD are intended to make it easier for ADHDers to focus on one thing at a time, rather than relying on willpower, motivation, or self-control to reduce distractibility. Dr. Edward Hallowell, a psychiatrist who has written extensively about ADHD, likened ADHD to nearsightedness. Just as nearsighted eyes have trouble focusing, so does the ADHD brain. One solution is to take medication, which he called "internal eyeglasses" because it allows the brain to filter out distractions and focus on the task at hand.

On the other hand, few people who start a medication hope to be on it forever. So if your child has not learned any non-medication strategies, what happens if he stops his medication? Developing the skills to set goals and stick with them despite setbacks is important for a successful life. In a number of studies, the ability to work hard has been demonstrated to be at least as important as IQ in determining success—not only in school, but also in "real life." As David Brooks writes in his book *The Social Animal*, "Those who have habits and strategies to control their attention can control their lives."

Using medication without working toward personal growth is artificial and unlikely to yield permanent benefits. It's like fertilizing and watering a plant that also needs to be staked—but forgetting the stakes. The plant will grow, but flop all over the ground. Consciously learning strategies will optimize your child's performance and keep him from falling back into old habits. Then, if he stops his medication, he will have developed skills and strategies that help him remain successful.

Therefore, medication should be viewed as part of an overall strategy, not as the only route to take. The MTA (Multimodal Treatment of ADD) study was the largest study to address the question, "Is medication alone better than behavioral therapy alone, or is a combination of medication and behavioral therapy best for ADHD?" The study began in the 1990s and enrolled approximately 600 children. Follow-up studies were done for years after the initial study. Medication was found to be very effective, but on several outcome measures, the combination of medication and behavioral therapy was found to be the best. Behavioral therapy alone was initially felt to be less effective than medication therapy alone, but a follow-up study eight years later raised questions about how persistent the effects of medication were. That is, the long-term benefits of medication over behavioral treatments were not as clear.

Medication should never be used as the "easy way out." As mentioned in Chapter 1, medications can have a "zombie effect" on children, where they become quiet to the point of losing their personality. This will certainly make a classroom or home quieter, but it's not fair and unpleasant for the child. The goal is to balance your child's energy and creativity with the desired amount of impulse control. Sometimes it's a matter of changing the dose or trying a different medication altogether.

Coaching Corner

Many studies in psychiatry have demonstrated that in general, the combination of medication plus nonmedication treatments is most effective at eliminating symptoms and maintaining behavioral and psychological well-being over time. This is true for ADHD as well.

It is also important to note that, just as with the training strategies in this book, medications work best if the person taking them is "on board" and not resistant to taking them. If your child only grudgingly agrees to take medication initially, he may become more enthusiastic about continuing to take it if it works well for him. It is always important to listen to your child's concerns about taking medication. Some children with ADHD may view medication as validation that they are a failure—instead of as a way *out* of failure. It's critical to convey that starting medication does not mean that your child has failed as a person and that you're not trying to change who he is (and, in fact, you love who he is!). Starting medication means that he faces some challenges that have not been solved in any other way, and medications might help specifically address these challenges.

Medications should be considered after weighing the following questions: What methods have already been attempted? And to what extent are your child's ADHD behaviors truly impairing his ability to succeed? A key consideration should be whether your child's inability to focus is so severe that he cannot effectively use the strategies in this book. In that event, you may have to try medication in order to make progress with behavioral techniques.

There are two basic classes of medications for ADHD: stimulants and non-stimulants. For each class of medication, we will look at the common drugs in that category, how they work, and their potential benefits and side effects. We will first discuss stimulants, usually the doctor's first choice for treating ADHD. We then will take a look at non-stimulant options.

> **Coaching Corner**
>
> *It would be easy if we doctors could name and prescribe the "one" medication that is best for everybody! (Or the one that has "the least side effects.") Everyone is different! Even in the same family, different medications work (or have different side effects) for different people.*

STIMULANTS

The stimulant class of ADHD drugs consists of Ritalin and Ritalin-based medications (including Focalin). Stimulants also include the amphetamine-based Adderall, Dexedrine, and Vyvanse. Ritalin is not exactly an amphetamine, but it behaves very similarly to amphetamines. All of these medications work by increasing the amounts of two chemical transmitters in the brain (dopamine and norepinephrine). The names of the different stimulant medications and how they are organized can get confusing, because each has both a brand name and a generic name.

Below are some of the more common names. A short-acting medication requires more frequent dosages (two or three a day), while one dose of a long-acting medication is usually effective for the entire day.

Common Stimulant Medications for ADHD

Generic Name	Brand Name	Duration
Amphetamine	Evekeo	Short-acting
Dexmethylphenidate	Focalin	Short-acting
	Focalin XR	Long-acting
Dextroamphetamine	Adderall	Short-acting
	Adderall XR	Long-acting
	Dexedrine	Short-acting
	Dexedrine spansule	Long-acting
	Zenzedi	Short-acting
Lisdexamfetamine	Vyvanse	Short-acting
Methylphenidate	Concerta	Long-acting
	Daytrana	Long-acting (patch)
	Metadate CD	Long-acting
	Metadate ER	Intermediate-acting
	Methylin	Short-acting
	Methylin ER	Intermediate-acting
	Quillivant XR	Long-acting (liquid)
	Ritalin	Short-acting
	Ritalin LA	Long-acting
	Ritalin SR	Intermediate-acting

Caffeine

Almost everybody knows from personal experience that caffeine is a chemical stimulant that increases alertness and energy. Given this fact, and given that many of the prescription medications used for ADHD also fall into the general category of "chemical stimulants," it is natural to wonder if caffeine can also improve symptoms of ADHD. Many adults who qualify for the diagnosis of ADHD seem to drink a lot of caffeine—and it has been suggested that this might be a form of "self-medication." These adult ADHDers may be using caffeine as a socially or more personally acceptable alternative to the prescription-only drugs that a doctor might offer them. Research on this topic, however, suggests that caffeine is less effective and has more side effects than most prescription ADHD medications. It is not a good option for the treatment of ADHD in children, and is problematic even in adults who have ADHD.

Caffeine can both improve and exacerbate ADHD symptoms. This could partly be a dosage effect—prescription medications may simply be stronger—but more likely, it is related to differences in the way in which caffeine "stimulates" the nervous system compared with prescription ADHD medications. Notably, although caffeine does lead to increased dopamine release in the brain, it does so via

Stimulants are generally the first line of treatment for most people considering medication for ADHD. They are effective about 70 to 80 percent of the time. It may seem paradoxical to give stimulants to a child who is already energetic, but studies have found that stimulants actually have a calming effect on most children who take them. Stimulant medications work right away. They are generally short-term medications—depending on the medication, they are effective only for the time they are in your child's system, about four to ten hours. Therefore, they can be taken "as needed," meaning that it is usually okay for your child to skip them on weekends or holidays if the primary issues are difficulty in school and with school-related work.

There are different medications available because there is not one an indirect mechanism. It also increases other neurotransmitters and hormones. It has other targets as well, which may produce opposing effects on ADHD symptoms. For example, caffeine leads to an increased release of epinephrine into the bloodstream. (Prescription stimulants, on the other hand, increase the brain's level of norepinephrine.) Because it is released into the bloodstream and carried throughout the body, epinephrine has more widespread effects on many organ systems, including increased heart and respiration rate, muscle contractions, and a generalized feeling of anxiety or nervousness ("caffeine jitters").

These effects of caffeine may not be desirable in a person with ADHD—particularly if the ADHDer is already struggling with hyperactivity or anxiety. Finally, the time-course of caffeine may be problematic. Medications prescribed by doctors for ADHD are designed to predictably increase and decrease in the body over time in order to "even out" their effects. Caffeine has a more rapid onset and offset, which may lead to an undesirable "yo-yo" effect on ADHD symptoms (many of us have felt the "crash" that comes immediately after a "jolt" of caffeine wears off). As appealing as the cost and accessibility of coffee or caffeine pills may be, we do not recommend using caffeine as a treatment for ADHD.

that works for everybody. There is not one that is "better" than the rest. Different ADHDers respond differently to these medications, probably because of differences in underlying brain chemistry.

How Stimulants Work

Before going further into how the medications work, it's important to state that the scientific community does not currently know how the brain works in sufficient detail to explain most human thought and behavior. Although this may change one day with further progress, it is not possible to fully understand how any medication specifically alters thinking or behavior.

ADHD may be caused by a physical difference in the brains of

ADHDers. Evidence suggests that two chemicals in the brain, norepinephrine and dopamine, are also central to the features of ADHD. Many brain cells (*neurons*) in areas of the brain most affected by ADHD (the frontal lobes and regions directly connected to them) use these two chemicals to communicate. Perhaps, in people with ADHD, these chemicals are present at lower levels or are less effective than they should be in some of these areas of the brain. However, it's important to note that norepinephrine and dopamine are found throughout the brain and are involved in a variety of different behavioral disorders and diseases that have nothing to do with ADHD, such as Parkinson's disease. (Refer back to Chapter 1 for more information about how the ADHD brain functions.)

> **Coaching Corner**
>
> *"Natural" or "non-prescription" treatment does not necessarily mean that the treatment is without side effects.*

Stimulant medications seem to increase the amount of norepinephrine and dopamine available to the brain. The medications tend to be most effective in brain areas such as the prefrontal cortex and some areas of the parietal cortex, which are brain regions that have been implicated in ADHD by other studies. Stimulants block the reuptake of dopamine at places where brain cells connect and communicate with each other (*synapses*). Reuptake is the way that brain cells dispose of neurotransmitters after they have done their job. By blocking reuptake of dopamine, stimulant medications increase the amount of dopamine present at these connections and make more available for brain cells to use when communicating with each other.

The Pros and Cons of Stimulant Medications

As previously mentioned, stimulant medications are often the first choice recommended by a doctor. Numerous studies have proven them to be safe and effective for the majority of children who take them. Many children who take stimulants experience marked improvements in the ability to focus; many also form better relationships with classmates and family. When stimulants are effective, they can cause a drastic drop in impulsivity and procrastination, among other disruptive behaviors.

It is unclear exactly what percentage of people taking ADHD medications will experience side effects. Stimulants are well-tolerated in general, but the long-term benefits and drawbacks have not been extensively studied. The most common reported side effects of stimulant medications are as follows:

- Loss of appetite

- Mild sleep disturbances (either insomnia or excessive sleepiness)

- Weight loss

- Irritability

- Emergence of tics

- Skin irritation

In addition, stimulants can cause growth retardation (usually minor) in children. There are two "black box" warnings from the FDA regarding stimulants. One states that they can cause serious cardiovascular complications due to an increase in blood pressure and heart rate. The other black box warning regards abuse potential. Stimulants are controlled substances by law because of their potential for physical and/or psychological dependence.

Most side effects taper off after a couple of weeks, or after an adjustment in dose. It's important to note that *all* medications, stimulant or non-stimulant, can cause unwanted mood changes. Children taking these medications can get grumpy, sad, anxious, or experience other unwanted mood effects. If your child starts a medication for ADHD and then starts acting negatively in some way, it might be a side effect of the medication. These types of side effects may improve as the child gets used to the medication over time, or can be improved through dose adjustments.

Coaching Corner

Just as finding the right ADHD coach may take time and several tries, so too is finding the best medication and dose a process of trial-and-error that may take time and several tries. Starting or stopping medication should only be undertaken in close cooperation with a well-trained physician, preferably one with significant expertise in treating children with ADHD.

With all kinds of medication, it's important to undergo monitoring by a physician. Doses often need to be modified, or a medication may need to be changed to a different one altogether. Sometimes side effects that seem quite challenging in the beginning can be overcome with a little adjustment, or even just advice. Depending on which medication your child takes, your doctor will need to monitor his vital signs, including blood pressure and pulse, weight, and height. Additionally, it will be important to discuss with the doctor how the medication makes your child feel—both the good and the bad.

NON-STIMULANTS

The second class of ADHD medication is the non-stimulants. There are some people for whom the stimulant medications don't work or aren't tolerated because of side effects, so having options is important. Non-stimulant medications that are FDA-approved for ADHD can be found in the table below.

Non-stimulant Medications for ADHD

Generic Name	Brand Name	Duration
Atomoxetine	Strattera	Long-acting
Guanfacine HCL	Intuniv	Long-acting
Clonidine HCL	Kapvay	Long-acting

In contrast to stimulant medications, non-stimulants take several weeks to work. Non-stimulants stay in the system twenty-four hours a day and should be taken every day—unlike stimulants, it is not practical to take "holidays" off because they take longer to leave the body and may cause withdrawal symptoms. However, because non-stimulants stay in the bloodstream for a longer time, their beneficial effects are longer-lasting than those of the stimulants. Non-stimulants may be the better choice if your child has significant anxiety or tics.

How Non-Stimulants Work

Non-stimulant medications work in a variety of different ways. Strattera is most like the stimulants in that it increases the availability of the same neurotransmitters in the brain, but unlike the stimulants, it works more strongly on norepinephrine instead of dopamine.

It's unclear how Intuniv and Kapvay work for ADHD. In fact, the active ingredient in each one started out as a treatment for blood pressure and only later was found to be helpful in ADHD. This type of drug "repurposing" is a common occurrence in pharmacology, and underscores how little scientists really understand about how chemicals work to alter behavioral or bodily symptoms.

There are other medications that physicians sometimes try to use for ADHD. There are short-acting versions of guanfacine and clonidine that are used, but are less effective than the long-acting versions listed on the previous page. Some patients have benefited from Provigil or Nuvigil (used mainly for treating daytime sleepiness), or antidepressants, such as Wellbutrin. Some antidepressants that are not generally used to treat ADHD work in part by raising norepinephrine in the brain. This does not necessarily mean that these antidepressants will also be effective in treating ADHD; rather, it is an example of how a single chemical (norepinephrine) can do distinct things depending on how, when, and where it is released in the brain (i.e., elevate mood versus increase attention). These are not FDA-approved treatments for ADHD and therefore won't be discussed further here, except to say that they work by other mechanisms to alter brain function.

Pros and Cons of Non-Stimulant Medications

Unlike stimulants, non-stimulants are not considered to have abuse potential by the FDA. Because non-stimulants typically have to be taken only once a day and stay in effect throughout the day, they may be a more feasible choice than the stimulants for many patients. Even the longest-lasting stimulant medications last just from the morning to the early evening, which leaves patients without medication during homework time. With stimulants there is also no medication in the body first thing in the morning, which often leads to a chaotic start to the day. Sometimes stimulants have to be taken more than once during the day because they wear off. It can be a challenge for some children to be take the additional dose when and where they need it (e.g., in the middle of the school day). For all these reasons, non-stimulants may be a better choice if your child has particular challenges with focusing in the morning or on his activities after school.

Non-stimulants have different side effects from stimulants. These include:

- Nervousness

- Disrupted sleep and alertness (insomnia, lethargy, and/or fatigue)

- Upset stomach or nausea

- Dizziness

- Dry mouth

- Liver injury or suicidal ideation (in rare cases)

YOUR CHILD'S CHANGING BRAIN

You may be wondering, "How long will my child have to stay on medication?" The answer is that there is never a "have to" about medications for ADHD. Taking medications for ADHD is different from taking medications for diabetes, heart trouble, or cancer, where a patient would suffer significant health issues and even death if he were to stop taking medication. It's optional to start medications for ADHD—and therefore, it's also optional to stop them whenever you want.

> ### Coaching Corner
> Medications for ADHD are optional to begin with, so likewise, they are optional to discontinue at any time—though always with a physician's advice and supervision. For some children, medication is a useful tool that can help a child focus effectively to learn behavioral and thinking strategies (as described throughout this book) to overcome the obstacles of ADHD. This is how we advocate using medication.

These kinds of medications are used to make life better. If your child's life isn't better on them, then you can stop them at any time. That said, it is important to note that for some medications it is safest to slowly taper off, whereas for others, it's okay to completely stop the entire dose all at once. (Consult your child's doctor before changing or stopping any medication.) Some children with ADHD take medication only for a year or two; some continue to take medication for many years. Some young adults continue to take medications through high school or early college, but as they develop more freedom to do what they really want with their time, they find they can concentrate without the medication. Some people take medications, particularly the stimulants, only when they are going to school regularly, and stop them on weekends or when they are "on vacation." In any case, the benefits should continue to outweigh the side effects for your child to keep taking the medication.

As mentioned earlier, medications serve as one piece of the puzzle. Every individual develops physically in a unique way; so too does the brain of every individual develop in a unique way. As your child matures, his biochemistry and the structure of his brain changes. It used to be thought that the structure of the brain was "fixed" in adolescence, but it is now understood that the brain continues to change throughout life. As areas of their brain continue to mature, some adolescents may need less medication. There is a theory that ADHD represents a delay in maturity of some areas of the brain, such as the frontal lobes. This immaturity may improve over time as these areas of the brain "catch up." In some people, the symptoms of ADHD may recede naturally with time, and the rationale for taking medication may cease for these individuals. This is not true of everybody with ADHD (as some adults continue to have ADHD), and at present there is no medical test that can predict whether this will happen to any individual child with ADHD.

Regardless of the biological causes of ADHD in your child, the human mind is flexible and can certainly improve its ability to perform a variety of tasks with training: That is the primary focus of this book. Tasks that are initially very challenging can become easier or even "second nature" to perform with proper practice supported by good coaching. This can be compared to your first experience behind the wheel of a car: At first, you need total silence to drive. At that stage, every aspect of driving takes intense, conscious focus; you cannot tolerate music or talking when you are trying to handle the myriad tasks required for success. However, with practice, you learn to drive without having to consciously think about it most of the time. In fact, this can become a new challenge itself when experienced drivers stop concentrating on driving and start trying to multitask while at the wheel (definitely a bad idea)!

The book *iBrain*, written by UCLA professor Gary Small and his wife Gigi Vorgan, details how exposure to digital technology (to the tune of over eight hours per day for most children and adolescents) is changing the way children's brains develop in modern society. Certain skills, such as multitasking and visuospatial skills (the ability to process visual information), are improving in the youngest population. However, there is a downside: Other skills, notably the ability to relate to people in real life, are on the decline, as is the ability to concentrate on one thing for a sustained time period. This trend may in part be responsible for the increasing diagnosis of ADHD. Digital technology may be contributing to shorter attention spans. However, if some experiences can rewire the brain to make ADHD worse, other types of experience, including committed training, can make ADHD better. Training will strengthen the connections you want your child's brain to make. With a healthy, focused training regimen—including a supportive, positive coach to keep your child on track toward his goals—medications may become supplemental or not necessary at all over time.

SUMMARY

We believe that the non-medication strategies outlined throughout this book are very valuable and should always be taught to children with ADHD. Medication can help a child who cannot otherwise focus long enough to work on these strategies and can bolster his concentration and self-esteem. However, while medication can be beneficial, it generally should not be relied on alone. A combination of behavioral therapy and medications seems to work best for children with ADHD, and it is good for your child to have strategies he can fall back on should he want or need to stop taking medication.

We recommend discussing medication further on an individual basis with your child's doctor. In general, medications for ADHD are divided into two classes: stimulants and non-stimulants. Taking medications for ADHD is always a choice and should be based on what actually helps your child. Once started, any medication can be discontinued at any time under the supervision of a doctor.

Conclusion

We began this book by saying that our approach is based upon the training techniques of world-class athletes. Not the physical training techniques—this book is not about coaching ADHDers to run a four-minute mile, shoot winning baskets, or land the perfect "ten" in gymnastics. However, the fact is that the techniques many athletes use to become great, such as focus and repeated practice, will help your child excel too. That is the simple message of this book.

Throughout this book, we have tried to provide you with the tools and principles that are needed to learn how to focus. However, it is not enough to simply do each exercise once or twice and then forget about it. As in sports, results will come only from *continual* practice and adherence to a routine—that is, from *training*. Just as you wouldn't expect a first-time runner to finish a marathon after one day of training, you cannot expect your child to have full concentration after going through this book with her one time. Your child may become frustrated if she feels she is not making any progress or that she is not able to keep up with her classmates. But as Derek Jeter once said, "There may be people that have more talent than you, but there's no excuse for anyone to work harder than you do." If your child gives 100 percent in overcoming the challenges of her ADHD, she will feel internal pride knowing that she is doing the best she can and trying her hardest.

There may be sections of this book you will have to return to more than once—for example, if your child just can't get used to working with a team, you may want to review Chapter 7 again—and some sections you might only have to read once or twice. If your child becomes bored with the exercises, you can adjust them to make them more challenging or thought-provoking. Whether it's coming up with goals or springing back from setbacks, each child has her own particular strengths. In reading this book and talking through its concepts with her, you will be able to better grasp what these talents are.

Your child is growing up in a society that is faster-paced and more technologically advanced than ever before. This can magnify her ADHD issues. It is important for her to be able to focus when she needs to; this will benefit her not only in school, but in life in general as she grows up and is faced with more responsibilities. There is a time for fun distractions, and there is a time for buckling down and getting to work. That is what the athletic mindset is all about: Developing skills through repeated training, identifying challenges, setting goals, and reflecting on progress and opportunities for improvement.

It is a great idea to seek outside help if you or your child feels overwhelmed—it is a big step to change habits that have been formed and practiced for years. There are always the options of hiring an ADHD coach to work with your child, or seeking a doctor's help in administering medication to your child. Remember, however, that while medication can sharpen your child's focus, it is not a cure-all: Your child should still practice the strategies outlined in this book in case that medication is ineffective or causes more problems than it solves. The strategies will also help prepare for a day when your child may no longer want to use medications and is ready to rely solely on this book's behavioral techniques.

Don't forget to reward your child when she achieves a goal or shows that she is putting time and effort into improvement—even if she has not progressed as far as you'd hoped. Whether this reward is praise, a pat on the back, or a special treat, it is important to show your child that you are proud of her and believe in her ability to create a Positive Cycle of Success! One mother-child team that exemplifies this unity is Deborah Phelps and her son, Olympic swimming champion Michael Phelps. As a child, Michael could not sit still in school and couldn't stay on task. Deborah, however, did not give up on him, even when teachers told her that her son would never be able to focus. After trying—and stopping—medication, Deborah noticed Michael's sharp concentration and effort when it came to swimming. Together, they worked on strategies for self-discipline that Michael could use in and out of the pool. The structure that swimming gave him allowed him to stay focused.

Lastly, this is not a quick fix by any means. There is a good chance that your child—and you, as well—may become frustrated as you practice some of the exercises. That is only human, and should be expected. Just keep providing encouragement and understand that change takes time; Rome wasn't built in a day. Over time, you will see how developing focus can make all the difference in the world for your child.

Our hope is that this book will make you and your child a team. Together, you can decrease the number of frazzled mornings and arguments over homework. Your child will be more likely to achieve the goals that she fully commits to, and you and your child can both be proud of the progress she makes.

And as a team, remember that the game is not over. At the dojo, we follow what we call "The Second Half Theory" and follow the mantra "*Finish Strong.*" The Second Half Theory states that even if you are losing the game at halftime, but then go on to win the second half, you win the entire game! So remember: Your child has time to get in there, play the rest of the game with all she's got, and win it.

Resources

There are many organizations, books, and websites that are dedicated to helping those with ADHD succeed in their everyday lives. The following list of resources can provide you and your child with strategies, tips, and ideas for becoming more organized and focused.

ORGANIZATIONS

Children and Adults with Attention Deficit-Hyperactivity Disorder (CHADD)
Multiple locations
www.chadd.org
(800) 233-4050
CHADD is a non-profit organization with chapters in many communities and over 12,000 members. Its mission is to improve the lives of people affected by ADHD using a set of core values. CHADD's website includes a page to search for the location closest to you.

The Hallowell Centers
The Hallowell Centers, named for Dr. Edward Hallowell, combine the latest research on the brain, body, and heart. To help their patients lead happier and more productive lives, the centers utilize positive psychology and their patients' strengths.

The Hallowell Center: California
425 Market Street, Suite 2200
San Francisco, CA 94105
(415) 967-0061
info@hallowellSFO.com
www.hallowellSFO.com

The Hallowell Center: New York
117 West 72nd Street, 3rd floor
New York, NY 10023
(212) 799-7777
info@hallowellcenter.org
hallowellcenter.org

The Hallowell Center: Seattle, Washington
5502 34th Ave NE
Seattle, WA 98105
(206) 420-7345
info@hallowelltodarocenter.org
www.hallowelltodarocenter.org

The Hallowell Center: Sudbury, Massachusetts
144 North Road, Suite 2450
Sudbury, MA 01776
(978) 287-0810
HallowellReferralsSudbury@
  gmail.com
www.drhallowellsudbury.com

The Hallowell Center: Hingham, Massachusetts
Center for Integrative Counseling
  & Wellness
62 Derby Street, Suite 6
Hingham, MA 02043
(781) 749-9227
info@CenterforIntegrative
  CounselingandWellness.com
www.centerforintegrative
  counselingandwellness.com

RECOMMENDED READING

Barkley, Russell. *Taking Charge of ADHD, Third Edition: The Complete, Authoritative Guide for Parents*. New York: The Guilford Press, 2013.

Cooper-Kahn, Joyce, and Laurie Dietzel. *Late, Lost, and Unprepared: A Parents' Guide to Helping Children with Executive Functioning*. Bethesda, MD: Woodbine House, 2008.

Hallowell, Edward, and John Ratey. *Driven to Distraction (Revised): Recognizing and Coping with Attention Deficit Disorder*. New York: Anchor Books, 2011.

Hartmann, Thom. *Attention Deficit Disorder: A Different Perception*. Nevada City, CA: Underwood Books, 1997.

Homayoun, Ana. *That Crumpled Paper Was Due Last Week: Helping Disorganized and Distracted Boys Succeed in School and in Life*. New York: Perigee Books, 2010.

Loehr, Jim, and Tony Schwartz. *The Power of Full Engagement: Managing Energy, Not Time, Is the Key to High Performance and Personal Renewal*. New York: Free Press, 2003.

McConnell, Kathleen, and Gail Ryser. *Practical Ideas that Really Work for Students with ADHD*. Austin: Pro-Ed, 2005.

Rief, Sandra. *How to Reach and Teach Children with ADD/ADHD: Practical Techniques, Strategies and Interventions*. San Francisco: Jossey-Bass, 2005.

Small, Gary, and Gigi Vorgan. *iBrain: Surviving the Technological Alteration of the Modern Mind*. New York: Collins Living, 2008.

WEB RESOURCES

ADD WareHouse

www.addwarehouse.com

ADD WareHouse holds the largest collection of ADHD-related books, videos, training programs, games, and assessment products in the world.

ADHD Coaches Organization (ACO)

www.adhdcoaches.org

The ACO is the worldwide professional membership organization for ADHD coaches. Their website provides information about ADHD coaches and helps clients select a coach.

Attention Deficit Disorder Association (ADDA)

www.add.org

The ADDA's mission is to work with adults who have ADHD to lead better lives. Their website provides information, resources, networking opportunities, and other tools for success.

Children and Adults with Attention Deficit-Hyperactivity Disorder (CHADD)

www.chadd.org
(800) 233-4050

CHADD is a non-profit organization with chapters in many communities and over 12,000 members. Its mission is to improve the lives of people affected by ADHD using a set of core values.

National Organization for Learning Disabilities (NCLD)

www.ncld.org

The NCLD, founded in 1977, sets to improve the lives of children and adults who have learning and attention disorders. It provides resources and advocates for equal rights for these individuals.

National Resource Center on ADHD

www.help4adhd.org

The National Resource Center on ADHD is a program of CHADD and seeks to provide the latest evidence-based information and science on ADHD.

Schwab Foundation for Learning—Internet Special Education Resources (ISER)

www.iser.com

ISER provides information, support, and hope for parents and educators helping kids with learning disabilities. Information about testing, treatments, programs, and more can be found on their website.

Understood for Learning and Attention Issues

www.understood.org/en

Understood provides resources to parents of children with learning disabilities from fifteen nonprofits. Resources include articles, quizzes, tips, research, and unique tools. Understood also has an active community on Facebook (www.facebook.com/understood).

HOMEWORK

Task	Sunday	Monday	Tuesday

PROGRESS

Sunday	Monday	Tuesday

Also see the section, "Tips for Parents with ADHD Children: At Home," on page 75 for more tips regarding checklists, progress logs, and calendars.

LOG

WEDNESDAY	THURSDAY	FRIDAY	SATURDAY

PROGRESS

WEDNESDAY	THURSDAY	FRIDAY

The reader is granted permission to reproduce this Homework Log above for his or her personal use only.

References

Chapter 1

Ceci, Stephen J, and Jayne Tishman. "Hyperactivity and Incidental Memory: Evidence for Attentional Diffusion." *Child Development* 1984; 55(6): 2192–2203.

Gilman, Lois. "Career Advice from the Corner Office: Famous People with ADHD." *ADDitude Magazine*, Dec–Jan, 2005.

Hartmann, Thom. *The Edison Gene*. Rochester, VT: Park Street Press, 2003.

Chapter 2

Curry, Stephen. "MVP Acceptance Speech." Speech, National Basketball Association, Oakland, CA, May 4, 2015.

Jenkins, Sally. "Only Medal for Bode Is Fool's Gold." *The Washington Post*, Feb. 26, 2006. www.washingtonpost.com/wpdyn/content/article/2006/02/25/AR2006022501546.html

Judd, Ron. "Apolo Ohno savors final chapter in storied Olympics career." *The Seattle Times*, Feb. 7, 2010. www.seattletimes.com/sports/olympics/apolo-ohno-savors-final-chapter-in-storied-olympics-career/

"Mr. Fariborz talks about 'how to WIN.'" YouTube video, 9:57, from introduction to "Hapkido Blend" Black Belt DVD series from Century Martial Arts. Posted by Fariborz Azhakh. Dec. 9, 2010. www.youtube.com/watch?v=a3H_Ozj9Vc4

Chapter 3

Doran, George T. "There's a S.M.A.R.T. way to write management's goals and objectives." *Management Review* 1981; 70(11): 35–36.

Locke, Edwin A. "Motivation Through Conscious Goal Setting." *Applied & Preventive Psychology* 1996; 5(2):117–124.

Chapter 4

Covey, Stephen. *First Things First*. New York: Fireside, 1994. 88–89.

Magness, Steve. "A Peek Inside—Training Log of Ciaran O'Lionaird in build up to 3:54 mile." *The Science of Running*, July 12, 2013. www.scienceofrunning.com/2013/07/ training-log-of-ciaran-olionaird-in.html

Matthews, Gail. "Goals Research Summary." *Dominican University*. Accessed August 13, 2015. www.dominican.edu/academics/ahss/undergraduate-programs/psych/faculty/ fulltime/gailmatthews/researchsummary2.pdf

"Superstar Interview: Michael Phelps." *Parenting.com*. Accessed August 17, 2015. www. parenting.com/article/superstar-interview-michael-phelps

Chapter 5

Hirshkowitz, Max, et al. "National Sleep Foundation's sleep time duration recommendations: methodology and results summary." *Sleep Health: Journal of the National Sleep Foundation* 2015; 1(1): 40–43.

Kim, Meeri. "Blue light from electronics disturbs sleep, especially for teenagers." *The Washington Post*, Sept. 1, 2014. www.washingtonpost.com/national/health-science/blue-light-from-electronics-disturbs-sleep-especially-for-teenagers/2014/08/29/3edd2726-27a7-11e4-958c-268a320a60ce_story.html

Murphy, J Michael, et al. "The Relationship of School Breakfast to Psychosocial and Academic Functioning: Cross-sectional and Longitudinal Observations in an Inner-city School Sample." *Archives of Pediatrics and Adolescent Medicine* 1998; 52(9): 899–907.

Pelsser, Lidy M, et al. "Effects of a restricted elimination diet on the behaviour of children with attention-deficit hyperactivity disorder (INCA study): a randomised controlled trial." *Lancet* 2011; 377(9764): 494–503.

Rommel, Anna-Sophie, et al. "Protection from Genetic Diathesis in ADHD: Possible Complementary Roles of Exercise." *Journal of the American Academy of Child and Adolescent Psychiatry* 2013; 52(9): 900-910.

Warner, Chuck. "Lessons From Legends: Jason Lezak & Seeds of Third Effort." *USAswimming.org*, Jan. 23, 2014. http://usaswimming.org/ViewNewsArticle.aspx?TabId=0&itemid =5837&mid=8712

Young, Janet A, and Michelle D Pain. "The Zone: Evidence of a Universal Phenomenon for Athletes Across Sports." *Athletic Insight: The Online Journal of Sport Psychology* 1999; 1(3): 21–30.

Chapter 6

Lofthouse, Nicholas, et al. "A Review of Neurofeedback Treatment for Pediatric ADHD." *Journal of Attention Disorders* 2012; 5(16): 351–372.

Ophir, Eyal, et al. "Cognitive control in media multitaskers." *Proceedings of the National Academy of Sciences of the United States of America* 2009; 106(37): 15583–15587.

Peale, Norman Vincent. *Treasury of Courage and Confidence*. Pawling, New York: Peale Center for Christian Living, 1969. 196.

Richardson, Alan. "Mental Practice: A Review and Discussion, Part II." *Research Quarterly* 1967; 38(2): 263–273.

Tian, Lixia, et al. "Enhanced resting-state brain activities in ADHD patients: A fMRI study." *Brain & Development* 2008; 30(5): 342–348.

Wais, Peter, et al. "Neural Mechanisms Underlying the Impact of Visual Distraction on Retrieval of Long-Term Memory." *The Journal of Neuroscience* 2010; 30(25): 8541–8550.

Chapter 7

Dweck, Carol. *Mindset: The New Psychology of Success.* New York: Ballantine Books, 2007.

Helmstetter, Shad. *What to Say When you Talk to Your Self.* New York: Pocket Books, 1990.

Riley, Pat. *Show Time: Inside the Lakers' Breakthrough Season.* New York: Grand Central Publishing, 1988.

Xenophon. "A Conference of Socrates with Aristippus Concerning Pleasure and Temperance." In *The Memorable Thoughts of Socrates,* edited by Henry Morley, 58–63. Oregon: Watchmaker Publishing, 2006.

Chapter 8

Conrad, Cheryl D. "What Is the Functional Significance of Chronic Stress-Induced CA3 Dendritic Retraction Within the Hippocampus?" *Behavioral and cognitive neuroscience reviews* 2006; 5(1): 41–60.

Covey, Stephen. *The Seven Habits of Highly Effective People.* New York: Free Press, 1989.

Helmstetter, Shad. *What to Say When you Talk to Your Self.* New York: Pocket Books, 1990.

Phelps, Elizabeth A. "Human emotion and memory: Interactions of the amygdala and hippocampal complex." *Current Opinion in Neurobiology* 2004; 14(2): 198–202.

Staff, Roger, et al. "Childhood Socioeconomic Status and Adult Brain Size: Childhood Socioeconomic Status Influences Adult Hippocampal Size." *Annals of Neurology* 2012; 71(5): 653–660.

Chapter 9

"About ADHD Coaching." *ADHD Coaches Organization.* Accessed Oct. 2, 2015. https://www.adhdcoaches.org/about-membership/about-adhd-coaching/

Frederickson, BL, and Christine Branigan. "Positive Emotions Broaden the Scope of Attention and Thought-Action Repertoires." *Cognition and Emotion* 2005; 19(3): 313–332.

Frederickson, BL, and M Losada. "Positive Affect and the Complex Dynamics of Human Flourishing." *American Psychologist* 2005; 60(7): 678–686.

Frederickson, BL. "The Role of Positive Emotions in Positive Psychology: The Broaden-and-Build Theory of Positive Emotions." *American Psychologist* 2001; 56(3): 218–226.

Hallowell, Edward. "Connectedness." In *Finding the Heart of the Child,* by Edward Hallowell and Michael Thompson. Washington DC: NAIS, 1997.

Losada, M. "The complex dynamics of high performance teams." *Mathematical and Computer Modelling* 1999; 30(9–10): 179–192.

McCarthy, Laura Flynn. "What You Need to Know about ADHD Coaching." *ADDitude Magazine.* Accessed Oct. 2, 2015. www.additudemag.com/adhd/article/4002.html

Rath, Tom. *StrengthsFinder 2.0*. New York: Gallup Press, 2007.

Rousey, Ronda. *My Fight/Your Fight*. New York: Regan Arts, 2015.

Snyder, CR. "Hope theory: Rainbows in the mind." *Psychological Inquiry* 2002; 13(4): 249–275.

Snyder, CR, et al. "The will and the ways: Development and validation of an individual differences measure of hope." *Journal of Personality and Social Psychology* 1991; 60(4): 570–585.

Trzesniewski, K. "Low Self-Esteem During Adolescence Predicts Poor Health, Criminal Behavior and Limited Economic Prospects During Adulthood." *Developmental Psychology* 2006; 42(2): 381–390.

Chapter 10

Brooks, David. *The Social Animal*. New York: Random House, 2012. Print.

Collingwood, Jane. "Side Effects of ADHD Medications." *PsychCentral,* July 9, 2010. http://psychcentral.com/lib/side-effects-of-adhd-medications/

Dalby, JT. "Will population decreases in caffeine consumption unveil attention deficit disorders in adults?" *Medical Hypotheses* 1985; 18(2): 163–167.

Elliott, Glen R, and Kate Kelly. "ADHD Medications, An Overview." *Attention Magazine,* October 2007.

Ferre, Sergi. "Role of the Central Ascending Neurotransmitter Systems in the Psychostimulant Effects of Caffeine." *Journal of Alzheimer's Disease* 2010; 20 Suppl 1: S35–49.

Garfinkel, BD, CD Webster, and L Sloman. "Responses to methylphenidate and varied doses of caffeine in children with attention deficit disorder." *Canadian Journal of Psychiatry* 1981; 26(6): 395–401.

Loh, Kep Kee, and Dr Ryota Kanai. "Higher Media Multi-Tasking Is Associated with Smaller Gray-Matter Density in the Anterior Cingulate Cortex." *Plos One* 2014; 9(9).

MTA Cooperative Group. "A 14-Month Randomized Clinical Trial of Treatment Strategies for Attention-Deficit/Hyperactivity Disorder. The MTA Cooperative Group. Multimodal Treatment Study of Children with ADHD." *Archives of General Psychiatry* 1999; 56(12): 1073–1086.

National Resource Center on ADHD. "Medications Used in the Treatment of ADHD." *CHADD*. Last modified May 2011. www.chadd.org/Portals/0/AM/Images/Understading/MedChart.pdf

Small, Gary. *iBrain*. New York: HarperCollins, 2008.

Stephenson, PE. "Physiologic and psychotropic effects of caffeine on man. A review." *Journal of the American Dietetic Association* 1977; 71(3): 240–247.

US Food and Drug Administration. "Dealing With ADHD: What You Need to Know." Last modified August 6, 2015. www.fda.gov/ForConsumers/ConsumerUpdates/ucm269188.htm

Conclusion

Dutton, Judy. "ADHD Parenting Advice from Michael Phelps' Mom." *ADDitude Magazine,* Apr–May, 2007. www.additudemag.com/adhd/article/1998.html

About the Authors

Dr. Sarah Cheyette is a physician who specializes in pediatric neurology and treats ADHD medically, and is the mother of four children with co-author Dr. Benjamin Cheyette. She has been in private practice since 1998. She has seen many children and adults with ADHD, and feels that while medication can sometimes be helpful, the non-medication strategies outlined in this book are *always* helpful and may be the most important component of successfully treating ADHD. She met coauthor Peter Johnson while training in a form of kickboxing called Tae Bo® at his dojo—and additionally watched him train her kids in karate—and was very impressed by how he has motivated all kinds of people to work hard to meet their full potential. She realized that the ideas that a coach routinely instills in his athletes can also apply to the treatment of ADHD, and she would like her ADHD patients and others to be able to internalize these strategies to be the most successful they can be. These strategies, as well as an FAQ about ADHD and a blog about additional management techniques, can be found on the authors' website at www.adhdandthefocusedmind.com.

Karate master *Peter Johnson* is a seventh-degree black belt in karate and also a master of Tae Bo®. He has been teaching students in the martial arts since 1993. Over time, he has seen the number of his students diagnosed with ADHD rise. This has been accompanied by a rise in the frequency of inquiries from parents and school counselors who are interested in karate as a way to help kids with ADHD build "mental discipline muscles." Indeed, martial arts have had a dramatic effect on the lives of many people with ADHD (based on statistics from the National Association of Professional Martial Artists on the positive scholastic benefits of karate in children's lives). Peter has seen many of his karate students shift from having lackluster academic performance to achieving honor student status. Peter's philosophy is that martial arts is not simply about acquiring physical skill, but more importantly, is about acquiring a drive for excellence in all areas of life. Along these lines, Peter is also an ultra-endurance athlete and runner, and he uses personal lessons he has learned in that setting to help his students feel fully engaged in the moment.

Dr. Benjamin Cheyette, Sarah's husband, is a professor of psychiatry at the University of California San Francisco, where he sees patients, teaches medical students and psychiatric residents, and runs a scientific laboratory exploring the molecular origins of psychiatric illness. In his clinical practice he has treated patients with ADHD, including professionals who qualify for this diagnosis. He is also a black belt student of Peter Johnson, and has witnessed the transformative power of successful coaching strategies on goal-setting, focus, and achievement in the dojo— as well as the generalization of such strategies beyond athleticism to other spheres of life.

Index